Public Policy and the Neo-Weberian State

T0270898

The neo-Weberian state constitutes an attempt to combine the Weberian model of administration with the principles laid down during the retreat from the bureaucratic management paradigm (new public management and public governance). The concept of neo-Weberian state involves changing the model of operation of administrative structures from an inward-oriented one, focused on compliance with internal rules, into a model focused on meeting citizens' needs (not by resorting to commercialisation, as is the case with new public management, but by building appropriate quality of administration).

This book discusses the context of the neo-Weberian approach and its impact on the processes of societal transformation. Further, it identifies and systematises the theoretical and functional elements of the approach under consideration. This volume includes comparative analyses of the neo-Weberian state and public management paradigms. In the empirical part of the work, its authors review selected policies (economic, innovation, industrial, labour, territorial, urban management, and health) from the perspective of tools typical of the neo-Weberian approach. This part also includes a critical scrutiny of changes which have taken place in the framework of selected policies in recent decades. The study assesses the appropriateness of the neo-Weberian approach to the management of public affairs regarding countries which have modernised their public administrations in its spirit. One of the aims of this analysis is to answer the question whether the application of neo-Weberian ideas may result in qualitative changes in the context of public policies. The final part of the book covers implications for public management resulting from the concept of neo-Weberian state.

Public Policy and the Neo-Weberian State is suitable for researchers and students who study political economy, public policy and modern political theory.

Stanisław Mazur is Professor at the Cracow University of Economics, Faculty of Public Economy and Administration, Poland, and is Dean of the Faculty of Public Economy and Administration.

Piotr Kopyciński is Assistant Professor at the Cracow University of Economics, Faculty of Public Economy and Administration, Poland, and is an expert in more than 20 research and implementation projects in the analysis of public policy, innovation, local and regional development.

Routledge Frontiers of Political Economy

For a full list of titles in this series please visit www.routledge.com/books/series/ SE0345

Public Policy and the Neo-Weberian State

Edited by
Stanisław Mazur
and Piotr Kopyciński

LONDON AND NEW YORK

First published 2018 by Routledge

2 Park Square, Milton Park, Abingdon, Oxfordshire OX14 4RN

52 Vanderbilt Avenue, New York, NY 10017

Routledge is an imprint of the Taylor & Francis Group, an informa business

First issued in paperback 2020

British Library Cataloguing-in-Publication Data
A catalogue record for this book is available from the British Library

Library of Congress Cataloging-in-Publication Data
Names: Mazur, Stanisław (Economist), editor. | Kopyciński, Piotr, editor.
Title: Public policy and the neo-Weberian state / edited by Stanisław
    Mazur and Piotr Kopyciński.
Description: Abingdon, Oxon ; New York, NY : Routledge, 2017. |
    Includes index.
Identifiers: LCCN 2017013298 | ISBN 9781138732834 (hardback) |
    ISBN 9781315187945 (ebook)
Subjects: LCSH: State, The. | Public administration. | Economic policy. |
    Social policy. | Weber, Max, 1864–1920.
Classification: LCC JC11 .P83 2017 | DDC 320.6—dc23
LC record available at https://lccn.loc.gov/2017013298

ISBN: 978-1-138-73283-4 (hbk)
ISBN: 978-0-367-59481-7 (pbk)

Typeset in Times New Roman
by Book Now Ltd, London

Contents

Illustrations

Figures

Tables

Boxes

Contributors

Paweł Białynicki-Birula PhD, Cracow University of Economics, Faculty of Public Economy and Administration

Marek Ćwiklicki Professor, Cracow University of Economics, Faculty of Public Economy and Administration

Maciej Frączek PhD, Cracow University of Economics, Faculty of Public Economy and Administration

Tomasz Geodecki PhD, Cracow University of Economics, Faculty of Public Economy and Administration

Jakub Głowacki MA, Cracow University of Economics, Faculty of Public Economy and Administration

Jacek Klich Professor, Cracow University of Economics, Faculty of Public Economy and Administration

Piotr Kopyciński PhD, Cracow University of Economics, Faculty of Public Economy and Administration

Michał Kudłacz PhD, Cracow University of Economics, Faculty of Public Economy and Administration

Łukasz Mamica Professor, Cracow University of Economics, Faculty of Public Economy and Administration

Stanisław Mazur Professor, Cracow University of Economics, Faculty of Public Economy and Administration

Michał Możdżeń MA, Cracow University of Economics, Faculty of Public Economy and Administration

Marek Oramus MA, Cracow University of Economics, Faculty of Public Economy and Administration

Michał Żabiński MA, Cracow University of Economics, Faculty of Public Economy and Administration

Introduction

Stanisław Mazur and Piotr Kopyciński

In *Public Policy and the Neo-Weberian State*, we address an intriguing, but still under-researched phenomenon – the application of neo-Weberian ideas in public management. The neo-Weberian approach is rooted in the continental European concept of the state and in its dominant political and administrative culture. To a certain extent, it stands in opposition to the neo-liberal socio-economic agenda and new public management (NPM). It also remains at odds with public governance, which is conceptually rooted in neo-liberal ideology. This is not tantamount to a complete rejection of the achievements of NPM and public governance – inspirations for the neo-Weberian approach can be sought in certain attributes of both of the above-mentioned coordination mechanisms.

Owing to the prevailing disappointment with the neo-liberal socio-economic agenda and its associated management models, the neo-Weberian state has gained in attractiveness and importance both as an object of study and a set of governance rules and mechanisms.

The main reason for our interest in public policy and the neo-Weberian state is our belief, as members of the team of authors, that it is high time to consolidate the scattered knowledge of the neo-Weberian approach in public management and reflect on it critically, especially in the context of its practical application possibilities. This approach emerges as an interesting vantage point from which to explain the rules and mechanisms of operation of public administrations in countries belonging to the continental European cultural circle. It also offers valuable practical tips for those who attempt to modernise the public sector not only in continental Europe but also in other countries, including those rooted in the Anglo-Saxon tradition and in NPM.

The book consists of two main parts, with a total of ten chapters, followed by a Conclusion. Part I, 'The neo-Weberian state: fundamental principles', outlines the constitutive issues of the concept. At the beginning of Chapter 1, 'The origins of and trends in the neo-Weberian approach', M. Ćwiklicki and S. Mazur list the sources of the neo-Weberian approach and discuss them briefly. Next, they outline three basic ways of understanding the neo-Weberian approach and describe their respective characteristics. In the final section, they present the ways of understanding such categories as the neo-Weberian model of state, the neo-Weberian public management model and neo-Weberian public sector reform.

In Chapter 2, 'The social and political context of the neo-Weberian state', M. Możdżeń and M. Żabiński review the main challenges that trigger change in the role of the modern state and ways of exercising public authority in a globalised world. They conclude that responding to such challenges effectively requires at least a modification of certain public management rules and instruments.

In Chapter 3, 'The neo-Weberian state and paradigms of public management', S. Mazur and M. Oramus compare the neo-Weberian approach with the competing public management paradigms, such as the classic model of public administration, NPM and public governance. At the outset, they identify the similarities and differences that exist among these models, discussing their advantages and limitations both in theoretical and in practical terms. They deal with the following spheres: management tools, public policy implementation, forms of public service provision, organisational structures and mechanisms of organisational learning.

Part II, 'The neo-Weberian state and public policies', is devoted to the analysis of selected public policy types with a view to categorising their rules and mechanisms in neo-Weberian terms.

In Chapter 4, 'The neo-Weberian approach in economic policy', T. Geodecki attempts to answer the question concerning the possible transition from the neo-liberal to the neo-Weberian model of economic policy. For this purpose, the author compares the approach characteristic of public choice theory with the approach based on an active role of the state in the sphere of economic policy. The author raises a number of important issues, including the justification for such a role of the state, particularly in promoting the expansion of domestic industry and in protecting it from external competition.

In Chapter 5, 'The neo-Weberian approach in innovation policy', P. Kopyciński deals with the issue of coordination mechanisms as applied to innovation policy. First, the author charts the evolution of the understanding of innovation policy, which reflects the increasing complexity of public affairs. He then goes on to identify the weaknesses inherent in the previously used policy coordination mechanisms, indicating that an interesting remedy for these failures may be offered by the neo-Weberian approach. These theoretical considerations are supported by an analysis of coordination mechanisms applied in the implementation of smart specialisation strategies in Scotland and in Poland, respectively.

In Chapter 6, M. Frączek examines the neo-Weberian public management model in the context of labour market policy in Poland. He begins his analysis with a set of categories specific to the neo-Weberian public management model devised by the author. He observes that labour market policy exhibits a number of features typical of the neo-Weberian approach, but also notes the presence of attributes of other public management models. This leads him to conclude that the current model applied in this sphere is a hybrid one with a tendency to evolve towards the neo-Weberian approach.

The issues of industrial policy evolution are considered in Chapter 7, 'The neo-Weberian approach in industrial policy'. Its author, Ł. Mamica, attempts to assess the impact of the neo-Weberian approach on industrial policy, noting that it leads to the departure from horizontal policy in favour of sectoral policies.

The author points out that after 2008, the neo-liberal free-market approach lost the status of the only system capable of efficiently allocating of resources. Instead, the state began to be perceived as an entity that can effectively oppose the global, transnational corporations which often act against its vested interests.

In Chapter 8, 'The neo-Weberian approach in health policy in selected countries', J. Klich offers a comparative analysis of health policies pursued in Germany, the United Kingdom, France, Denmark and the Netherlands from the perspective of the neo-Weberian public management model. These countries were selected due to their rich experience in the field of public management reform and a considerable diversity of their healthcare systems. The neo-Weberian public management model emerges as an inspiration for health sector reform.

The issue of territorial policy is undertaken by P. Kopyciński in Chapter 9, 'The neo-Weberian approach in territorial policy'. The author traces its evolution towards an integrated approach to territorial development and argues that it makes more sense to talk about territorial policy rather than about regional one. He notes that such an evolution is not accompanied by a serious reflection on the usefulness of the currently dominant coordination mechanisms. In his opinion, neither NPM nor public governance provides adequate mechanisms for managing territorial policy, hence the perceived advantages of the neo-Weberian approach.

In Chapter 10, 'The neo-Weberian approach as a public management model in urban areas', M. Kudłacz tackles the issue of urban management. Recognising the complexity of large urban agglomerations, the author discusses the relevant styles of management with a special focus on their richness and diversity. He attributes these differences to distinct historical, cultural and socio-economic developments. His reflections on the possibilities of applying the neo-Weberian approach to urban management figure prominently in the analysis.

In the Conclusion, P. Białynicki-Birula, J. Głowacki and J. Klich take a broader look at the implications of the neo-Weberian approach for public management. They begin their considerations by invoking the neo-Weberian concept of state, and then investigate its relevance to public management in relation to selected public policies. In the final part, they outline the most important theoretical and methodological challenges facing the neo-Weberian approach as applied in the sphere of public management.

The authors of this book are public management scholars co-operating with the Department of Public Economy and Administration at the Cracow University of Economics. They represent a multidisciplinary team of economists, lawyers and specialists in the field of management sciences, which makes them uniquely qualified to undertake such complex theoretical issues as the neo-Weberian approach to public management. The authors appreciate the assistance of Anna Chrabąszcz (managing editor) and Rafał Śmietana (translator).

The authors would like to thank everyone involved in preparing this publication for their critical remarks, comments and tips, which enriched it with new insights and lines of thought.

Part I

The neo-Weberian state

Fundamental principles

1 The origins of and trends in the neo-Weberian approach

Marek Ćwiklicki and Stanisław Mazur

The rationale behind the emergence and development of the neo-Weberian approach

The neo-Weberian approach as a public management model is a relatively new phenomenon in the theory of public administration. However, the first attempts to define it in practical terms were made several decades ago in the administrations and economies of European countries, mainly in continental Europe. Specifically, the roots of the approach in question date back to enlightened absolutism, to the beginnings of the formation of a democratic law-governed state, and to the modern Weberian bureaucracy. The key aspects of this heritage have survived to the present day and can be found in a number of European countries. This testifies to the viability of the concept despite its absence from the mainstream academic discourse and public debate. It has become, among other things, the source of remedies for the adverse socio-economic effects of globalisation, such as the erosion of sovereignty of nation-states and the undermining of their position in international relations with respect to transnational actors. The second category of reasons which contribute to the increased interest in the neo-Weberian principles includes not only the adverse consequences of the 'hollowing-out of the state,' but also the unsatisfactory results of reforms based on the principles of NPM and public governance. The third group of factors includes attempts to capture public resources by interest groups and the dismantling of the welfare state.

The developments listed above have led to the belief that the state must regain its socially and economically important functions which determine the degree of its democratic legitimacy, and mitigate certain adverse effects brought on by previous coordination mechanisms, including the uncritical adaptation of market-based management methods by public sector organisations. Such a line of thinking is consistent with the ingrained belief of the political élites of continental European countries that the state is a political union whose natural duty is to work for the community of citizens and contribute to their welfare by actively influencing the socio-economic processes.

The birth of the neo-Weberian state – a literature review

The presentation and discussion of the development of the neo-Weberian approach in a chronological order draws extensively on the literature review. For the most part, it is based on sources cited in the most recent, third edition of the book *Public Management Reform: A Comparative Analysis* (Pollitt, Bouckaert 2011). This reference was selected as the leading one, since in its 2004 edition the phrase *neo-Weberian state* (NWS) appeared in print for the first time. The term was first used to describe the reforms typical of European countries, but different from those undertaken in New Zealand and the United States (Pollitt, Bouckaert 2011, p. 3). It should be noted that the term NWS is often used in the literature without any explanation of its meaning. As a result, the references to the Weberian model in comparative analyses comprise not only the machinery of government, power relations in administrative systems or instrumental rationality, but also the negative perception of the NWS as a threat to liberal democracy. The negative import of the NWS is attributed to the study of organisations, where it is associated with the dominance of informal practices and the exploitation of the system for particularistic purposes.

The present analysis of the origins of the NWS shall be limited to publications in which the object of research includes the state and/or public administration.

The cited authors (Pollitt, Bouckaert 2011, pp. 19, 22) in their characteristics of the NWS make passing references to the previous (second) edition of the book, specifically, to its Chapter Four devoted to the trajectory of modernisation and reform, as well as to the publications by W. Drechsler and R. Kattel (2008/2009), and L. E. Lynn (2008). We shall start our discussion from there, noting the way in which the NWS is understood in each one.

In the first publication, Drechsler and Kattel refer to the 2004 edition of *Public Management Reform* and conclude that the NWS is a political orientation which results from the reforms implemented in Europe at the turn of the 20th and 21st centuries, empirically rooted in the structure of the Weberian bureaucracy supplemented with elements of NPM. These authors perceive the NWS model as the basis, as the necessary condition for effective implementation of reforms in line with NPM. For this reason, their proposals are addressed not only to the developing countries. Drechsler and Kattel perceive the NWS as a concept linking the Weberian principles with sustainable economic development, appropriate for managing complex, innovation-based societies. The authors note that: 'Criticism towards the NWS that it is too close to NPM is justified to the extent that it does co-opt positive elements of NPM, but on a Weberian foundation, i.e. that both are asymmetrically aufgehoben' (Drechsler, Kattel 2008/2009, p. 98).

L. E. Lynn (the second source cited by Pollitt and Bouckaert), when discussing the NWS, drew primarily on the second edition of *Public Management Reform* and based his considerations on other works as well. The term *neo-Weberian approach* has been used in political science, sociology and public administration works since the 1970s. As an example of such an interpretation, Lynn gives H. Brown's treatment of bureaucracy published in 1978. Lynn also refers to a supplementary source (L. Seabrooke 2002), in which the author also refers to M. Mann and T. Skocpol as neo-Weberians. Noting the terminological confusion, Lynn treats the NWS as a state-centred concept and cites the following definition of the state formulated by M. Mann in 1986: 'A territorially demarcated, differentiated set of institutions and personnel with a centre that exercises authoritative rulemaking backed by the coercive powers of the state' (2008, p. 4).

Lynn goes on to explain that the neo-Weberian approach reflects the continuity of evolutionary development of the state in accordance with norms and material interests. The formulation of general theories or models contributes to an isomorphism of administrative systems and to a more uniform perception of the state. This can be easily noticed in the idea of the European Union and in the drive to achieve convergence among European economies and societies. These unifying pursuits (isomorphism, convergence) strongly contrast with the different evolutionary paths taken by individual state systems throughout Europe. An example of the latter is the following observation made by Lynn, which derives from analyses of public management in Europe and in the United States in 2008:

> Germany evolves only slowly from its Rechtsstaat and corporatist traditions, France combines old and new traditions, albeit in some tension with one another; the emergence of managerialism in Napoleonic Spain is embryonic; and the United Kingdom, the most aggressive NPM reformer, may be breaking ground for a 'new public governance' paradigm.
>
> (p. 9)

An analysis of the contents of the two major sources in Pollitt and Bouckaert (2011) reveals that they refer to an earlier edition of their book *Public Management Reform*. We have also queried the phrase 'neo-Weberian state' in such databases as Scopus and Web of Science – it contains publications treating the NWS as a concept or a paradigm referring to public management which were not mentioned in the third edition of Pollitt and Bouckaert's book.

These sources include an article by W. N. Dunn and D. Y. Miller (2007), most frequently cited in Scopus (as at 2 November 2016). In their paper, the authors present the NWS as Europe's critical response to NPM. In their analysis of the concept, they make references to three literature sources: the second edition of B. G. Peters' monograph *The Future of Governing* (2001), the second edition of C. Pollitt and G. Bouckaert's *Public Management Reform* (2004), and an article by W. Drechsler (2005b). Of these references, the latter two are the most important ones for the tracing of relevant inspirations and contexts. Only the last one has not yet been discussed in this study.

Drechsler's (2005b) characteristic of the NWS is based on the definition provided by Pollitt and Bouckaert (2004),[1] which mentions the distinction between the 'neo-Weberian' and 'Weberian' features, respectively. Drechsler complements the NWS functions listed by Pollitt and Bouckaert to arrive at an analytical model endowed with a normative function. In his view, 'an administrative system generally works better, of course depending on time and place, the closer it is to the NWS' (Drechsler, 2005b). As a result, the NWS, owing to its strong normative and empirical foundations, constitutes a reliable basis for reform efforts.

Unlike Dunn and Miller, Drechsler notes that the NWS is not in opposition to NPM, but rather constitutes its corollary with the benefit of hindsight, and as such can be called post-post-NPM. He supports his reasoning by reiterating his own previously published arguments (Drechsler 2003). He shows that traditional administration derived from the Weberian bureaucracy predominates in South-Eastern European countries. This observation reflects the classical approach to administration present in Weber's work published in 1946.[2]

In his analysis of European reforms, which he considers to be representative of NPM, Drechsler claims that the strong position of traditional public administrations across Europe can be consistently documented by research findings. In support of his assertion, Drechsler compares the Weberian bureaucracy with the European Administrative Space and European public administration standards included in the OECD study of 1999 (OECD 1999). He also emphasises the role that a stable state plays in economic development based on innovation understood in the Schumpeterian sense (Drechsler 2005a, p. 96).

The chronological analysis of citations presented above demonstrates that the main source of the NWS as an idea should be sought in Pollitt and Bouckaert's work (2004). These authors were the first to develop a framework for the description of reforms with five basic components related to finance, personnel, organisation, performance measurement, transparency, and open government. An analysis of data from twelve countries[3] on the ways and extent of implementation of reforms since the 1980s reveals certain differences among their groups. Recognising these differences, the authors used the term neo-Weberian state to refer to certain solutions typical of Western European countries.

Based on the discussion above, one may define the neo-Weberian approach as a reform model followed by certain continental European countries, which includes the preservation of positive attributes of the Weberian bureaucracy in the modernisation of the state apparatus (or traditional administration). A schematic diagram of these sources is shown in Figure 1.1.

Clearly, the NWS draws on a variety of cultural, doctrinal, management, and empirical sources. The first one reflects the criticism of progressive convergence

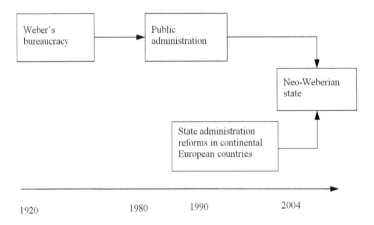

Figure 1.1 Origins of the neo-Weberian approach.

Source: Own study.

of states, societies, economies, and administrations as a result of globalisation processes. The second one refers to the backlash against the neo-liberal global vision of international order with its attendant proposals to limit state functions and to reduce its activity. The management aspect focuses on the distrust of the primacy of market-based solutions over other models managing public affairs emphasised by NPM, and overlaps with the last, empirical aspect in that there is insufficient empirical evidence to confirm of the superiority of market-based management mechanisms over other approaches.

The NWS can thus be understood in the following ways:

1   as a model of state which includes a set of specific values, institutions, struc-
     tures, and functions of a democratic, capitalist law-governed state embedded
     in European culture;
2   as a public management model with a relatively consistent set of concepts,
     theories and ideas about the rules, structures and mechanisms of governance
     drawing on the works of Max Weber;
3   as a specific category of reforms characterised by changes in state structures
     and public management mechanisms consistent with the assumptions of the
     neo-Weberian paradigm.

The aforementioned distinction is largely conventional and, as such, serves ana-lytical purposes rather than reflects the actual internal diversity of the approach in question. Its aspects overlap and mutually influence one another, which, in turn, makes it problematic to clearly mark their boundaries. In subsequent sections of this chapter, the ways of understanding the NWS are discussed in more detail.

The Neo-Weberian model of state

Understanding the nature of the NWS requires a reference to its underlying con-ceptual foundations. For very obvious reasons, these should be sought in the works of Max Weber. In his reflections on the modern state, he placed a particu-larly strong emphasis on the following issues relevant to the modern state:

- monopoly on legitimate coercion;
- legitimacy of power;
- territory;
- sovereignty;
- constitutionalism;
- non-personal power;
- bureaucracy;
- citizenship (Pierson 2004, pp. 5–6).

Weber recognised the monopoly on the legal use of violence to be one of the constitutive features of the modern rational state. In doing so, he invoked a long and rich tradition, for example the views of N. Machiavelli and T. Hobbes, who regarded such a monopoly as the basic principle of state-building. The idea materialised in the Treaty of Westphalia (1648) and in the concept of the modern nation-state. Weber defined the state as follows, adding a reference to the monopoly of power:

> Today, however, we have to say that a state is a human community that (successfully) claims the monopoly of the legitimate use of physical force within a given territory. Note that 'territory' is one of the characteristics of the state. Specifically, at the present time, the right to use physical force is ascribed to other institutions or to individuals only to the extent to which the state permits it. The state is considered the sole source of the 'right' to use violence.
>
> (Weber 1946, p. 78)

The above definition should be supplemented with Weber's comment concerning power. It reads: '[the] probability that one actor within a social relationship will be in a position to carry out his own will despite resistance, regardless of the basis on which this probability rests' (Weber 1978, p. 53). K. Tribe suggested one of the more recent translations of the definition: 'the chance, within a social relationship, of enforcing one's own will against resistance, whatever this chance might be based on' (Swedberg 2005, p. 205). However, it should be borne in mind that Weber did not advocate excessive use of force by the state. He claimed that violence is not a normal means of administration, and the threat to use it can be resorted to only if other options have failed.

For Weber, apart from the monopoly on legal violence, an equally important issue was the legitimisation of state power. He expressed it as follows: 'If the state is to exist, the dominated must obey the authority claimed by the powers that be' (Weber 1946, p. 78). At the same time, he asked: 'When and why do men obey? Upon what inner justifications and upon what external means does this domination rest?' In response, he described the following commonly cited types of power:

- traditional – 'eternal yesterday,' i.e. of the mores sanctified through the unimaginably ancient recognition and habitual orientation to conform;
- charismatic – the authority of the extraordinary and personal gift of grace, the absolutely personal devotion and personal confidence in revelation, heroism, or other qualities of individual leadership;
- legal – domination by virtue of 'legality,' by virtue of the belief in the validity of legal structure and functional 'competence' based on rationally created rules (Weber 1946, p. 79).

In the case of the third type of power, Weber explained that:

> obedience is determined by highly robust motives of fear and hope – fear of the vengeance of magical powers or of the power-holder, hope for reward in this world and in the beyond – and besides all this, by interests of the most varied sort.
>
> (Ibid.)

As a result, the modern state ruled by a legal authority is characterised by an administrative and political order subject to change through legislation, an administrative and political apparatus operating in accordance with the law, a supreme authority and the right to use force. Today, they can be considered as features of neo-bureaucracy (Ćwiklicki 2015).

The legitimacy of the legal order is thus based on the benefits that accrue from it, e.g. in the form of legal protection of private property, or ultimate ones expressing the will of God (Weber 1946, p. 51 ff.). Such a legitimacy results from the internalisation of power by both the rulers and the ruled.

The third important theme for Weber in the context of the state, essential for our understanding of the foundations of the state model based on the idea of NWS, is its duty expressed in terms of responsibilities. Weber saw the state as an entity responsible mainly for maintaining order and guaranteeing the security of citizens through the rule of law. This involved, first and foremost, the protection of private property and creating conditions conducive to the realisation of citizens' economic interests. The economic context in his thought included the state's monetary and economic policies which favour domestic producers by facilitating doing business.

Finally, according to Weber, the state should not be defined by its objectives and functions, but rather by specific means: '[O]ne can define the modern state sociologically only in terms of the specific means peculiar to it, as to every political association, namely, the use of physical force' (Weber 1946, p. 78).

Before we proceed to discuss the links between the NWS and Weber's perception of the state, it should be made clear that not all the views held by the German sociologist are clearly manifest in the NWS concept. One may rather notice certain elements, expressions, symptoms, and fragments of his thinking about the state, including mainly the issues related to the state as a political union, which has a strong impact on social and economic relations, uses various tools to manage them, and strives for sovereignty in international relations.

A significant impact on the conceptual foundations of the neo-Weberian state was exerted by such scholars as P. Evans, D. Rueschemeyer and, F. Block, T. Skocpol, Ch. Tilly, and S. Skowronek. Drawing on Weber's work, especially on his concept of the state, they developed it by emphasising the role of the state as an autonomous entity and a major causative factor driving social and economic change.

Recognising the power of capital, they hold that the state still enjoys a significant autonomy in terms of policy formulation and implementation (Block 1987). They perceive the state as an independent power in the process of socio-economic change, advocating the adoption of a 'state-centred perspective,' thereby undermining the Marxist narrative about the class nature of society:

> In contrast to most (especially recent) Marxist theories, this view refuses to treat states as if they were mere analytic aspects of abstractly conceived modes of production, or even political aspects of concrete class relations and struggles. Rather it insists that states are actual organisations controlling (or attempting to control) territories and people.
>
> (Skocpol 1979, p. 31)

For Skocpol, 'the state organisations ... have a more central and autonomous place', because just as Block does, she sees in the state 'potential autonomy of action over ... the dominant class and existing relations of production' (ibid.).

Just as Weber did, the scholars mentioned above emphasise the legitimacy of the state to exercise power, including the use of coercion. In their reflections, they appear to adopt a more minimalist understanding of legitimacy than Weber. Tilly defines the concept as 'the probability that other authorities will act to confirm the will of a given authority' (Tilly 1985, p. 171).

These researchers have devoted a lot of attention to analysing contingent relationships between the state and society, the nature and the extent state autonomy. They raise questions about the origins of state power and its potential for autonomous action, even if it is pursued in opposition to interest groups and social classes. They argue that a strong administrative apparatus developed in response to industrialisation and the fact that industrial relations grew more complex (e.g. in the United States, cf. Skowronek 1982). For a wider discussion of the views of researchers associated with the conceptualisation of the NWS, see Evans *et al.* (1985).

The foregoing discussion justifies the conclusion that the NWS is based on the idea of special importance of the state in social life and its unique role in solving collective problems. This model of the state is founded on the rules of representative democracy and procedural legitimacy, and, in the process of applying administrative law, shapes the relationships between citizens and the state (represented by its civil service).

From the NWS perspective, the desired model of the state results from the transformation of the neo-liberal vision of social order and the restoration of the strong position of the state in its dealings with the civil society sector and the market sector. However, it should be emphasised that the state does not enjoy an absolute autonomy and unlimited sovereignty in these relations, e.g. in its internal contacts with influential interest groups, or in the external ones, such as its membership in defence alliances.

The state can thus be a sovereign actor both in internal and in external (international) relations, and, as such, become an active participant in social and market processes. Yet the scope of state intervention may – under certain circumstances – lead to its omnipotence, which may threaten civil liberties and contribute to statist practices in the economy.

This raises the question of how to counteract the above-mentioned trends which invariably have negative effects on society and on the economy. The apologists of the NWS believe that a strong commitment of the state apparatus to the idea of democratic rule of law may constitute a viable safeguard. The descriptions of the state's role in socio-economic processes focus on its duty to coordinate rather than to command.

Consequently, the most important responsibilities of the NWS are based on the following expectations:

- to solve problems arising from globalisation processes, technological and demographic change, and environmental degradation, to counteract the destructive influences of globalisation;

- to create an institutional order which facilitates the achievement of critical social and economic goals;
- to pursue policies that respond to the needs of society.

The neo-Weberian public management model

The second perspective arising from the analysis of the NWS literature is the public management model, which draws on the Weberian tradition, particularly in the area of modern bureaucracy and the way it is organised according to the principles of scientific management. Furthermore, it invokes the idea of political neutrality of the civil service as understood by W. Wilson (separation of policy-making from administration). Important components of this model include aspects of NPM and public governance.

First, we shall discuss the issues of bureaucracy and bureaucratisation of social life in political theory pioneered by Weber, who saw in it a sign of modern times. The ideal type of bureaucracy presented in his works permits us to make an organised attempt to understand the process of rationalisation of social life and the legally authorised ways of exercising political power.

According to Weber, bureaucracy is a rational and objective structure. The bureaucratic state order is the most rational one and constitutes an important characteristic of the modern state (Weber 1946, p. 196ff.). Weber's notion was based on an analogy with the operation of complex machinery and reflected instrumentally conceived effectiveness modelled on Frederick II's Prussian army, as well as the mechanisation associated with the industrial revolution (Morgan 1986, pp. 21–22).

The adaptation of the scientific achievements of management research in public administration manifested itself in attempts to standardise the work of officials in order to develop a single best way of performing one's duties and supervising the observance of appropriate standards (Hughes 1994). Standardisation and regular inspections fit in well with the Weberian bureaucracy, because they ensure professional and efficient operation of the administrative apparatus in accordance with the law.

Weber believed that the modern bureaucracy operated efficiently:

> Precision, speed, unambiguity, knowledge of files, continuity, discretion, unity, strict subordination, reduction of friction and of material and personal costs – these are raised to the optimum point in the strictly bureaucratic administration and especially in its monocratic forms.
>
> (Weber 1946, p. 214)

The modern bureaucracy is primarily characterised by a monocratic official hierarchy, reliance on impersonal rules, documenting activities, separation of officials from ownership, stability of employment, qualifications, impartiality, political neutrality, and centralised control. The list also includes such auxiliary features as impersonality, rationality, specialisation, a civil service focused on achievement free of arbitrariness and the discretion that characterised earlier ways of organising bureaucracy. This is what Weber wrote about officials in the bureaucratic model:

According to his proper vocation, the genuine official – and this is decisive for the evaluation of our former régime – will not engage in politics. Rather, he should engage in impartial 'administration.' This also holds for the so-called 'political' administrator, at least officially, in so far as the raison d'état, that is, the vital interests of the ruling order, are not in question. *Sine ira et studio*,' without scorn and bias,' he shall administer his office. ... The honour of the civil servant is vested in his ability to execute conscientiously the order of the superior authorities, exactly as if the order agreed with his own conviction. This holds even if the order appears wrong to him and if, despite the civil servant's remonstrances, the authority insists on the order. Without this moral discipline and self-denial, in the highest sense, the whole apparatus would fall to pieces.

(Weber 1946, p. 95)

Weber believed that the effectiveness and rationality inherent in the bureaucratic model were universal, hence a global convergence of public administration towards a bureaucratic fashion would follow. In this way, it was supposed to be possible to rationally manage the processes of social change.

Some scholars choose not to mention the fact that although Weber considered bureaucracy to be a model solution, he was also concerned about its potentially devastating impact on individuals and their communities. His fears are reflected in the metaphor of the iron cage as the consequence of the bureaucratisation of the social world, in which bureaucracy appears to be an instrument of a dominant power over its members. He expressed this concern as follows: 'The individual bureaucrat cannot squirm out of the apparatus in which he is harnessed' (Weber 1946, p. 228). Referring to the potential consequences of the development of a rational bureaucracy in the area of technicisation and reification of social reality, Weber formulated a diagnosis with a great predictive power:

This living machine is creating the housing of future servitude. Like the fellahin [peasants] in the Ancient Egyptian state, people may one day have no option but to fit into this housing a purely technical – i.e. a rational – civil service administration and provision affords the final and only value determining the manner in which their affairs are to be conducted.

(Bellamy, Ross 1996, p. 324)

When trying to identify the effects of bureaucratisation, one may quote the observation made by A. de Tocqueville on 19th-century America:

[I]t covers the surface of society with a net-work of small complicated rules, minute and uniform, through which the most original minds and the most energetic characters cannot penetrate, to rise above the crowd. The will of man is not shattered, but softened, bent, and guided: men are seldom forced by it to act, but they are constantly restrained from acting: such a power does not destroy, but it prevents existence; it does not tyrannize, but it compresses, enervates, extinguishes, and stupefies a people, till each nation is reduced to be nothing better than a flock of timid and industrious animals, of which the government is the Shepherd.

(Tocqueville 2002, p. 663)

When analysing the consequences of the operation of a bureaucratic apparatus, Weber asks a fundamental question '[w]ho controls the existing bureaucratic apparatus?' In his view:

Under normal conditions, the power of a fully developed bureaucracy is always overtowering. The 'political master' finds himself in the position of the 'dilettante' who stands opposite the 'expert,' facing the trained official who stands within the management of administration.

(Weber 1946, p. 233)

The issue of preserving control over the administrative apparatus is also the subject of debate on the neo-Weberian public management model. It is argued that the capacity to do so depends on a strict observance of the legal order, and on the process of socialisation of officials construed as societal control over them.

Weber perceived administration mainly through the prism of legal regulations and procedures with all the aspects of operation of the executive branch being subordinated to the law. It should be noted that these issues constituted a key aspect of the modern forms of statehood dating back to the Middle Ages and referred to as the *rule of law* in England or *Rechtsstaat* in continental Europe (Izdebski 1997). However, they focused exclusively on the issues of constitutional guarantees pertaining to civil rights, while avoiding organisational issues and those related to the provision of public services. The emphasis on efficiency of administration in the theory of bureaucracy, in addition to legalistic considerations, made bureaucracy a powerful instrument in the hands of the state.

The neo-Weberian public management paradigm emphasises such features as a professional civil service, the rational organisation and operation of the state administrative apparatus, specialisation and professionalisation, formalisation, hierarchy, and procedures. These are also the characteristics that follow from the previously discussed ideal bureaucracy model and are listed in the document titled *European Principles for Public Administration* (OECD 1999). They also include reliability, predictability (legal certainty), openness and honesty, responsibility, efficiency and effectiveness. The cited document introduces the European administrative space and constitutes an example of increasing convergence of systems, structures, rules and mechanisms of public administration in Europe. This phenomenon leads to the consolidation of the European administrative space reflecting the history, identity and institutional specificity of each country, based on the tradition of European public law and the classic concept of public management. Such a convergence, however, does not lead to a complete uniformisation of rules, structures, and mechanisms in force in the administrations of individual EU member states, which continue to retain their distinctive features.

When discussing the neo-Weberian bureaucracy, one should mention the fact that it was considerably influenced by Wilson's work on the separation of politics and administration. Wilson explicitly stated that '[A]dministration lies outside the proper sphere of politics. Administrative questions are not political questions. Although politics sets the tasks for, it should not be suffered to manipulate its offices' (1887, p. 210). Thus administration emerges as a mechanism for the implementation of political decisions, which is reflected in the following statements made by Wilson: 'The broad plans of governmental action are not administrative; the detailed execution of dry plan is administrative' (ibid., p. 212) and 'public administration is detailed and systematic execution of public law' (ibid., p. 212).

These considerations lead to the identification of political and administrative positions in the public management system and to the introduction of parliamentary responsibility of ministers for the actions of their subordinate officials. The emphasis on staff professionalisation leads to the adoption of merit-based recruitment and the founding of a non-political civil service.

A review of the inspirations behind the NWS leads to the conclusion that the approach emerged in opposition to NPM, especially as regards the belief in a progressive convergence of governance mechanisms. The NWS is thought to address the theoretical and empirical shortcomings of solutions transferred to public administration from the business world. It assumes that the public sector has a specific organisational culture; as a result, the management methods developed to meet its needs do not fit any other type of organisation. Public organisations operate in accordance with the precepts of professionalism, modernity, efficiency, flexibility, and responsiveness rooted in the civil service ethos. The NWS stands in opposition to NPM, especially to the latter's supremacy of market-based management methods, which marginalise the value of solutions proposed by the state and its administrative apparatus. This mainly applies to the mechanisms introduced in the UK since the late 1970s, which contributed to undermining the classically understood civil service ethos.

However, the neo-Weberian public management model also comprises features characteristic of the market-based approach, including concern for the quality of public services and aspects of performance such as efficiency and effectiveness. Moreover, the outcomes of all the actions taken by public administrations are subject to evaluation.

The incorporation of NPM elements into the NWS may be construed as an attempt to eliminate the weaknesses of the bureaucratic model, such as its low efficiency, lack of flexibility, primacy of procedures over performance, and weak organisational learning mechanisms.

It appears, then, that the NWS is usually characterised in comparison with NPM. Its relationships with public governance have already been covered in this section.

The features typical of the latter concept include consultative and participatory mechanisms, which may be interpreted as an intention to address the defects of procedural democracy inherent in the Weberian model. These developments should be perceived as attempts to respond to an increasing empowerment of citizens and their communities, which is manifested by their desire to influence the shape of public decisions. Citizen participation in the decision-making process determines the extent to which the ensuing state actions are considered to be legitimate.

The neo-Weberian type of public sector reform

The third way of understanding the NWS – as a specific type of reform aimed at restructuring the state administration – includes the following aspects:

- professionalisation of the civil service;
- improving the efficiency of public administration, including public services;
- strengthening the public service ethos;
- bolstering the mechanisms for legitimising state actions;
- strengthening citizens' trust in the state;
- increasing the transparency and responsiveness of the state.

These reforms are implemented on an ongoing basis since the state apparatus is always considered to be in need of improvement. The emphasis on the modernisation of state administration is due to the reservations concerning the suitability of business methods for solving various problems faced by the modern state. These doubts grew out of the observations of the effects of market-oriented reforms, such as the fragmentation of the administrative system, the primacy of technologically conceived public management and public governance over their strategic and cultural aspects, insufficient compatibility of solutions devised using business tools, the blurring of rules and accountability mechanisms, the erosion of the civil service idea, and an excessive focus of the state on economic and financial aspects of its activities.

The reforms based on the principles of public governance have also been criticised, among others, for eroding the idea of democratic representation, diminishing accountability, disintegration of public management mechanisms, asymmetrical relations among the participants in the process of managing public affairs, and protracted decision-making. These ills are expected to be remedied by the Weberian model in combination with selected elements of NPM and public governance; Figure 1.2 shows that the neo-Weberian public sector reform constitutes an attempt to combine the advantages of the original Weberian model, NPM and public governance.

Countries which have undertaken reforms in the neo-Weberian spirit include Finland, the Netherlands, Sweden (Northern Europe) as well as Belgium, Germany, and Italy (Western and Southern Europe), but they all differ with respect to the substance, scope, and pace of change. The reforms were initiated in the Scandinavian countries followed by Western Europe. In recent years, their implementation began in Central and Eastern Europe (Kickert 2007, p. 47).

Interesting research into administrative reforms is being conducted by the European Group for Public Administration. Its members discuss, among other things, ways of strengthening the capacity of the public sector entities in order to solve certain problems related to the functioning of the economy and public service provision (Ongaro 2014).

The kinds of reforms implemented in these countries enable us to identify three types of trends in neo-Weberian reforms (they are presented synthetically in Table 1.1).

The third type of reform requires an additional comment. In countries representing the third group, one may observe the process of intense and simultaneous amalgamation of rules and mechanisms typical of different public management

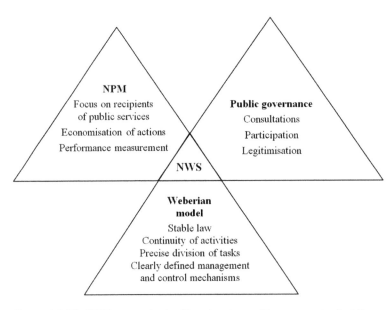

Figure 1.2 The NWS as a synthesis of the advantages of three concepts of public management.
Source: Own study.

Table 1.1 Types of neo-Weberian reform

Type	Features	Countries
1	• Improving citizen participation mechanisms • Strengthening the legitimacy of state actions • Improving the legal and law-enforcement systems	Finland, Sweden
2	• Professionalisation of the civil service • Management flexibility • Integration of strategic and financial management	Germany, Spain, Portugal
3	• Reorganisation of governance mechanisms and structures • Improving the efficiency and effectiveness of coordination of public actions • Improving the quality of law, democratisation of state–citizen relationships • Development of e-government	Poland, Czech Republic, Hungary, Slovakia, Estonia

Source: Own study.

models. After a period of rapid and sometimes chaotic implementation of reforms associated with NPM and public governance, these countries turned their interest to the neo-Weberian public management paradigm. This shift of focus was due to two reasons. First, it was a response to the prevailing disappointment with the consequences of the implementation of solutions offered by NPM and public governance. Second, it resulted from path dependence understood as a strong cultural impact of the German administrative tradition on the public administrations of Central European countries.

Conclusion

The origins of the neo-Weberian approach should be sought in a tradition that dates back to the era of enlightened absolutism, when the foundations of a democratic law-governed state were shaped. Later inspirations can be found in the Weberian conceptualisation of modern bureaucracy with its idea of a politically impartial administration and the principles of scientific management. Its more contemporary sources include the criticism of the neo-liberal vision of international order in its globalised form, challenging the perceived limitations on the functions of the state and its activities, and the rejection of the primacy of market-based solutions over other coordination mechanisms of collective action championed by neo-liberal public management models.

The neo-Weberian approach to the extent considered in this book may be understood as a form of state, a public management model, and as a type of administrative reform.

The neo-Weberian state can be defined as a democratic law-governed state with a market economy, whose government plays a central role in shaping socioeconomic processes and assumes the responsibility for providing citizens with a fairly broad range of public services. It employs diverse governance mechanisms, particularly those rooted in administrative law that serve to ensure equality before the law and to protect against arbitrary state actions. The basic form of legitimacy of the neo-Weberian state is a representative democracy.

The neo-Weberian public management model can be described as a way of managing public affairs that reconciles the values typical of the Weberian bureaucracy (e.g. hierarchy, specialisation, standardisation, depersonalisation, stability, non-involvement in politics) with those promoted by modern economics and management science (efficiency, effectiveness, quality, subjectivity). The distinguishing features of such a management model include a fairly powerful and stable corps of officials, a strong proceduralisation of activities rooted in administrative law, and an extensive use of hierarchical coordination mechanisms.

Finally, the neo-Weberian public sector reforms comprise changes whose normative layer is rooted in the values embodied in the neo-Weberian state and in the objectives that it intends to pursue. In their instrumental layer, the reforms transfer the economic rules and public management mechanisms fundamentally typical of the market-based approach to the neo-Weberian model of managing public affairs in a way that does not undermine the axiological or instrumental integrity of the latter.

Notes

1 Discussed in this monograph in Chapter 3.
2 Drechsler refers to Weber's original work of 1922 titled *Economy and Society* (published in English in 1946).
3 Finland, Australia, the Netherlands, United States, Canada, the United Kingdom, Sweden, New Zealand, France, Italy, Germany and Belgium.

Bibliography

Bellamy, R., Ross, A. (eds) (1996). *A Textual Introduction to Social and Political Theory.* Manchester University Press.

Block, F. (1987). *Revising State Theory: Essays in Politics and Postindustrialism.* Philadelphia, PA: Temple University Press.

Brown, R. H. (1978). Bureaucracy as praxis: Toward a political phenomenology of formal organisations, *Administrative Science Quarterly*, 23 (3), p. 365. http://doi.org/10.2307/2392415

Ćwiklicki, M. (2015). Towards neo-bureaucracy: bureaucracy in contemporary public management concepts, in: R. Wiszniowski, K. Glinka (eds). *New Public Governance in the Visegrád Group,* Vol.4. Toruń: Adam Marszałek, pp. 15–26.

Drechsler, W. (2003). *Managing Public Sector Restructuring: Public Sector Downsizing and Redeployment Programs in Central and Eastern Europe. Inter-American Development Bank.* Retrieved from https://publications.iadb.org/bitstream/handle/11319/4469/Managing%20Public%20Sector%20Restructuring%3a%20Public%20Sector%20Downsizing%20and%20Redeployment%20Programs%20in%20Central%20and%20Eastern%20Europe.pdf?sequence=2

Drechsler, W. (2005a). The re-emergence of 'Weberian' public administration after the fall of new public management: the central and eastern European perspective, *Halduskultuur*, (6), pp. 94–108.

Drechsler, W. (2005b). The rise and demise of the new public management, *Post-Autistic Economics Review,* 33. Retrieved from www.paecon.net/PAEReview/issue33/Drechsler33.htm

Drechsler, W., Kattel, R. (2008). Towards the neo-Weberian State? Perhaps, but certainly, adieu, NPM!, *NISPAcee Journal of Public Administration and Policy,* Special Issue: 'A Distinctive European Model? The Neo-Weberian State', 1 (2), pp. 95–99.

Dunn, W. N., Miller, D. Y. (2007). A critique of the new public management and the neo-Weberian state: advancing a critical theory of administrative reform, *Public Organisation Review,* 7 (4), 345–358. http://doi.org/10.1007/s11115-007-0042-3

Evans, P., Rueschemeyer, D., Skocpol, T. (eds) (1985) *Bringing the State Back In.* Cambridge: Cambridge University Press.

Hughes, O. E. (1994). *Public Management and Administration.* New York: Palgrave Macmillan.

Izdebski, H. (1997). *Historia administracji* [The History of Administration], vol. 4. Warsaw: Liber.

Kickert, W. (2007). Public management reforms in countries with a Napoleonic state model: France, Italy and Spain, in: C. Pollitt, S. Van Thiel, V. Homburg (eds), *New Public Management in Europe. Adaptation and Alternatives.* New York: Palgrave Macmillan, pp. 26–51.

Lynn, L. (2008). What is a Neo-Weberian state? Reflections on a Concept and its Implications, *NISPAcee Journal of Public Administration and Policy,* Special Issue: 'A Distinctive European Model? The Neo-Weberian State', 1 (2), pp. 17–30.

Mann, M. (1986). *The Sources of Social Power* (vol. 1). Cambridge: Cambridge University Press.

Mazur, S. (2016). The neo-Weberian approach – its origins, understanding of the term, and trends, in: S. Mazur (ed.) *The Neo-Weberian Approach in Public Management. From a Model to a Paradigm?* Warsaw: Scholar, pp. 15–26.

Morgan, G. (1986). *Images of Organization.* Beverly Hills, CA: Sage.

OECD (1999). European principles for public administration, SIGMA Papers, no. 27, OECD Publishing. http://dx.doi.org/10.1787/5kml60zwdr7h-en

Ongaro, E. (2014). The changed EU governance and administrative reforms in Member States under fiscal stress: Making the case for learning from similar countries, EGPA Policy Paper.

Peters, B. G. (2001). *The Future of Governing* (2nd ed., rev.). Lawrence: University Press of Kansas.

Pierson, Ch. (2004). *The Modern State*, 2nd ed. London and New York: Routledge.

Pollitt, C., Bouckaert, G. (2004). *Public Management Reform: a comparative analysis* (2nd ed.). Oxford and New York: Oxford University Press.

Pollitt, C., Bouckaert, G. (2011). *Public Management Reform: a Comparative Analysis: New Public Management, Governance, and the neo-Weberian State* (3rd ed.). Oxford and New York: Oxford University Press.

Seabrooke, L. (2002). *Bringing Legitimacy Back in to neo-Weberian State Theory and International Relations.* Canberra: Australian National University, Dept. of International Relations, Research School of Pacific and Asian Studies.

Skocpol, T. (1979). *States and Social Revolutions: A Comparative Analysis of France, Russia, and China.* Cambridge: Cambridge University Press.

Skowronek, S. (1982). *Building a New American State.* Cambridge: Cambridge University Press.

Swedberg, R. (2005). *The Max Weber Dictionary. Key Words and Central Concepts.* Stanford, CA: Stanford University Press.

Tilly, C. (1985). War making and state making as organized crime, in: P. Evans, D. Rueschemeyer and T. Skocpol (eds) *Bringing the State Back In.* Cambridge: Cambridge University Press.

Tocqueville, A. (2002). *Democracy in America.* Chicago: The University of Chicago Press.

Weber, M. (1946). Economy and society, in: H. H. Gerth, C. Wright Mills (eds), *From Max Weber: Essays in Sociology.* Oxford: Oxford University Press.

Weber, M. (1978). *Economy and Society: An Outline of Interpretive Sociology.* Berkeley, CA: University of California Press.

Wilson, W. (1887). The study of administration, *Political Science Quarterly*, 2 (2), pp. 97–222.

2 The social and political context of the neo-Weberian state

Michał Możdżeń and Michał Żabiński

The context of functioning of a modern developed state

It would be a truism to say that the contemporary state is facing challenges of an enormous magnitude. Due to the need (1) to manage the increasingly complex interdependences amongst the actors, both nationally and internationally, and (2) to strategically anticipate and respond to changes in the international environment, solving the problems of coordinating collective action appear to overwhelm the states managed through the traditional governance mechanisms. As one of the eminent Polish sociologists observed, 'the globalisation processes, once started, hold all the states hostage to the globalised market' (Marody 2014, p. 300). Indeed, numerous contemporary researchers argue that the coexisting processes of accelerating societal evolution and changes in the market and technology pose a serious challenge to the structures of the nation-state, which, it must be remembered, emerged in a completely different reality (Bauman 2000; Polanyi 2001; Dunsire 1996; Jessop 1998).

However, the structures created for the purpose of building a nation-state have not lost their usefulness. Their long-term relevance, despite the perceptible processes of hollowing-out of the state (Milward, Provan 1993) is confirmed time and again. An obvious example is, of course, the period of economic crisis, when the support provided by state institutions turns out to be crucial to maintaining the relative stability of the entire economic system. In a sense, crises reinforce the legitimacy of the state with respect to supranational organisations (cf. the relative effectiveness of US vs. EU policies after 2008), but naturally, the situation is far more nuanced. To paraphrase Mark Twain, 'the reports of the death of the state are greatly exaggerated'.

At the same time, one cannot fail to notice that the state is evolving in the face of external pressures. The fascination with reforms implemented in the spirit of NPM (which resulted in the hollowing-out of the state), and later, those based on public governance, resulted in conspicuous changes in the mechanisms of operation of the developed countries. They have also spread virtually throughout all the countries with what is known in the literature on the varieties of capitalism (VoC) as *dependent market economies* (Nölke, Vliegenthart 2009). Incidentally, in the case of the latter, this 'spread' often appears to occur in a distorted way.

Jessop (2007, p. 8) writes: 'the difficulty arises when it turns out that the discourse associated with 'good governance' often serves to legitimise neo-liberalism, justifying, in fact, a non-egalitarian and unjust economic and political project'.

In recent years it has become clear that political, social and economic changes have led to a situation in which the reforms implemented both in the spirit of the market and based on participatory mechanisms have failed to address external challenges. Such challenges often require strong and integrated action on the part of the public sector, yet the state – fragmented in terms of decision-making and access to capital – is not always capable of quickly mobilising adequate resources to counteract crises and alleviate their undesirable consequences. This is espe-cially painful for peripheral countries, according to a popular saying: when the US sneezes, the world catches a cold.

In this chapter, given the social, political and economic changes, which may, but need not, lead to a paradigm shift in the coordination of collective action, an attempt is made to draw a general picture of the situation of a developed country (an OECD or EU member state). The authors reflect on the consequences of the observed processes for the practice and philosophy of governance, among others, from the perspective of their capacity to reintegrate the idea of Weberian man-agement. It seems that several socioeconomic meta-processes particularly clearly affect the kinds of challenges faced by the state, including:

- global economic changes;
- social change and declining public safety (erosion of social safety nets);
- changes in international relations and shifting centres of sovereignty in favour of supranational organisations.

Naturally, the dimensions cited above do not exhaust the scope of change affecting the state (one may also mention e.g. the impact of non-state actors or advances in information technology). Besides, they are not analytically separable, but rather strongly interdependent. Still, for the sake of clarity of communication and limited space, the authors have decided to adopt such simplifying assumptions.

Economic changes and their consequences for the functioning of the state

At least since the beginning of the 20th century, social scientists have been aware of the fact that the development of markets is a process with a very high capac-ity to displace and subordinate various entities and institutions in other spheres of human activity (Weber 2012, p. 167). In the 1940s, Polanyi pointed to the changes which occurred in the 18th and 19th centuries in the political sphere under the influence of the markets' transformational potential. These changes included a clear definition of property rights (limiting the sphere of the commons), the freeing of the labour force by loosening the peasants' ties with the land, and the abolition of privileges of the political class, which led to the transformation of aristocratic relations into meritocratic ones (Polanyi 2001, pp. 36, 102, 162).

The transformation of the economic reality, which involved an unprecedented expansion of the market logic, does not seem to be subject to debate. Several interdependent trends observed internationally can be quoted in support of this view.

1   The progressive financialisation of the economy (Epstein 2005), which was not discernibly interrupted by the economic crisis, appears to proceed more and more independently of the efforts of individual states (Możdżeń 2016, p. 91).
2   In conjunction with the first process, there is an increasing scale of economic activity that manifests itself as the growing capitalisation rate and turnover of the world's largest enterprises (Flowers 2015). This process is possible owing to technological advances both in terms of communication and methods of managing complex global value chains (GVCs), which made it possible to integrate new economies within a complex network of dependencies (Grodzicki, Geodecki 2016). An additional factor which contributes to the increasing scale of economic activity is intensifying political globalisation (within just over 50 years, the number of intergovernmental organisations [IGOs] increased more than fiftyfold; cf. Table 2.1).
3   The monopolisation of large segments of the market, particularly striking in the area of IT products (explained in terms of returns to scale achieved by platforms operating on two-sided and multi-sided markets), the marked increase in economic and social disparities in developed countries, and the growing imbalance between the capital owners and the labour force are the consequences of interdependent processes of expanding business activity and advancing globalisation (Piketty 2014).
4   From the point of view of the business environment, there is the increasing importance of information technology in conjunction with innovations in management. This, in turn, results in changes in the manner and scale of service delivery thanks to flatter management structures (by facilitating the implementation of the democratic organisation principles also known as turquoise organisation or holacracy; cf. Laloux 2014; Varoufakis 2013; Robertson 2015), the blurring of boundaries among business partners, users, and employees (sharing or gig economy, crowdsourcing; cf. Allen, Berg 2014; Malone, Launbacher, Dellaroca 2009), or the emergence of network economies of scale in connection with the operation of platforms operating on two-sided and multi-sided markets constituting natural monopolies in the digital markets (Parker, Van Alstyne 2005; Rochet, Tirole 2006). At this point, one should also mention the potentially dangerous role of the

Table 2.1 Number of intergovernmental organisations in 1960–2013

Number of IGOs											
1960	*1966*	*1970*	*1976*	*1981*	*1986*	*1990*	*1996*	*2000*	*2006*	*2010*	*2013*
154	199	242	252	1,039	3,628	4,322	5,885	6,556	7,432	7,544	7,710

Source: UIA (2016).

rapidly improving quality of machine learning processes, which, in the long run, may further increase the imbalance between capital owners and labour (Brynjolfsson, McAfee 2016).

The above-mentioned changes justify the observation that business activity is undergoing a radical transformation. This carries considerable, both direct and indirect, implications for public management, which must be able to anticipate social change and respond to it in an active and decisive manner. The consequences include:

- the growing imbalance between the nation-state and the sphere of the economy resulting from the financialisation and growing international impact of business – the latter gets out of the state's control and is only efficiency-driven, not subject to democratic pressures;
- the emergence of tendencies which oppose the increasing scale of business operations (the expansion of transnational corporations), the rise of religious fundamentalism (the problem of terrorism), and the revival of nationalist sentiment;
- the precarisation of work resulting from the processes of globalisation and technological change, which leads to economic instability of hired labour and the increasing capacity of companies to exploit co-production in developing their products – users, who supply their personal data in the process, contribute to make the products more attractive (social networks operate according to this principle),
- the potential of technologies and new management methods to make public management more flexible (agile) and anticipatory (according to the concept of digital-era governance; cf. Dunleavy *et al.* 2006), which embodies the ideal of organisational and systemic learning in the public sector.

The increasing uncertainty of social actors

People always tend to perceive the times in which they live as tumultuous, while idealising the allegedly peaceful and stable past. References to this common belief can be found both in art (cf. Woody Allen's *Midnight in Paris*) and in popular collocations such as 'auld langsyne' or the 'good old days.' Man usually idealises the past, escapes into good memories from the hardships of the present and fears the future. For the citizens of Western European countries, the good old days are the period of prosperity in the 1990s, for Central and Eastern Europeans it is the turn of the century, the moment of their triumphant entry into the European Union, whereas for a considerable number of Russians they are the glory days of the Soviet Union. Each country and each generation chooses a different moment in its history to remember with nostalgia. In this respect, society of the second decade of the 21st century is not unique. However, in many other respects, it is unique. What makes our age exceptional is the technical and technological progress and the changes in the ethical standards, as well as the political and economic processes.

This is undoubtedly significant from the perspective of the shape of the modern society in the so-called developed countries, and from the point of view of the problems and social challenges facing the modern state. The democratic, liberal state, formed in the 20th century and changing under the influence of crucial historical events – such as World War II, the rise of the European Union, the Cold War, the crisis of the 1970s, the collapse of communism and the unification of Europe – is currently facing another serious challenge. A number of scholars (e.g. Goodhart, Taninchev 2011) argue that the state as we know it can no longer continue to exist and must change in response to the needs of society.

Sociology provides us with a number of definitional planes from which to explore society, its specific aspects, or even to question its existence (Giddens, Sutton 2014; Marody 2014). From the vantage point of analysing social processes, its main problems and their importance for the state, it appears appropriate to adopt an event-driven approach, according to which society is a constantly changing space filled with social events (Sztompka 2012, pp. 36–37). It allows us to capture the relationships between the society as a whole, individuals, the state, and the economic environment. However, any analysis of such complex phenomena requires a key which would allow for a consistent and logical presentation of contemporary society and the challenges that it poses to the state. Such phenomena as terrorism, growing social inequalities, the radical revival of nationalism and xenophobia across Europe and in the US, as well as immigration, or the economic crisis and the associated internal problems that affect the European Union, seem to indicate that such a key can be provided by the sense of security. Inspired by the list of the main challenges facing governments and states compiled by McNabb (2007, pp. xiii–xiv), we propose the following categorisation of problems:

1   *Security in the social sphere:* related to the issue of belonging, trust and sense of community, but includes also uncertainty and changing norms of social life, specifically:

   * loss of public trust in the power élites and in the capacity of the state to control capital;
   * increased uncertainty in the face of the impossibility to anticipate economic and political phenomena.

2   *Security in the economic sphere:* issues related to regulating the economy, including:

   * inequality of wealth and poverty;
   * increasing social stratification;
   * responsibility for managing the market sphere – increased expectations to regulate.

3   *Security in the political sphere:* seen through the prism of the role of the state and myths which assert the existing political order, currently threatened by:

   * the crisis of trust in the state;
   * the revival of nationalist movements.

Security in the social sphere

Society means people, their actions, culture, and interactions. Our behaviour is conditioned by the institutional structure in both of its aspects: the formal one (laws, money) and the informal one (norms and customs). Thanks to them we know how to proceed in a given situation, and formulate our expectations as to how others may behave. We observe these behaviours, but at the same time, we perpetuate and co-create them. They allow us to pursue our individual (although, in fact, universal) transactional needs: (1) to prove oneself; (2) to obtain positive feedback (benefits) within the interaction framework; (3) to enjoy a sense of group affiliation; (4) to experience trust; (5) to have a sense of existence (facticity) (Turner 2002, pp. 99–100; 2007, pp. 124–125).

Our capacity to meet these needs determines our desire to belong to a given social group. Further, group membership reflects our need to interact both with other people and other groups (institutions: representing the state, the social or market sectors, respectively). These interactions are based on trust. The higher the level of trust, the more frequent the interaction and the lower the transaction costs, and vice-versa (Uslaner 2002, pp. 17–23; Kramer 2004, pp. 153–156). Moreover, we grade trust from our closest relatives up to the level of the state (Sztompka 2007, pp. 103–105), and the shape of these relationships depending on the level of trust is of great importance in the economic and political dimension (Czapiński, Aksamit 2015; Hardin 2002, pp. 186–191; Krastev 2013, pp. 39, 49; Turner 2002, pp. 98–147; Sztompka 2007, pp. 245, 293, 303–304). Hence trust determines our sense of security with respect to other people, to the institutions of the state, and to the law.

According to OECD data (2015, p. 128), the level of trust has been increasing since the shock of the 2007/2008 economic crisis, but we tend to place more trust in others than in our national governments. Trust in others does not translate into public trust, i.e. in the state and public institutions, or in the political parties in particular. We shall discuss the issue in more detail in the section devoted to political security.

The critical importance of trust is associated with the problem of uncertainty (Sztompka 2007, pp. 67–70). Uncertainty in this context is defined as the impossibility to anticipate the future, and therefore to plan. Faced by this, we lose our comfort rooted in the belief that it is possible to prepare for future events (Beck, Giddens, Lash, 1994, p. 16; Taleb 2010). The complexity of the modern world, the fluid post-modernity (Bauman 2000, pp. 6–15), in which it is impossible not just to associate causes with effects, but even to distinguish the former from the latter, increases the decision-making complexity in the face of problems and ethical dilemmas (the so-called wicked problems; cf. Rittel, Webber 1973, pp. 160–161). Thus, it is increasingly difficult to estimate risk, with each subsequent decision only deepening the state of uncertainty (Beck, Giddens, Lash 1994, p. 20; Bell 1978, p. 98; Bauman 2000, pp. 132, 212–213). When faced with this phenomenon, society resorts to three main coping strategies: hope, belief, and trust – which constitute the only way in which man can actively cope with uncertainty (Sztompka 2007, pp. 67–70). An important factor influencing trust is the stability of social roles (Sztompka 2007, p. 97), which allows us to formulate clear expectations of individuals performing these roles, and thus to reduce uncertainty. However, an inherent part of our reality is the variability of these social roles, which results in the lack of their stable rooting in social structures (Bauman 2000, pp. 6–15). Accordingly, trust declines, risk grows, including the risk of social conflict, and society becomes even more alienated and atomised (Beck *et al.* 1994, pp. 21–23, 27; Bell 1978, pp. 88–91). All these elements reduce our sense of security.

Security in the economic sphere

The societal sense of security is undoubtedly affected by its economic situation, which, in turn, is significantly influenced by the level of inequality and poverty (Wilkinson, Pickett 2011). The importance of this issue was emphasised by Christine Lagarde, Managing Director of the IMF, who spoke at length about the process of accumulation of wealth, increased social stratification, and income inequality at the conference Inclusive Capitalism in 2014. According to data from the Oxfam Report (Hardoon, Ayele, Fuentes-Nieva 2016), in 2016 the total assets held by the 62 richest people in the world were greater than the combined wealth of the poorer half of humankind, i.e. 3.6 billion people (the year before it was the 80 richest). These 62 people constitute only 0.000001% of the world's population. Moreover, the process of capital concentration is inexorably progressing. In nominal terms, the assets of those 62 richest people in the last five years have increased by 44%, while at the same time, the assets of the poorer half of humanity have decreased by 41%. This phenomenon has had a damaging effect on the global economy, which is clearly supported both by IMF data (Dabla-Norris *et al.* 2015) and the findings of research conducted by Wilkinson and Pickett (2011) or Bagchi and Svejnar (2013), who have demonstrated a correlation between poverty/increasing wealth inequality and diminishing economic growth.

When discussing the role and functions of the state, it is particularly important to mention the fact that a significant negative impact on economic growth is exerted by wealth inequality resulting from politically motivated reasons (Bagchi, Svejnar 2013). The state must indeed implement fiscal and regulatory measures in order to reduce the level of inequality, yet public institutions of inferior quality may, paradoxically, strengthen the position of oligarchs, thus increasing the said inequality.

More importantly, wealth inequality weakens social ties, leading to an increase in crime, decline in the quality of life, inequalities in access to education and health care (Wilkinson, Pickett 2011). These disparities keep a substantial part of society in poverty understood as a limitation on the opportunities available to individuals to fully and valuably participate in social life (Giddens 2009, pp. 517, 530–531, 542–548). In consequence, the higher the poverty level, the more social conflict, and thus the lower the level of trust, which plays a key role in economic processes (Akerlof, Shiller 2009).

Security in the political sphere

Challenges to security in the social and economic spheres, however, do not always lead to changing the way the state operates. Indeed, history provides us with many examples of social inequalities and widespread poverty which did not trigger change. At this point, it is worth invoking Akerlof and Shiller's (2009) concept of narrative. Society needs a myth that justifies the hardships suffered by it or offers hope for the future, thus reinforcing the existing order of things. In the past, myths included such great ideas as Roosevelt's New Deal or the American Dream (USA), West German ordoliberalism, lasting peace and joint development (EU member states), the construction of a new socialist world (the Soviet Union), or even Bill Clinton's slogan 'It's the economy, stupid' so strongly associated with the belief in Fukuyama's 'end of history' and the absolute triumph of liberal capitalism (Blyth 2002).

In today's post-crisis world, it is no use looking for great, unifying myths; we find ourselves caught in a moment of discontinuity characterised by the loss of legitimacy of the hitherto universal order. It seems that we are dealing with systemic perturbations that will last until the world finds or develops a new global (?) modus operandi, or the countries forming individual communities agree on where they want to go together. Armed conflict still remains an alternative. This problem clearly applies to the European Union, which, nearly a decade after the outbreak of the economic crisis, is experiencing the greatest identity crisis in its history.

The growing distrust of globalisation, the weakness of the state which is incapable of responding to social and economic problems, is accentuated by its apparent lack of ability to tax transnational corporations and capital holders. This kind of fiscal incapacity leads to the radicalisation and polarisation of political attitudes (Krastev 2013, pp. 74–75).

These phenomena demonstrate the weakness of state institutions and undermine not only the existing order, but also question the existing mechanisms of power. The capacity of the state to collect taxes is, in fact, essential for public finances, which constitute an extremely important means of shaping society (Bell 1978, pp. 195, 208, 222). The global financial market is so influential that it can impose its logic on the economy and society, while the nation-states appear to be powerless (Castells 2009, pp. xviii, xxi, 104–105, 142, 147). All this contributes to an atmosphere of distrust towards the state and political parties, which are increasingly treated as agents representing international corporations, not the citizens (Krastev 2013, pp. 52–59). These views have been substantially influenced by the events surrounding such projects as the Anti-Counterfeiting Trade Agreement (ACTA), the Transatlantic Trade and Investment Partnership (TTIP), or the recent Comprehensive Economic and Trade Agreement (CETA).

All this results in increased distrust of state institutions, and thus contributes to undermining the legitimacy of the existing order. It manifests itself as decreased citizen involvement in the democratic processes, such as participation in the elections, social and political activity (Giddens, Sutton 2014, pp. 400–405), or the tendency to criticise such institutions and organisations as the police, schools, or local governments (Sztompka 2007, p. 107). Citizens are losing confidence in public authorities which cannot implement effective public policies and are incapable of preventing negative economic phenomena or mitigating their consequences, the best example of which is the economic crisis and the subsequent recession both in the US and in Europe (Krastev 2013, pp. 20–21, 24–25, 39, 61).

This should not be surprising since the contemporary political parties grow increasingly distant from the concerns of citizens who often find it difficult to identify the interests represented by those organisations (over 100 years ago, Weber expressed the same concerns regarding professional politicians). A particularly negative manifestation of this phenomenon is the revolving door between the worlds of politics, business, and administration. Perhaps its best illustrations are the careers of the former German Chancellor Gerhard Schröder in Gazprom, the Russian energy giant, and of the former European Commission President José Manuel Barroso, who, after his term in office, was employed by Goldman Sachs.

The absence of a pan-European or even broader global ideology in place of the outdated and outmoded slogans of neo-liberal capitalism and liberal democracy contested by ever-widening anti-establishment circles underlies the rebirth of nationalist trends which challenge the existing order, including the democratic rule of law (Krastev 2013). A revival of nationalist attitudes, of radical and populist parties is becoming more and more apparent throughout Europe. These groups, by denying the democratic legitimacy of the current élites, fuel distrust of the state and its institutions, as evidenced by both Brexit and the consistently increasing clout of anti-EU and right-wing parties (see Figure 2.1).

This phenomenon is visible both in the old democracies, such as the United Kingdom (United Kingdom Independence Party, UKIP) and France (Front National, FN), and in young democratic countries, such as Hungary (Fidesz – Hungarian Civic Union [Magyar Polgári Szövetség], or the Movement for a Better Hungary – Jobbik [Magyarországért Mozgalom]) and Slovakia (Ordinary People and Independent Personalities [Obyčajní Ľudia a nezávislé osobnosti, OĽaNO, or the radical-nationalist People's Party – Our Slovakia [Ľudová strana – Naše Slovensko]). Actions undermining the existing democratic standards have been undertaken in Hungary and in Poland. These processes are driven by the lack of trust in the democratic state in its current form.

The radical renewal movements – which demand a departure from the existing order, expect flexibility on the part of public institutions and a push for a public sector more attuned to social needs – may strengthen social ties and reduce uncertainty (Bell 1978, pp. 225–226), but they may just as well dismantle the democratic rule of law.

Shifting and centralisation of collective action coordination process

Mindful of the inevitability of the changes described above and their negative impact on the traditional instruments of the nation-state, individual countries

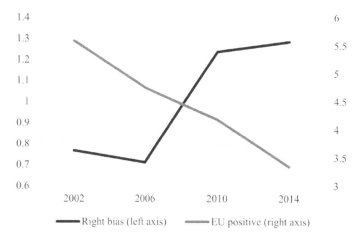

1.4   6
1.3   5.5
1.2
1.1   5
1   4.5
0.9
0.8   4
0.7   3.5
0.6   3
    2002   2006   2010   2014

━━━Right bias (left axis)   ━━━EU positive (right axis)

Figure 2.1 Right bias and support for European integration among parties participating in parliamentary elections in European countries (support-weighted). Values shown were calculated by standardising two variables from the Chapel Hill Survey: LRGEN, which assesses party position in terms of its overall ideological stance, and POSITION, which assesses the overall orientation of the party leadership towards European integration by setting the neutral position at zero and dividing it by 5 (for LRGEN), or by 4 (for POSITION) in order to normalise the scale to the range <–1, 1>. Indicators of ideological positions of each party in the database thus obtained were weighted via multiplying them by the amount of support for the party in the previous elections. In the next step, both ratios were averaged for each year and each country. As a result, the average was calculated for all the countries surveyed in a given year.

Source: Based on Bakker *et al.* (2015a, 2015b).

implement consolidation measures aimed at promoting all kinds of associations, unions, and societies, whose crowning example is the European Union (see Table 2.1). By doing so, they hope to balance out the growing domination of markets and maintain their own capacity to take pre-emptive action. The formation of these associations constitutes another process which strongly affects the capacity of the state as traditionally understood, even though sometimes (e.g. in the free-trade zones) it strengthens market actors with respect to the state ones. International governmental organisations seem to represent an attempt to respond to the expansion of the market sphere with a view to regulating it and bringing it under control.

    This process of shifting the coordination centres of collective action towards international bodies has its natural and clear implications for the capacity of national governments to act autonomously. Not only is the scope of their discretion diminished by certain obligations (e.g. to observe the World Trade Organisation agreements), but quite often, the decisions concerning the desired policy course related to matters traditionally considered as domestic ones tend to be made at the supranational level, which is more and more often the case in the EU. To a certain extent, progressive interdependence frees the state from internal pressures and encourages it to take creative action in order to adapt: 'The linkage of states into transnational structures and into international flows of communication may encourage leading state officials to pursue transformative strategies even in the face of indifference or resistance from politically weighty social forces' (Skocpol 1985, p. 9).

A good solution that facilitates tracking the shift in coordination centres to the supranational level is the European Semester introduced in 2011 as a consequence of the adoption of the Europe 2020 Strategy. It involves the annual monitoring of key development indicators covering social, economic, fiscal, political and administrative issues, and assists the member states in aligning their policies with the objectives and rules agreed at the EU level. National governments, as a consequence of the directions of change, are required to annually update the so-called National Reform Programme, in which they take into account the Commission's recommendations.

As a result of the above-mentioned processes, the centres of sovereignty undergo fundamental shift, especially in the case of less-developed countries, which benefit from development funds. These relationships, however, are not hierarchical, but rather transactional and delegational in nature (the EC delegates tasks to national governments, offering appropriate financial incentives). The system resembles in many ways the political process in a decentralised national system and has two major consequences: first, it puts pressure on the centralisation of political and administrative decisions at the national level, and second, it significantly hinders the use of various democratic mechanisms, since political guidelines are 'imposed from above.'

If the processes leading to centralised coordination of collective action at the international level continue (which is by no means certain), the legitimacy and effectiveness of actions taken by state authorities will have to be strengthened. This can be achieved by partially rehabilitating hierarchical management supported by representative democracy mechanisms instead of the sometimes specious public governance and decentralisation mechanisms. In other words, public management cannot function in a state of permanent imbalance between the actually used coordination mechanisms and the pressure of the political environment.

Conclusion

Doubtlessly, the above-mentioned trends emerging in the environment of the modern state have a huge impact on its capacity to act and on the desired form of interventions. They drive change in the institutional system in an attempt to ensure that the instruments and influence mechanisms in the public sphere remain compatible (association with technology intended) with the processes which occur in other areas. Without doubt, various countries, owing to the nature of their environment (position in global value chains, varieties of capitalism, level of social destabilisation, degree of political integration), react institutionally to the trends discussed above in different ways, especially if their respective path dependencies are taken into account. As argued by Pollitt and Bouckaert (2011, pp. 118–122), continental European countries naturally tend to strengthen their traditional forms of activity, which may be collectively called the neo-Weberian public management model (or the neo-Weberian state).

It appears that the challenges discussed above, although their selection may be considered somewhat biased, should be addressed in the neo-Weberian spirit. In our view, an effective response to them ought to comprise the following: (1) strengthening the role of the state in relation to private organisations; (2) promoting the redistributive function and ensuring an equal start in the face of growing socio-economic inequality; (3) making the democratic process more representative; and (4) improving the performance of state agencies by reducing the fragmentation of their activities and by using modern information and management technologies.

The discussion above is not meant to imply that the NWS is the only way to react to these pressures. Without doubt, however, its main advantage consists in the fact that it fits in well with the evolving economic and socio-political context, since it reaffirms representative democracy supported by modern public management instruments while strongly drawing on the Weberian model of administration.

Bibliography

Akerlof, G., Shiller, R. (2009). *Animal Spirits: How Human Psychology Drives the Economy and Why It Matters for Global Capitalism*, Princeton, NJ: Princeton University Press.

Allen, B., Berg, C. (2014). *The Sharing Economy. How Over-Regulation Could Destroy an Economic Revolution*, Melbourne: Institute of Public Affairs.

Bagchi, S., Svejnar, J. (2013). Does wealth inequality matter for growth? The effect of billionaire wealth, income distribution, and poverty. *Discussion Paper No. 7733.* The Institute for the Study of Labour (IZA).

Bakker, R., Edwards, E., Hooghe, L., Jolly, S., Koedam, J., Kostelka, F., Marks, G., Polk, J., Rovny, J., Schumacher, G., Steenbergen, M., Vachudova, M., Zilovic, M. (2015a). 1999–2014 Chapel Hill Expert Survey Trend File. Version 1. 1. Available on chesdata. eu. Chapel Hill, NC: University of North Carolina.

Bakker, R., de Vries, C., Edwards, E., Hooghe, L., Jolly, S., Marks, G., Polk, J., Rovny, J., Steenbergen, M., Vachudova, M. (2015b). Measuring party positions in Europe: The Chapel Hill expert survey trend file, 1999–2010, *Party Politics,* vol. 21, no. 1, 143–152.

Bauman, Z. (2000). *Liquid Modernity*, Cambridge: Polity Press.

Beck, U., Giddens, A., Lash, S. (1994). *Reflexive Modernization. Politics, Tradition and Aesthetics in the Modern Social Order,* Cambridge: Polity Press.

Bell, D. (1978). *The Cultural Contradictions of Capitalism*, New York: Basic Books.

Blyth, M. (2002). *Great Transformations: Economic Ideas and Institutional Change in the Twentieth Century*, Cambridge: Cambridge University Press.

Brynjolfsson, E., McAfee, A. (2016). *The Second Machine Age: Work, Progress, and Prosperity in a Time of Brilliant Technologies*, New York and London: W. W. Norton & Company.

Castells, M. (2009). The rise of the network society: the information age. In: *Economy, Society, and Culture,* Volume I, 2nd edition, Wiley-Blackwell.

Czapiński, J., Aksamit, B. (2015). Nieufny jak Polak. Z psychologiem społecznym Januszem Czapińskim rozmawia Bożena Aksamit [Distrustful like a Pole. Social psychologist Janusz Czapiński talks to Bożena Aksamit], *Duży Format*, 29 October, pp. 6–7.

Dabla-Norris, E., Kochhar, K., Ricka, F., Suphaphiphat, N., Tsounta, E. (2015). *Causes and Consequences of Income Inequality. A Global Perspective.* IMF.

Dunleavy, P. Margetts, H., Bastow, S., Tinkler, J. (2006). New public management is dead – long live digital-era governance, *Journal of Public Administration Research and Theory*, vol. 16, no. 3, pp. 467–494.

Dunsire, A (1996). Tipping the balance: autopoiesis and governance, *Administration and Society,* vol. 28, no. 3, pp. 299–334.

Epstein, G. A. (ed.) (2005). *Financialization and the World Economy*, Cheltenham and Northampton, MA: Edward Elgar.

Flowers, A. (2015). Big business is getting bigger, FiveThirtyEight Portal, http://fivethirty eight. com/datalab/big-business-is-getting-bigger/ (accessed 21 October 2016).

Foster, J. B., McChesney, R. W., Jonna, R. J. (2011). Monopoly and competition in twenty-first century capitalism, *Monthly Review*, vol. 62, no. 11, http://monthlyreview. org/2011/04/01/monopoly-and-competition-in-twenty-first-century-capitalism/ (accessed 22 October 2016).

Giddens, A. (2009). *Sociology,* 6th edition. Cambridge: Polity Press.

Giddens, A., Sutton, P. (2014). *Essential Concepts in Sociology*, Cambridge: Polity Press.

Goodhart, M., Taninchev, S. B. (2011). The new sovereigntist challenge for global governance: democracy without sovereignty, *International Studies Quarterly*, vol. 55, no. 4, pp. 1047–1068.

Grodzicki, M., Geodecki, T. (2016). New dimensions of core-periphery relations in an economically integrated Europe: the role of global value chains, *Eastern European Economics*, vol. 54, no. 5, pp. 377–404.

Hardin, R. (2002). Cooperation. In: R. Hardin. *Trust and Trustworthiness*, New York: Russell Sage Foundation, pp. 173–200.

Hardoon, D., Ayele, S., Fuentes-Nieva, R. (2016). *An Economy for the 1%. How privilege and power in the economy drive extreme inequality and how this can be stopped.* Oxfam International.

Jessop, B (1998). The rise of governance and the risks of failure: the case of economic development, *International Social Science Journal*, issue 155, pp. 29–46.

Jessop, B. (2007). Promoting good governance, disguising governance failure: reflections on policy paradigms and policy narratives in the field of governance, *Zarządzanie Publiczne* no. 2/2007, pp. 5–26.

Kramer, R. (2004). Collective paranoia: distrust between social groups. In: R. Hardin (ed.). *Distrust*, New York: Russell Sage Foundation, pp. 136–166.

Krastev, I. (2013). *In Mistrust We Trust: Can Democracy Survive When We Don't Trust Our Leaders?* TED Conferences.

Laloux, F. (2014). *Reinventing Organisations. A Guide to Creating Organisations Inspired by the Next Stage of Human Consciousness*, Brussels: Nelson Parker.

Malone, T. W., Laubacher, R., Dellaroca, C. (2009). Harnessing crowds: mapping the genome of collective intelligence, *MIT Sloan Research Paper*, no. 473–09.

Marody, M. (2014). *Jednostka po nowoczesności. Perspektywa socjologiczna* [The Individual after Modernity: A Sociological Perspective], Warsaw: Wydawnictwo Naukowe Scholar [Scholar Publishing House].

McNabb, D. (2007). *Knowledge Management in the Public Sector. A Blueprint for Innovation in Government*, Armonk, NY: M. E. Sharpe.

Milward, H. B., Provan, K. G. (1993). The hollow state: private provisions of public services. In: H. Ingram, S. Smith (eds), *Public Policy for Democracy*. Washington, DC: The Brookings Institution, pp. 213–235.

Możdżeń, M. (2016). The state – transformation and pressure from the environment. In: S. Mazur (ed.). *The Neo-Weberian State. Towards a New Paradigm of Public Management?* Warsaw: Scholar Publishing House.

Nölke, A., Vliegenthart, A. (2009). Enlarging the varieties of capitalism: the emergence of dependent market economies in East Central Europe, *World Politics*, vol. 61, no. 4, pp. 670–702.

OECD (2015). *How's Life? 2015: Measuring Well-being*. Paris: OECD Publishing.

Parker, G., Van Alstyne, M. (2005). Two-sided network effects: a theory of information product design, *Management Science*, vol. 51, no. 10.

Piketty, T. (2014). *Capital in the Twenty-First Century*, Cambridge and London: Belknap Press.

Polanyi, K. (2001). *The Great Transformation. The Political and Economic Origins of Our Time*, Boston, MA: Beacon Press.

Pollitt, C., Bouckaert, G. (2011). *Public Management Reform: A Comparative Analysis – New Public Management, Governance, and the Neo-Weberian State*, Oxford: Oxford University Press.

Rittel, H., Webber, M. (1973). Dilemmas in a general theory of planning, *Policy Sciences*, vol. 4, pp. 155–169.

Robertson, B. J. (2015). *Holacracy: The New Management System for a Rapidly Changing World*, New York: Henry Holt and Company.

Rochet, J. C., Tirole, J. (2006). Two sided markets: The progress report, *The RAND Journal of Economics*, vol. 37, no. 3.

Skocpol, T. (1985). Bringing the state back in: Strategies of analysis in current research. In: P. B. Evans, D. Rueschemeyer, T. Skocpol (eds). *Bringing the State Back In*, Cambridge: Cambridge University Press.

Sztompka, P. (2007). *Zaufanie. Fundament społeczeństwa* [Trust: The Foundation of Society], Cracow: Znak.

Sztompka, P. (2012). *Socjologia. Analiza społeczeństwa* [Sociology. An Analysis of Society], Cracow: Znak.

Taleb, N. (2010). *The Black Swan: Second Edition: The Impact of the Highly Improbable*, New York: Random House Trade.

Turner, J. H. (2002). *Face to Face. Toward a Sociological Theory of Interpersonal Behavior,* Stanford, CA: Stanford University Press.

Turner, J. H. (2007). *Human Emotions. A Sociological Theory*, Abingdon, Oxon: Routledge.

UIA (2016). Union of International Associations Statistics, www.uia.org/publications/statistics_(accessed 21 October 2016).

Uslaner, E. M. (2002). Strategic trust and moralistic trust. In: *The Moral Foundations of Trust*, Cambridge: Polity Press, pp. 14–50.

Varoufakis, Y. (2013). Varoufakis on value, spontaneous order, and the European crisis, EconTalk episode (recorded interview), 25 February 2013, www.econtalk.org/archives/2013/02/varoufakis_on_v.html (accessed 4 October 2016).

Wallerstein, I. (2004). *World-Systems Analysis: An Introduction*, Durham, NC: Duke University Press.

Weber, M. (2012). *The Theory of Social and Economic Organisation*, Eastford, CT: Martino Fine Books.

Wilkinson, R., Pickett, K. (2011). *The Spirit Level: Why Greater Equality Makes Societies Stronger*, New York: Bloomsbury Press.

3 The neo-Weberian state and paradigms of public management

Stanisław Mazur and Marek Oramus

Introduction

The neo-Weberian concept of state shall be compared with the basic public management paradigms – Weber's original, new public management (NPM), and public governance – along the following dimensions: the origins of the paradigm, functions of public administration, management instruments, public policy design and implementation, forms of public service provision, organisational structures, relationships between the administration and the social and economic actors, civil service models, mechanisms of organisational and systemic learning, and decision-making procedures.

Sources of the paradigm/concept

Traditional public administration

Fundamentally, the paradigm of the traditional public administration was influenced by three intellectual currents. The first one focused on building a professional and politically neutral corps of officials (Northcote, Trevelyan 1854; Wilson 1887). The second one relied mainly on the application of sound management principles (Fayol 1949; Gulick, Urwick 1937). The third one involved the principles of organisational governance and the operation of the state administrative apparatus. A prominent representative of the last trend is Max Weber, who considered bureaucracy to be the most rational organisational and functional form of administration.

To all intents and purposes, Weber's administration relies on a precise division of responsibilities complete with their detailed description, on a formalised system of orders and sanctions and a hierarchical division of roles based on specialist skills tested in the course of formal verification procedures. In his view, bureaucracy is characterised by efficiency, precision, speed, professionalism control, continuity, discretion, and the desire to maximise performance in relation to the invested funds. Qualified officials act according to general, abstract, and precisely defined rules. The bureaucratic organisation rests on a rationalised and impersonal nature of its structural elements and objectives that unite them (Weber 1946). Officials are expected to be competent, objective, impartial and loyal, guided by concern for the public interest.

Public administration is supposed to serve socially legitimised objectives in a way that respects the procedural order of the democratic law-governed state. However, this is not always the case. Already in the 1950s, social scientists wrote a lot about bureaucracy and formal organisation contributing to alienation and psychological dysfunctions (Gerth, Wright Mills 1953; Argyris 1957).

Bureaucracy exerts a significant negative impact on social life owing to the way it exploits the available resources (knowledge, information, expertise, secrecy) in order to appropriate part of the domain traditionally assigned to politicians. The process of autonomisation of bureaucracy results in such adverse phenomena as capturing public resources, securing illicit gains by interest groups, and maximising the budgets of public organisations.

Researchers who identify themselves with the communitarian approach emphasise the negative impact of bureaucracy on the fundamental values of a democratic society, such as freedom, equality, and justice. They point out, among other things, the inherent weakness of bureaucratic organisations, namely their inadequate responsiveness understood as the lack of capacity to make accurate social diagnoses, the inability to read societal preferences, and the inability to satisfy them.

In turn, the proponents of systemic theories, especially J. Habermas, imply in no uncertain terms that the world of systems rationalises social reality and subsequently colonises the world of life. Administration is also criticised by NPM, normatively correlated with the theory of public choice. Its theorists accuse administrations of taking over too much responsibility, wasteful spending of public resources, and poor performance.

The distinctive features of the traditional (classical) model of public administration are shown in Table 3.1.

New public management

The conceptual and ideological foundations of NPM can be traced back to public choice theory, neoclassical economics, and the neo-liberal doctrine. A market-oriented administration is conceptually rooted in economic theories which emphasise efficiency and effectiveness of public institutions. The ideological basis for reforms aimed at building such an administration was provided on the one hand, by the belief in the inability to perpetuate the too costly and highly inefficient welfare state model, and on the other hand, by the neo-liberal view that the public sector needed free-market mechanisms.

This model of public administration was promoted especially vigorously during the past thirty years by researchers and politicians espousing neo-liberal ideas. Its prominent representatives include such politicians as Margaret Thatcher, John Major and Ronald Reagan. Its conceptual foundations are based on the works of D. Osborne and T. Gaebler (1992), and C. Hood (1991). Their intellectual sources can be found in the writings of public choice theory precursors, e.g. A. Downs (1957, 1967), G. Tullock (1965), M. Olson (1965), and W. Niskanen (1971).

Table 3.1 Distinctive features of the Weberian administration

Dimension	Constitutive features
Role of government	'Rowing'
Management principles	Hierarchy
Management mechanisms	Legislation, regulation
Ways of defining public interest	Politicians supported by experts
Nature of public service ethos	Technocratic subordination to political superiors
Constitutive values of public service ethos	Hierarchy, neutrality, effectiveness, efficiency, loyalty, objectivity, responsibility
Rationality	Formal
Key resources	Public
Success criteria	Procedural perfection
Organisational structure	Bureaucratic
Relations with the environment	Exclusive
Nature of learning	Individual
Learning objectives	Literal adherence to procedures
Dominant public policies	Distribution, redistribution

Source: Own study.

The wave of market-oriented reforms swept through public management in the late 1970s and the 1980s, initially in the English-speaking and the Scandinavian countries. This type of reforms is usually defined as NPM. The key distinguishing market features in the operation of public administration included recognising market mechanisms as essential for the coordination of public activities and public service provision, orientation towards the customer (conceived as a recipient of public services), and the privatisation of a significant portion of the public sector. Equally distinctive features were deregulation, decentralisation and de-bureaucratisation, economisation of activities, and performance orientation (Bresser-Pereira 2004).

It is difficult to objectively assess the outcomes of reforms attributed to NPM, which is in part due to the lack of comparable and reliable international comparisons. However, their positive consequences included decentralisation of the administrative system, lower costs of public service provision and their improved quality, strengthened control mechanisms and accountability of public decision-makers, improved effectiveness and efficiency in managing public affairs.

On the other hand, the negative consequences resulting from the implementation of NPM-inspired reforms in the public sector included the weakened capacity of the state to solve structural problems both within and outside it, the primacy of technologically understood governance and public management over their strategic and cultural aspects, low compatibility of management tools adapted from

Table 3.2 Distinctive features of new public management

Dimension	Constitutive features
Role of government	'Steering'
Management principles	Exchange
Management mechanisms	Economic
Ways of defining public interest	Aggregation of interests and needs of citizens-consumers carried out by officials supported by experts
Nature of public service ethos	Management by objectives, standardisation of public services, quality measurement, privatisation, deregulation, contracting, public–private partnership, vouchers
Constitutive values of public service ethos	Efficiency, effectiveness, responsiveness, subordination
Rationality	Economic
Key resources	Economic
Success criteria	Effectiveness and efficiency of allocation of goods and quality of public services
Organisational structure	Decentralised
Relations with the environment	Partially inclusive
Nature of learning	Team-based
Learning objectives	Problem-solving based on economic criteria
Dominant public policies	Regulatory

Source: Own study.

the commercial sector with the public sector's requirements due to their inherent cultural differences, the fragmentation of the administrative system (numerous executive agencies) which hindered effective coordination and blurred the rules and mechanisms of accountability for the quality of governance, neglecting the broader context of activities undertaken by the state and public authorities by narrowing them down to the economic and financial dimension.

The main features of the market-oriented model of administration are shown in Table 3.2 above.

Public governance

The intended and unintended consequences of market reforms prompted reformers and researchers to explore new ways of modernising the state and its administration. The starting point for their search was the belief that administrative reforms based on the logic of NPM were 'instrumentally fetishised.' In other words, the approach in question emphasised the instrumental and technological aspects of managing public affairs without giving due regard to the systemic aspects of governance in a complex social reality.

The basic premises behind the development of the public governance paradigm included the development of multi-level governance (MLG) mechanisms and the limited capacity of public authorities to solve social and economic problems in a complex social reality in an imperative and hierarchical manner, as well as the unpredictability of problems and threats whose resolution or elimination requires the cooperation of the state with various social actors. The concept of public governance was based on: networking, MLG, reconciliation, deliberation, participation, partnership, dialogue, consensus, autonomy and responsibility (these distinctive features can be found in other paradigms; in this case, however, they are quite often found in combination with other features).

Public governance is thus founded on the following beliefs:

- Public values and objectives are established in the process of communication conceived in a manner corresponding to the principles of a republican democracy.
- Social actors share the belief in the importance of public affairs.
- Public objectives are achieved thanks to the synergistic integration of resources held by different social actors with different statuses.
- Public actions are evaluated using such criteria as responsiveness, concern for the public interest, justice, quality of cooperation with stakeholders.
- The state and social actors evaluate the ways of achieving specific goals and their associated mechanisms in order to improve them (Mazur 2011b).

The model of public governance is characterised in Table 3.3.

The critics of public governance focus on problems related to accountability, which arise from the dispersal of powers, the illusory possibilities of exercising control by politicians whose actual capacity to act has been substantially circumscribed. They also indicate the low level of steerability of governance processes resulting from the participation of numerous actors with different statuses, goals and interests. Moreover, public governance mechanisms are thought to be costly and involve protracted decision-making processes due to extensive consultation and bargaining procedures.

The neo-Weberian concept of state and public management

The neo-Weberian approach, when perceived as an intentionally constructed public management model, is a relatively new phenomenon. However, its inherent mechanisms have been applied in the administrations and economies of European countries for decades. Its cultural legacy has survived in many European countries and sustained its vitality, even if academic discourse and public debate seemed to be oblivious to its role or marginalised its validity.

The growing interest in the NWS can be interpreted as an attempt to remedy certain negative consequences of globalisation, including the erosion of sovereignty of nation-states and the undermining of their position in international

Table 3.3 Distinctive features of public governance

Dimension	Constitutive features
Role of government	'Mediation'
Management principles	Network
Management mechanisms	Debate, reconciliation, compromise
Ways of defining public interest	Dialogue of politicians, officials and citizens in search of satisfactory solutions
Nature of public service ethos	Public governance
Constitutive values of public service ethos	Dialogue, compromise, reconciliation, integration of resources held by social partners to further public affairs, participation, responsiveness, inclusion
Rationality	Reflexive
Key resources	Sharing (public, private, social)
Success criteria	Implementation of arrangements made by consensus
Organisational structure	Smooth, task- and process-based
Relations with the environment	Inclusive
Nature of learning	Organisational
Learning objectives	Innovative problem solving based on economic and social criteria
Dominant public policies	Regulatory, institutional

Source: Own study.

relations in comparison with transnational actors. The neo-Weberian approach has also gained in importance as a reaction to the 'hollowing-out of the state' and the adverse consequences of MLG. Its positive perception also results from the belief prevailing in numerous European countries that the state must curb the activities of various interest groups attempting to capture public resources, and return to those socially and economically important functions that determine its democratic legitimacy (e.g. the welfare state).

It is also possible to seek the origins of the neo-Weberian approach in the belief that the state must actively influence socio-economic processes, which is firmly rooted in the thinking of the political élites of continental Europe. It reflects the traditional understanding of the state as a political union whose natural duty is to work for the community of citizens and look after their well-being. The concept also offers a counterweight to the glorification of market management methods and their uncritical transfer into the public sector. Arguments that lend credence to the proponents of this position are provided by the unsatisfactory outcomes of reforms introduced under the aegis of NPM, and by the often criticised results of modernisation activities carried out in the spirit of MLG.

In summary, the sources of the neo-Weberian approach can be traced back to the following kinds of factors:

- *cultural* – questioning the belief in a gradual convergence of countries, societies, economies and governments induced by globalisation processes;
- *doctrinal* – a critique of the neo-liberal, global vision of the international order, of the proposals to constrain state functions and responsibilities;
- *managerial* – rejection of claims about the primacy of market management over other models of managing public affairs typical of NPM;
- *empirical* – lack of conclusive empirical evidence in favour of the superiority of market management mechanisms over other approaches.

The NWS opposes the Anglo-Saxon solutions, which promote the hegemony of market-based management methods, disparage the state with its administrative apparatus and undermine the classically understood civil service ethos so rigorously introduced into the public sector in the United Kingdom since the late 1970s. The NWS challenges the belief in a gradual convergence of market-oriented management mechanisms associated with NPM.

The nature, level and dynamics of neo-Weberian reforms in these countries vary. Initially, reforms in this spirit were undertaken in Northern European countries (Finland, the Netherlands, Sweden), and later, in Western and Southern European ones (Belgium, Germany, Italy). In recent years, they have been implemented in Central and Eastern Europe (Pollitt, van Thiel, Homburg 2007, p. 47). Generally speaking, there are three trends of reform within the neo-Weberian approach. The first one focuses on improving civic participation mechanisms, on strengthening the legitimacy of actions undertaken by the state and its administration, and on improving the legislation and enforcement systems. By and large, this path was followed by the Scandinavian countries. The second trend accentuates the issues related to the professionalisation of the civil service, management flexibility, and integration of strategic and financial management (e.g. Germany, Spain, Portugal). The third aims to reorganise the governance mechanisms and structures, to enhance the efficiency and effectiveness of coordination of public activity, to improve the quality of law, democratise the relationships between the state and citizens, and to develop e-government (e.g. Poland, the Czech Republic, Hungary, Slovakia, Estonia). In countries representing the third group, one may observe a radical and simultaneous amalgamation of rules and mechanisms typical of different public management models. After a period of extreme receptiveness to NPM and MLG with a somewhat chaotic transfer of the attendant mechanisms, Central European countries are now starting to show more and more interest in the neo-Weberian public management paradigm. This appears, in part, to be due to the prevailing disappointment with the effects to date of the implementation of NPM and MLG solutions, and in part, results from path dependence understood as a strong cultural impact of the German administrative tradition on the public administrations of Central European countries.

The characteristics of the neo-Weberian model are presented in Table 3.4.

Table 3.4 Distinctive features of the neo-Weberian model

Dimension	Constitutive features
Role of government	'Steering'
Management principles	Law
Management mechanisms	Hierarchy, reconciliation, compromise
Ways of defining public interest	Aggregation of citizen interests and needs made by politicians
Nature of public service ethos	Legalist and economic
Constitutive values of public service ethos	Legalism, efficiency, effectiveness, subordination
Rationality	Legalistic
Key resources	Economic
Success criteria	Compliance with the law, effectiveness and efficiency of allocation of goods and public service quality
Organisational structure	Centralised
Relations with the environment	Partially inclusive
Nature of learning	Team-based
Learning objectives	Problem-solving based on legal and economic criteria
Dominant public policies	Regulatory

Source: Own study.

A comparative analysis of public management models

Roles attributed to public administration

We shall begin our discussion of public management models with a review of functions that each of them attributes to public administration. This issue comprises primarily the relationships within the classic triangle, whose vertices are occupied by the public sector, the market, and civil society, respectively, whereas its sides represent the relationships among them (Hausner 2005, pp. 81–82). The division of functions and roles also determines the tasks for which actors representing different sectors are responsible, and, therefore, is crucial for the entire public management system.

The neo-Weberian public management model largely constitutes a response to the weakened role of the state, which resulted, among other things, from the domination in recent decades of NPM. The latter approach promoted market-oriented solutions, the broadest possible freedom to conduct business, in other words, it placed a great deal of trust in the private sector. The state and its administration became a secondary actor – it tried not to interfere too much in the functioning of the markets, and acted predominantly as an observer whose task was to remove the unnecessary administrative barriers. The state's role was to create institutional conditions conducive to an efficient and effective use of market mechanisms for managing public affairs. The state was also responsible for facilitating the cooperation of public and non-public entities for public purposes.

Recent years have shown, however, that this approach fails in the event of serious financial crises. When faced with severe economic turbulences, social actors (including business people) expect the state to intervene and thereby to mitigate their unfavourable effects (Oramus 2016, p. 44).

Consequently, the proponents of the neo-Weberian approach attempted to restore the primacy of the state in line with Weber's original recommendations. The neo-Weberian approach treats the state as a sovereign actor both in internal and in international relations. The NWS is based on the belief in a special importance of the state in social life and its unique role in solving collective problems. The model is founded upon the rules of representative democracy and, as such, has procedural legitimacy. The representatives of the state can exert pressure on other actors in order to resolve deadlocks and contribute to a more efficient achievement of the set objectives. It is worth noting that to that end, officials must exhibit a series of features listed by Weber, including expertise, precisely defined responsibilities, commitment to work, etc. (Weber 1946).

In summary, in the neo-Weberian public management paradigm, the state is not just an observer of the processes which occur in the socio-economic environment, as was the case under NPM. Neither is it a moderator cooperating on an equal footing with other stakeholders, which was advocated by public governance. Instead, it becomes the key actor responsible for coordinating collective action using diverse instruments, including the imperative ones.

Instruments for managing public affairs

Another feature that differentiates the various models of public management are the tools and mechanisms used by the administrative apparatus in order to perform its tasks efficiently. For example, the list of typical instruments advocated by NPM includes:

- contracting for public services (with entities operating both within the public sector and outside);
- establishment of executive agencies;
- analysing the feedback of service recipients and taking it into account in the management processes;
- emphasis on cost-effectiveness;
- performance-related remuneration;
- emphasis on organisational development and learning;
- implementation of management through quality;
- dissemination of strategic planning and management methods;
- higher turnover of employees in senior management positions;
- implementation of a number of programmes to measure administrative performance (Zawicki 2007, pp. 144–147).

The list above shows how many mechanisms characteristic of NPM were actually adopted in the neo-Weberian model. To mention just a few, opinion surveys among recipients and emphasis on the outcomes of actions taken, particularly in relation to the expenses incurred, are associated with the use of instruments intended to improve the management of public affairs through the implementation of quality management systems, outcome evaluations and motivating employees to perform better by means of a bonus system.

By comparison, the public governance model emphasises the mechanisms of network and non-hierarchical management. It is based on the assumption that the role of public authorities is to integrate the resources belonging to various autonomous actors (public, private and social) in order to solve collective problems (Mazur 2015). The model employs a broad set of instruments. They are not imposed by the authorities; instead, they are rooted in the interactions between the state and social actors. It is through this process that these instruments are produced, reproduced and improved. They can be divided into four categories: information, reconciliation, implementation and reflection (Mazur 2011a, pp. 21–22).

Improving public management mechanisms

Another issue is the way in which institutional change is implemented in the various models of public management. The most common dichotomous division in this respect is the distinction between evolutionary and revolutionary changes. The former assumes a gradual transformation of a given institution. The foundations remain essentially unchanged with modifications affecting other parts of the structure. Conversely, revolutionary changes require the institution to abandon its existing fundamental operating principles in order to build a completely new order. In a similar way, one may describe changes as complex (affecting the entire institution) or fragmentary (affecting only a selected part of the existing institutional structure) (Mazur 2011a).

If we look at the different public management models through the prism of the distinction mentioned above, it is worth considering whether changes in the existing procedures in public administration should be implemented incrementally, or any change in paradigm inevitably leads to the dismantling of the existing institutional order and to its fundamental reconstruction. In general, strategic planning plays an equally important role in each of these models. Certain difficulties are also associated with the implementation of change in a complex structure, such as a public administration system. Therefore, it appears that Pollitt and Bouckaert's proposal also leans towards evolutionary reforms. Fundamental reforms that are too radical may undermine trust in the state, yet the neo-Weberian public management model is expected to respond to the lack of trust not only in the market, but also in the state in its present form. Given these rigid and well-established structures, even an attempt to implement revolutionary change is likely to result in a hybrid solution containing undesirable elements of the rejected structure

(Mazur 2011a). The evolutionary approach to the implementation of change appears to be consistent with the neo-Weberian public management model. The proponents of this concept point out that the pro-market and pro-social solutions developed over the years should not be radically discarded in favour of the dominance of the state. Instead, the state should have its original role gradually restored by eliminating those elements of the previously existing models that have failed.

Public policy design and implementation

Another element that demands attention is the role of the neo-Weberian public management model in the design and implementation of public policies. It is one of the areas of state operation with a considerable impact on how other social actors perceive its effectiveness.

Public policies carried out in accordance with the Weberian model employ procedural and centralised tools based on hierarchical control mechanisms. They are founded on the belief that central planners and decision-makers can accurately define the problems, select appropriate measures to solve them and effectively supervise the implementation process. The basic mechanisms of public policy implementation include law, regulations, distribution and redistribution of national income. A special role is attributed to legal norms, which are believed to be capable of solving social and economic problems and of triggering positive change. This management model predominantly involves distributive and redistributive public policies implemented through vigorous legislative activity.

Under the NPM model, public policies are intended to achieve objectives usually expressed in economic terms. The policies themselves are decentralised and hybrid. They are based on transactional mechanisms rather than on hierarchical or imperative ones. The dominant type of public policy is regulatory. The strategic public policy directions are set in a centralised manner. However, the selection of operational goals as well as the mechanisms and instruments for achieving them is left to individual public offices and agencies equipped with a considerable autonomy. Public policies are carried out in a fairly decentralised organisational environment. Customers and stakeholders are actively involved in their implementation, particularly in the sphere of determining public service standards. This approach promotes flexible organisational forms such as contracting for services, internal competition mechanisms in the public sector, privatisation and deregulation.

Under the public governance model, public policies are based on network management mechanisms which take advantage of consultations, dialogue and compromise as the primary instruments for coordinating collective action. Public authorities are expected to integrate the resources belonging to various autonomous actors (public, private, social) to facilitate collective problem-solving. They primarily act as mediators. The key processes include regulatory and institutional policies based on consensual reconciliation mechanisms.

Public entities conducting public policies extensively use instruments that facilitate obtaining feedback from stakeholders and policy recipients. The latter are also often involved in the programming and execution of public policies. An important place in public governance is occupied by reflection on the outcomes of the implemented policies, which has led to the emergence of a new standard, namely evidence-based public policies.

In the neo-Weberian model, the state occupies a central position. It is seen as an entity equipped with the resources which enable it to conduct public policies effectively through legal regulations and the redistribution of national income. In the process of designing and implementing public policies, the state and its agencies cooperate closely with non-state actors on programming arrangements, on the implementation of public policies and on evaluating their outcomes. Despite the highly complex participatory and consultative mechanisms, the state assumes full responsibility for the effects of public policies and programmes.

The key features of public policies in the neo-Weberian model include both their strong reliance on law (legal procedures) and focus on performance. The practical consequence of the latter is the application of measurement systems to parametrise the actions undertaken by public authorities and to evaluate them in a fairly objective manner.

In summary, public policies under the neo-Weberian model are characterised by a relatively high degree of centralisation of programming, fairly centralised implementation mechanisms, the dominance of the state and its agencies in the sphere of public policies, broad participation of non-state actors in programming (especially in the Northern European countries), legalism, procedural exactitude, and the use of mechanisms for monitoring and evaluation in order to improve these policies and programmes.

Forms of public service provision

Another area which offers a distinct analytical perspective on the neo-Weberian public management model is the form of public service provision, which depends, among other things, on the legal status of the provider, payment type and schedule, or the kind of service. These forms may include:

- private firms (usually operating on a commercial basis);
- public enterprises;
- public institutions, local government bodies, and associations (Kożuch, Kożuch 2011).

The first legal form mentioned above (private firms) is characteristic of NPM. Public services are often purchased from entities representing this sector. According to the proponents of NPM, the provision of services by the public sector is, by definition, inefficient due to its lower motivation to perform given a stable inflow of public funds, overemployment and difficulties in keeping up with the prevailing market trends. The focus on the delivery of public services by private entities can be considered as the first wave of their de-statisation. It was thought that commercial entities offered the best response to these problems, but the role of the public interest in the entire process was underestimated. The private sector demonstrated yet again that it was primarily interested in maximising profits and in securing other advantages. The widespread disappointment with the market-based model of public service provision brought about the second wave of de-statisation, which took the shape of their communalisation. One of the foundations of the public governance model is public implementation of joint actions by the administration, bodies representing civil society, as well as the recipients of services. In co-production, there are no contractual relationships (ordering party – contractor). Citizens are involved in the production of goods/provision of services. The fact that they are not merely passive recipients encourages them to be more involved in the affairs of the local community and to contribute to social capital. It should be remembered that the discharge of public contracts by NGOs is not considered co-production. Note, however, that at the stages of organising, financing and monitoring the process of public service provision, the overall responsibility still rests with the state, even though it involves the other stakeholders in the system of public consultation or institutional communication platforms (Sześciło 2015, pp. 278–281).

The neo-Weberian public management model shows a clear preference for the delivery of public services by public institutions and firms (including utilities). NPM emphasised high quality of services while taking into account their cost-effectiveness. The former feature also fits in with the neo-Weberian public management model.

It should be remembered that in the neo-Weberian model, the state has a number of important responsibilities, which include those fulfilled through the provision of public services. The state is expected to solve the problems arising from globalisation, technological and demographic change, and environmental degradation. It is also expected to create an institutional order conducive to the achievement of important social and economic goals. Under the neo-Weberian approach, the state not only establishes the rules and makes sure that they are observed, but also becomes an active participant in social and market processes, apart from being the fund-holder and the service-provider.

Preferred organisational structures

Weber's original model is a rigid bureaucratic structure which excludes all the relationships of a personal nature and extra-rational reasons (Weber 1946). It is dominated by narrow, multi-level organisational structures with a limited remit. NPM advocates a more decentralised approach with a greater role played by local and regional levels, hence quite often decisions are made at lower organisational levels whose managers enjoy a greater autonomy. By contrast, public governance makes use of fluid organisational patterns, e.g. by teams responsible for solving specific problems. There is no uniformity in their management, and binding decisions are made by different people depending on the issue at hand (no uniform chain of command).

This aspect of the neo-Weberian public management model has not been char-acterised in detail, but given its embeddedness in the bureaucratic system, the presence of professional managers and the involvement of external actors in the decision-making process (including experts and civil society representatives), it seems fair to assume that it employs the linear-staff structure. The structure relies on the presence of advisory bodies attached to the most important managerial positions and responsible for, among other things, feeding the necessary informa-tion into the decision-making process (Nalepka, Kozina 2007, p. 91).

Such a structure appears to reflect the neo-Weberian public management model. Although it provides for the existence of a dominant power centre with an emphasis on hierarchy, it also appreciates the contribution of advisory bodies, which may include the representatives of academia, the private sector and civil society. Thus, to a certain extent, public administration is open to the outside world while retaining the monopoly on making final decisions.

When discussing the dominant organisational forms in different models of public management, one should remember that public administration is a very complex structure, whose constituent elements may vary between countries. Hence the linear-staff structure should not be treated as the only determinant of the neo-Weberian public management model; moreover, public administrations tend to employ hybrid solutions that combine elements of various models – their modifications reflect both historical and cultural factors.

Relationships with other actors

Another dimension of the public management models analysed here is the way in which they shape the interactions between the entities representing the state and other actors. While the neo-Weberian approach widely employs the solutions associated with the classical bureaucracy conceptualised by Weber, and to a lesser extent draws on NPM, in terms of relationships with other actors it tends to be based on public governance.

In order to illustrate these differences more clearly, we shall refer to the dis-tinction between imperative vs. interactive governance, which reflects the position taken by the state when attempting to influence other actors. The former implies the use of coercion in relation to subordinated entities in order to push through a decision deemed not to require consultation with stakeholders (Oramus 2015, p. 185). This approach can be controversial, given the complexity of the mod-ern world characterised by dynamics (changes in the system due to interactions), complexity (of relationships amongst the various elements of the system) and diversity (of elements in the system), all of which affect the very fabric of society and the socio-political systems (Kooiman 1993, pp. 35–43), as well as the limited capacity for knowledge acquisition by centralised power centres.

The advocates of the interactive model take a different approach to the issue of governance. The involvement of numerous actors and building strong relationships with the state should result in improved cooperation and greater benefits for all the stakeholders. In the interactive model, all the entities involved are treated as autonomous. No coercive measures are applied, since they would only serve to emphasise the differences, instead of helping to reach a consensus. Success depends primarily on the ability of all participants to assimilate the new rules for mutual interaction and to create effective solutions within a shared space (Oramus 2015, pp. 185–186).

The imperative model is characteristic of Weber's ideal bureaucracy. The state and its administrative apparatus have the monopoly on legislation and issue directives to other social actors. The state, owing to its extensive administration and a complex system of regulations, is the dominant architect of public actions and their main executor. Under this approach, the contribution of social and economic actors as partners of administration to the process of creation and execution of public policies is relatively small.

Over time, the preference for a more interactive approach culminated in public governance. This concept reflects the focus on the way in which the actors of different statuses, participating in the process of public decision-making, interact (Rhodes 1994). These interactions are not determined by state power, but by its ability to control the network relationships which mirror the dynamic interdependence of actors in the governance system (Chhotray, Stoker 2009). Power is dispersed and fluid, based on the reliance of actors on the resources held by others, which are deemed necessary for the achievement of the set objectives. Relationships are dynamic, constantly modified to respond to new expectations and challenges. In this approach, the problems of the state and its administration go beyond the boundaries of offices and public organisations, 'spilling out' into the territories belonging to other social actors (Stoker 1998). Thus, the approach emphasises the coordinating functions of the state acting in an environment of empowered stakeholders (Kooiman 2003; Rhodes 2007).

The neo-Weberian public management model allows for a certain degree of interaction with external actors, but the imperative approach remains its core feature. If we were to accept the opposite assumption, it would be difficult to reconcile the resulting contradiction with the neo-Weberian return to state monopoly in the area of law. Besides, the foregoing analysis has shown that strong legalism is one of the fundamental aspects of this model. In terms of the role of citizens, the approach in question appears to be most closely related to Weber's original concepts in that citizens are primarily voters who legitimise the state and the actions of its apparatus. The eight attributes of the neo-Weberian model proposed by Pollitt and Bouckaert include an orientation to the needs and desires of citizens (Pollitt, Bouckaert 2011, pp. 118–119), but the perception of stakeholders as partners is not likely to play a dominant role in the entire model.

The civil service model

The Weberian model of administration also gives rise to a specific bureaucratic public service ethos, associated with effectiveness, efficiency, specialisation, loyalty and neutrality. Apart from drawing on the constitutive features of the Weberian bureaucracy, it is rooted in Wilson's distinction between politics and administration (Wilson 1887), Taylor's scientific management theory (Taylor, 1911), and rationalism present in the works of Goodnow (1900) and Willoughby (1919).

The bureaucratic public service ethos corresponds with the procedural model of democracy and the logic of action typical of a technocratic administration. It is based on the assumptions that public objectives are established in the political process conceived in a manner corresponding to the rules of procedural democracy, and the means of achieving these objectives are instrumental and rational. Consequently, actions of officials are judged primarily by the criterion of legality and compliance with official procedures. In this approach, officials loyally, impartially and honestly serve their political superiors in achieving the goals formulated in a democratic political process (Mazur 2011a).

Under NPM, the market-oriented public administration developed its own unique ethos based on the belief in the central position of the citizen – understood as a customer – with respect to public sector organisations. The ethical conduct of a public official consisted in efficiency and effectiveness, rationality in public spending and maximisation of the quality of services offered by the public sector. The ethos of such an administration manifested itself in a pluralistic approach, which accentuated the importance of multiple centres of power, competition and rivalry in order to reduce the negative consequences and to instil a sense of public mission. The conceptual roots of this approach can be found in the theories of pluralism (Dahl 1961; Polsby 1963) and neo-pluralism (McFarland 2004).

The community-oriented public service ethos is based on the process of communication through which social actors (politicians, civil servants, citizens) define public problems and discuss ways to solve them. Once a course of action has been developed, they jointly participate in its implementation, contributing resources, and deal with the consequences of their decisions (Mazur 2011b). These relationships are imbued with concern for the public interest and a tendency to seek solutions likely to gain widespread approval. In the case of such a public ethos, officials are not only the executors of decisions formulated by politicians elected in the democratic process or public sector managers driven by the logic of economic considerations. Their duties go much further and embrace participation in defining and redefining the public interest, proposing courses of actions and taking responsibility for their implementation. The possibilities of cultivating the community-oriented public service ethos are seen in the normative approach. It is based on the idea of the relative ineffectiveness of the classical, formal instruments of control. Instead, it underscores the importance of the moral dimension of control, i.e. the socialisation and internalisation of socially shared values by officials.

The reforms pursued in the neo-Weberian spirit are aimed at the professionalisation of the civil service corps. They are primarily founded on the assumption that the state apparatus needs to be constantly modernised, but they also reflect the belief that the mechanisms adapted from the business world are not the only way of solving the central problems faced by the modern state.

Mechanisms of organisational and systemic learning

In Weber's management model, the mechanisms of organisational and systemic learning in public policies are reactive by nature. One of their characteristics is the small potential to take pre-emptive action. Adaptation consists mainly in improving organisational procedures, whereas their literal observance constitutes the basic criterion for on-the-job evaluation. An indirect effect of such an approach is that officials are not really motivated to innovate, because there are not expected to go beyond their strictly delineated responsibilities (Mazur, Olejniczak 2012, pp. 28–32).

The concept of organisational learning was made popular by NPM. The basic success criteria for officials and public organisations include effectiveness and efficiency in the allocation of goods and the quality of public services. The practice of systemic and organisational learning focuses on solving problems based on economic criteria. This change manifests itself, among other things, in recognising the importance of feedback provided by employees, which contributes to reflection and sometimes leads to the modification of the rules and mechanisms of managing public affairs. In this case, organisational learning is considered to be a team effort (Mazur, Olejniczak 2012, pp. 32–36). By comparison, the public governance model views producing solutions as a social learning process. Apart from the representatives of public administration, it involves broad stakeholder groups. Knowledge generated in this way is thus jointly produced by all the actors (ibid., pp. 36–41).

Organisational learning, which figures prominently in the neo-Weberian model, is believed to offer an opportunity to build a competent and professional clerical corps. The practice, however, tends to vary by country. In countries thought to represent this particular public management model (e.g. France, Germany, Spain, Portugal), the organisational learning mechanisms are similar to those characteristic of the Weberian model. Other countries (such as Norway, Sweden, Denmark, Finland) tend to follow patterns typical of the market-based approach combined with public governance (e.g. evaluation research, diffusion of innovations, measuring public service quality).

The role of administrative law

The dimensions through which we chose to characterise the individual models also include the role of legislation and regulation, which is reflected in Pollitt and Bouckaert's call to reform administrative law and to improve its enforcement as one of the eight major distinctive features of the neo-Weberian model (Pollitt, Bouckaert 2011, pp. 118–119). It should be read as an attempt to rehabilitate the importance of legal norms in the management of public affairs.

Weber's original approach is characterised by an essentially legalistic attitude to administration as the domain governed by regulations and procedures. It implies that all the aspects of functioning of the executive branch are subordinated to the law. It should be noted that these issues constituted a key aspect of the modern forms of statehood dating back to the Middle Ages and referred to as the *rule of law* in England or *Rechtsstaat* in continental Europe (Izdebski 1997). They focused on the issues of constitutional guarantees pertaining to civil rights, while avoiding organisational matters and those related to the provision of public services.

In this respect, the neo-Weberian model significantly differs from NPM (with its emphasis on management by objectives, deregulation, privatisation and public–private partnerships) and from public management (reaching consensus by debate). The dominant idea underlying the neo-Weberian model is the concept of a democratic law-governed state which guarantees legal security and legality of public administration activities. Such a strong role of the state may, under certain circumstances, lead to its omnipotence being seen as a real threat to civil liberties and freedoms, as well as to statist practices in the economy. According to the proponents of the neo-Weberian approach, such detrimental behaviours can be countered by a strong commitment of the state apparatus to the idea of the democratic rule of law.

The strong emphasis on the role of administrative law in the neo-Weberian model causes a certain dissonance in the context of the previously mentioned focus on results rather than on the primacy of procedures. This is another instance where one gets the impression that Pollitt and Bouckaert attempted to aggregate the positive elements of the other three models without paying sufficient attention to the contradictions among them. The neo-Weberian public management model focuses on administrative law and the procedures rooted in it as the main source of legitimacy for officials, which means that particular attention should be paid to optimising such procedures and tools as quality management systems or analyses and evaluations of public programmes. But in general, public opinion resents rigid adherence to rules and procedures, which partly results from the fact that Weber's original model led to a significant expansion of the bureaucratic apparatus and to an inefficient allocation of public resources (Niskanen 1971). However, such one-sided criticism seems to be incorrect. Accentuating the role of administrative law and its reform may be associated with a number of potential benefits, which include e.g. greater trust of citizens in officials resulting from improved control of their decisions and a greater impartiality owing to the need to rely on the binding interpretation of the law, not on one's own interests. Thanks to the precise delineation of responsibilities, it is also easier to avoid the duplication of procedural responsibilities, and, if need be, to take appropriate measures against individual officials.

Decision-making

The features of the individual public management models presented so far also affect what decision-makers actually do, which, in turn, translates into the operation of the entire public administration (for the purpose of this text, we identify decision-making with choosing among the available options). In practice, theoretical inquiry focuses on situations in which the decision-maker must select one of at least two options associated with a particular decision problem (Clemen, Reilly 2014, pp. 27–28).

The first important factor characterising the public management models under discussion, which has an impact on the decision-making process in the public sector, is the perception of the role of government. It may focus on solving social and economic problems through the direct performance of public tasks ('rowing'), it may develop public policies and engage in strategic planning ('steering'), or integrate the resources held by different stakeholders, including the private sector ('mediating') (Stoker 1998). Accordingly, this division determines whether the rulers themselves make decisions on public matters, or try to delegate them to other actors while adopting the role of facilitators. 'Rowing' plays an important role in the ideal bureaucracy model, but it is also present in the neo-Weberian approach, where it appears together with 'steering' (attributed to NPM).

Thus, under the hierarchical approach, the decision at issue, depending on how consequential it is, is taken at a particular organisational level, so, in principle, the situation of the decision-maker is always clear. In the case of management by exchange, the decision-maker is guided by market principles, i.e. by the desire to make public spending as cost-effective as possible. Finally, in the public governance model dominated by networks, decisions are taken on the basis of dialogue, negotiation and consultation, and result in reaching a consensus. Regrettably, the process is often adversely affected by problems typical of collective decision-making, such as the group-thinking syndrome (also called herd thinking), which was noted and described by Irving Janis, who analysed the behaviour of a number of decision-making bodies. The researcher came to the conclusion that decisions taken by such groups tend to be irrational, making little or no use of the expertise and authority of their individual members, which is reflected in the overestimation of group strength and morality, narrow thinking and a pressure towards unity (Janis 1972).

The most important features of decision-making in successive public management models include their success criteria. In Weber's ideal bureaucracy, the model public servant rigorously adheres to the existing procedures. In contrast, NPM focuses on the verification of the efficiency and effectiveness of decision-making. Eventually such an approach also began to be perceived as controversial, since it tended to measure everything in terms of material values and marginalise the interests of citizens. In response, public governance emphasised social participation and decision-making within networks involving the representatives of all the sectors, who had the opportunity to make a substantial impact on the choices eventually made by the representatives of the state. In this area, the neo-Weberian model seeks a compromise among the three solutions which seem to place fundamentally irreconcilable demands on the potential decision-makers. Thus, the ideal decision-maker should simultaneously observe the existing procedures, retain flexibility and avoid grossly inefficient decisions resulting from poorly designed regulations, while bearing in mind the opinions of the stakeholders participating in the process. Such a trilemma appears to be unsolvable, hence policymakers should strive for a compromise – by trying to negotiate a kind of golden mean amongst these values.

These aspects of decision-making are directly related to yet another factor, namely the nature of relationships with the environment in the process of making choices. Depending on the adopted approach, the representatives of the rulers may prevent third parties from expressing their opinions (exclusivity), allow them to have their say, but without having to take their opinions into account when making the actual decisions (partial inclusiveness), or ensure their full involvement in the decision-making process (inclusiveness). Both in the ideal bureaucracy model and in the neo-Weberian approach, an important role is played by the idea that representatives of the state apparatus serve society. Under NPM, the role of decision-makers in certain countries was significantly reduced due to the primacy of market-based solutions deemed to be more efficient in comparison with the fossilised and slow public administration. Under public governance, as shown in the section discussing the relationships between decision-makers and other actors, all the partners engaged in dialogue are equal in principle, but in practice, this assumption must be considered quite utopian.

Conclusion

The analysis presented in this chapter demonstrates that even though the constitutive features of individual public management models are quite distinct, they have certain attributes in common. This is due to the fundamentally evolutionary and incremental nature of the transformation of public management concepts, models and paradigms, with the exception of countries undergoing systemic transformation, such as the Central and Eastern European ones.

In the process of their evolutionary transformation, public management paradigms build up and amalgamate. Their individual characteristics combine, which leads to the presence of sometimes mismatched features in a single model, and to the emergence of internally diverse, often eclectic constructs. These components are partly complementary and partly antagonistic, or even mutually exclusive (e.g. this is how the heterogeneous public service ethos devoid of axiological clarity is shaped). Despite the problems with their unequivocal interpretation, it is still possible to identify their boundaries and their *differentia specifica*.

Finally, the process of convergence of public management paradigms usually involves the flow of certain specific characteristics among the paradigms in ways which do not undermine their basic structures or values in which they are rooted.

Bibliography

Argyris, C. (1957). *Personality and Organisation: The Conflict between System and the Individual*. New York: Harper.

Bresser-Pereira, L. C. (2004). *Democracy and Public Management Reform. Building the Republican State*. Oxford: Oxford University Press.

Chhotray, V., Stoker, G. (2009). *Governance Theory and Practice. A Cross-Disciplinary Approach*. London: Palgrave Macmillan.

Clemen, R., Reilly, T. (ed.) (2014). *Making Hard Decisions with DecisionTools,* 3rd ed. Mason, OH: South-Western, Cengage Learning.

Dahl, R. A. (1961). *Who Governs? Democracy and Power in an American City.* New Haven, CT: Yale University Press.

Downs, A. (1957). *An Economic Theory of Democracy.* New York: Harper and Row.

Downs, A. (1967). *Inside Bureaucracy.* Boston: Little, Brown and Company.

Fayol, H. (1949). *General and Industrial Management.* New York: Martino Fine Books.

Gerth, H., Wright Mills, C. (1953). *Character and Social Structure.* New York: Harcourt, Brace & Co.

Goodnow, F. J. (1900). *Politics and Administration: A Study in Government.* New York: Russell and Russell.

Gulick, L., Urwick, L. (1937). *Papers in the Science of Administration.* New York: Institute of Public Administration.

Hausner, J. (ed.) (2005). *Administracja publiczna* [Public Administration]. Warsaw: Wydawnictwo Naukowe PWN.

Hood, C. (1991). A public management for all seasons?. *Public Administration,* 69 (spring), 3–19.

Izdebski, H. (2007). *Doktryny polityczno-prawne. Fundamenty współczesnych państw* [Political and Legal Doctrines. Foundations of Modern States]. Warsaw: LEXISNEXIS.

Janis, I. (1972). *Victims of groupthink: a psychological study of foreign-policy decisions and fiascoes.* Boston: Houghton Mifflin Harcourt.

Kooiman, J. (ed.) (1993). *Modern Governance: New Government-Society Interactions.* London: Sage.

Kooiman, J. (2003). *Governing as Governance.* London: Sage.

Kożuch, B., Kożuch, A. (ed.) (2011). *Usługi publiczne. Organizacja i zarządzanie* [Public Services. Organisation and Management]. Cracow: Instytut Spraw Publicznych UJ.

Mazur, S. (2011a). *Władza dyskrecjonalna wysokich urzędników publicznych. Perspektywa nowego instytucjonalizmu* [Discretionary Authority of High-Ranking Public Officials: The Perspective of New Institutionalism]. Cracow: Cracow University of Economics Publisher.

Mazur, S. (2011b). *The Resource-Integrating State: Development Potential vs. the Quality of Public Regulations.* Cracow: MSAP.

Mazur, S. (ed.) (2015). *Public Governance.* Warsaw: Scholar Publishing House.

Mazur, S. (ed.) (2016). *The Neo-Weberian State. Towards a new paradigm of public management?* Warsaw: Scholar Publishing House.

Mazur, S., Olejniczak, K. (2012). Rola organizacyjnego uczenia się we współczesnym zarządzaniu publicznym [The role of organisational learning in contemporary public management]. In: K. Olejniczak (ed.), *Organizacje uczące się. Model dla administracji publicznej* [Learning Organisations. A Model for Public Administration]. Warsaw: Wydawnictwo Naukowe Scholar [Scholar Publishing House].

McFarland, A. S. (2004). *Neo-pluralism, The Evolution of Political Process Theory.* Lawrence: University Press of Kansas.

Nalepka, A., Kozina, A. (2007). *Podstawy badania struktury organizacyjnej* [Fundamentals of Organizational Structure Study]. Cracow: Wydawnictwo Akademii Ekonomicznej.

Niskanen, W. (1971). *Bureaucracy and Representative Government.* Chicago: Aldine Press.

Northcote, S. H., Trevelyan, C. E. (1854). *Report on the Organisation of the Permanent Civil Service.* London: House of Commons.

Olson, M. (1965). *The Logic of Collective Action: Public Goods and the Theory of Groups.* Cambridge, MA: Harvard University Press.

Oramus, M. (2015). Model współzarządzania (governance) i problemy dotyczące jego wdrażania w administracji publicznej [Governance and its implementation problems in public administration]. *Rocznik Administracji Publicznej* 2015 (1), pp. 179–195.

Oramus, M. (2016). Neoweberowskie państwo w kontekście globalnego kryzysu ekonomicznego [The neo-Weberian state in the context of the global economic crisis]. *Myśl Ekonomiczna i Polityczna* 1 (52), pp. 37–55.

Osborne, D., Gaebler, T. (1992). *Reinventing Government: How the Entrepreneurial Spirit is Transforming the Public SectorFrom Red Tape to Results: Creating a Government That Works Better and Costs Less,* 4th ed. Reading, MA: Addison-Wesley Publishing Company.

Pollitt, C., Bouckaert, G. (2011). *Public Management Reform A Comparative Analysis – New Public Management, Governance, and the Neo-Weberian State,* 3rd ed. Oxford: Oxford University Press.

Pollitt, C., Thiel, S. van, Homburg, V. (2007). *New Public Management in Europe. Adaptation and Alternatives.* New York: Palgrave Macmillan.

Polsby, N. W. (1963). *Community Power and Political Theory.* New Haven, CT: Yale University Press.

Rhodes, R. (1994). The Hollowing Out of the State: The Changing nature of the public service. *Political Quarterly,* 65 (2), pp. 138–151.

Rhodes, R. (2007). *Understanding Governance: Policy Networks, Governance, Reflexivity and Accountability.* Buckingham: Open University Press.

Stoker, G. (1998). Governance as theory: five propositions. *International Social Science Journal,* 50 (155), pp. 17–29.

Sześciło, D. (2015). Governance in public services. In: S. Mazur (ed.) *Public Governance.* Warsaw: Scholar Publishing House, pp. 275–291.

Taylor, F. W. (1911). *The Principles of Scientific Management.* New York, London: Harper & Brothers.

Tullock, G. (1965). *The Politics of Bureaucracy.* Washington, DC: Public Affairs Press.

Weber, M. (1946). Economy and Society. in: H. H. Gerth, C. Wright Mills (eds). *From Max Weber: Essays in Sociology.* Oxford: Oxford University Press.

Weber, M. (2002). *Gospodarka i społeczeństwo. Zarys socjologii rozumiejącej* [Economy and Society: An Outline of Interpretive Sociology]. Warsaw: Wydawnictwo Naukowe PWN.

Willoughby, W. F. (1919). *An Introduction to the Study of the Government of Modern States.* New York: The Century Co.

Wilson, W. (1887). The Study of Administration. *Political Science Quarterly.* 2 (2, June), pp. 197–222.

Zawicki, M. (2007). Instrumenty nowego zarządzania publicznego [The instruments of new public management]. *Zeszyty Naukowe Uniwersytetu Ekonomicznego w Krakowie,* no. 759, pp. 141–172.

Zawicki, M. (ed.) (2013). *Wprowadzenie do nauk o polityce publicznej* [An Introduction to Public Policy Sciences]. Warsaw: Polskie Wydawnictwo Ekonomiczne.

Part II

The neo-Weberian state and public policies

4 The neo-Weberian approach in economic policy

Tomasz Geodecki

Introduction

Until recently, the natural direction of the transformation of public management models was considered to involve the transition from the traditional Weber's model of administration, sometimes referred to as his model of ideal bureaucracy, to a new managerial solution in the spirit of new public management (NPM) and to public governance (Hausner 2008, p. 16; Mazur 2011, p. 215; Mazur 2016). The transformation was meant to reduce the involvement of the state administration in the provision of public services in order to achieve a greater flexibility and efficiency. It was recognised, however, that these reforms failed to solve a number important public policy problems (Białynicki *et al.* 2016); moreover, the withdrawal of the state from certain spheres of social and economic life had a number of negative consequences. The new, emerging management model reflects a more optimistic and trusting attitude towards the state apparatus (Pollitt, Bouckaert 2011).

This chapter constitutes an attempt to answer two related questions: Do the changing assumptions behind the operation of administration, endowed again with economic policy instruments, deserve to be called a transition to another, new model of public management? If so, can this new model be called the neo-Weberian state (NWS), as was suggested by Pollitt and Bouckaert? These questions are addressed by comparing:

- Weber's original model of administration as a frame of reference;
- the approach characteristic of public choice theory, which underlies the neo-liberal reforms in the spirit of the NPM (Bevir 2009);
- the evidence of a retreat from the managerial and free-market model and signs of a transition to another, new model of public management characterised by a more active role of the state in the sphere of economic policy (a kind of return to Weberian sources).

The analysis of views representative of the three perspectives addresses the three above-mentioned aspects of economic policy implementation, taking into account such criteria as economic effectiveness and public interest, specifically:

- the justification for an active role of the state in conducting economic policy, especially ways of supporting the expansion of domestic industry and of protecting it against competition from abroad;
- the involvement of interest groups in setting directions for economic policy;
- the effectiveness of incentives in the public sector.

The justification for pursuing a national economic policy

Max Weber's perspective

Max Weber did not share the optimism of his contemporaries regarding the peaceful nature of capitalism before World War I. He considered economic policies pursued by individual nation states to be necessary in the face of a growing economic competition among countries. In his lecture of 1895 ('Nation-State and National Economic Policy', in *Politics as a Vocation*, Weber 1998a) he argues that nations continue to struggle for a better position in the international division of labour, and this struggle is intensifying.

> Does anything change the fact that economic development began to affect the formation of a vast economic community of nations extending beyond national borders? Should we now abandon as useless the 'nationalistic' criterion of assessment, reject the 'national egoism' in economic policy? Did we really . . . overcome the need to fight that man wages for his economic self-sufficiency, for his woman and child? We know that is not so.
>
> (1998a, p. 168)

The economic interests of a country represent national interests to the extent that the nation is a vehicle for certain values recognised by Weber as universal and worthy of protection, such as thrift, diligence and business integrity, discussed later in his *Protestant Ethic and the Spirit of Capitalism* (2010). In Weber's view, the reference to a community of values constitutes a moral justification for the state pursuing a national economic policy. Shared values are what binds a political community together, hence the state should make economic decisions in order to preserve these values for the future generations: 'Our work, if it is to be meaningful, reflects concern about the future of our descendants' (1998a, p. 183).

The perspective of public choice theory

The assumptions and implications of public choice theory fit with the classical speculations concerning the reasons why individuals impose certain limitations on the market, as well as with the classical economists' call for these restrictions to be lifted. For example, according Adam Smith, customs duties reflect the merchants and manufacturers' concern for their business, which stands in opposition to the interests of the great masses of people.

In public choice theory, any limitations placed on the market (including free trade) by means of regulations is considered to be due to the activities of pressure groups. When regulations dictate how resources should be allocated, a certain proportion of activities in the economy is undertaken specifically with a view to securing favourable regulations. In an impersonal mechanism, resources are employed in order to maximise their utility to consumers, since this is the only way to achieve a greater profit. R. Tollison (1982) compares the cost of obtaining a favourable regulation to the cost of monopoly profits. Anne Krueger (1974) estimates that these costs are highest in the developing world, where the phenomenon of politically motivated rent-seeking is more widespread.

To all intents and purposes, public choice theory makes no mention of community interests, or else, it treats the concept only as a rhetorical device. Milton Friedman describes this mechanism as a reversal of Adam Smith's 'invisible hand:'

> There is, as it were, an invisible hand in politics that operates precisely in the opposite direction of Adam Smith's invisible hand. Individuals who intend only to promote the *general interest* are led by the invisible political hand to promote a *special interest* that they had no intention to promote.
>
> (Friedman, Friedman 1980, p. 281)

P. Krugman argues (1996) that economic policy aimed at achieving a better competitive position of the domestic economy is counterproductive. The very term *competitiveness* in relation to national economies is a 'dangerous obsession', because it suggests that trade restrictions can actually increase prosperity, while, as Krugman writes, we have known for 200 years why everyone benefits from free trade thanks to Ricardo's theory of comparative costs. For both of these reasons, interventions meant to improve the competitiveness of the national economy are considered to be inefficient. Gary Becker (1985) wittily summed up this view: 'The best industrial policy is none at all'. This postulate translated into the principles of the Washington Consensus marked 30 years of domination of market views on economic policy, defended, among others, by the World Bank (Wade 2012).

The reasons for and manifestations of departure from market-based public management models

The public sector appears to be back in order to play a more active role in economic policy. The concern for reindustrialisation and a bolder return to sectoral industrial policy are becoming visible (Gawlikowska-Hueckel 2014). The 'rehabilitation' of such an approach in the Western world is mainly due to the 2007/2008 crisis and several related circumstances:

- the pressure exerted on governments to protect employment and production;
- a precedent in the form of substantial aid to the financial sector (why not, then, support the real economy?);
- fewer and fewer segments of the market are thought not to require public intervention.

When analysed separately, certain activities do not appear to constitute a retreat from the principle of not distorting competition, but when they are interpreted together, they suggest a significant change in attitudes. The criticism of the so-called market fundamentalism (Wade 2012, 2015) seems to be gaining in popularity, especially in countries at an intermediate level of development, given their failure to catch up with the world leaders. The arguments quoted are based on the observation that due to free trade, only a few countries are allowed to specialise in high-growth production and generate technological improvements. Countries in whose economies no 'advanced' sectors exist are becoming more backward, while the rest of the world progresses technologically (Reinert 2007; Chang 2002). Owing to competition for the location of investment, postulated by the representatives of public choice theory, such countries are forced to make concessions to multinational corporations (Milberg, Winkler 2013). International tax competition thus triggered results in a reduction of social protection and poorer working conditions (Nölke, Vliegenthart 2009; Reinert, Kattel 2013). International integration paved the way to national disintegration, since the interests of the lower classes have been sacrificed on the altar of a narrowly conceived economic competitiveness. Paradoxically, such competitiveness may lead to underdevelopment. According to G. Myrdal (1958), economic underdevelopment results from a self-sustaining process of increasing inequality and exclusion of broad masses of society. Both market and political processes are aimed at maintaining the domination of élites. Since there is no global state or global solidarity, Myrdal argues, we are destined to build them on a smaller scale – as individual nation-states which conduct their policies according to the principle of patriotism. In this context, it constitutes a natural way of protecting the interests of all the citizens of a given country. The demand to curb class and other particularistic interests in the name of the common good is strongly reminiscent of Weber's ideas.

The responsibility for long-term economic growth and the well-being of citizens encourages governments to return to an active economic policy, which affects the allocation of resources among the individual sectors in the economy and influences the efficiency of manufacturing techniques (Stiglitz, Lin, Monga 2013 define industrial policy in these terms), because the markets fail to work effectively in these areas in times of crisis. In the United States, President Obama, in his 2013 State of the Union Address, said that his 'first priority is making America a magnet for new jobs and manufacturing'. The British Prime Minister in 2012 promised 'to have a proper industrial strategy to get behind the growth engines of the future' (Stiglitz, Lin, Monga 2013).

The European Commission drew attention to the issue of de-industrialisation, dedicating two of its flagship initiatives of the *Europe 2020 Strategy* (for 2010–2020) directly to industrial policy. It also launched the project 'An Integrated Industrial Policy for the Globalisation Era'. In 2012, A. Tajani, EU Commissioner for Industry, presented a programme for the reconstruction of European industry based on a number of key lines of support: R&D, SMEs in internationalisation, building human capital and improving access to finance.

In 2014, the European Commission urged to take 'immediate action for a European Industrial Renaissance'.

The development of manufacturing is important, because it constitutes an arena which reveals the comparative advantages of national economies in the production and exports of high value-added goods. In capitalism, profit and competitiveness of companies and nations result from their technological leadership (Schumpeter 1942; Fagerberg 1988). Those who witness the de-industrialisation of the West are seriously concerned about the fact that their economies are being deprived of sources of technological innovation, which entails the loss of good jobs and rising inequality (Rodrik 2015). In the European Union, one of these initiatives is the Innovation Union – a concept which refers not only to innovation in the economy as a whole (as was the case before 2010), but also distinctly emphasises the legitimacy of identifying those sectors in which support for R&D is likely to yield the greatest effect in the form of increased competitiveness (smart specialisations) (Foray *et al.* 2009; Commission 2012).

The demand for re-industrialisation and support for innovation has gained special traction in countries at risk of becoming stuck in the so-called middle development trap. This term reflects the persistence of the international division of labour and refers to the observation that in the last half-century (1960–2008), very few countries at an intermediate level of development made it to the high-income group. It was observed that out of more than 100 countries (Economist 2012) at an intermediate level of development in 1960 (in relation to the United States), only 13 managed to advance to the high-income group (including Greece, Israel, South Korea, and Taiwan).

Public administrations of these countries are becoming increasingly active in the sphere of economic policy. As was documented in the OECD annual review of economic reforms *Going for Growth,* countries which pursue the most vigorous economic policy include those in which slowing growth threatened income convergence (OECD 2015).

It was in the context of an active administration that economic policy came to the fore. In the 1980s, administrations started to gradually regain their place as key players in this area, but the overall trend was still barely perceptible. The first scholars to have noticed it were P. Evans, O. Rueschemeyer and T. Skocpol (1985). In their collection of essays, they pointed to the renaissance of Weber's concepts. The state was seen:

- not only as a form of societal organisation and reconciliation of interests of various groups competing for 'allocations,' but also as an institution that promotes a focus on production as a primary feature with respect to redistribution (Skocpol 1985);
- as the main actor that enables the developing countries to escape from the underdevelopment trap by focusing their efforts on accumulating capital and on negotiating favourable conditions for foreign investors, as evidenced by the East Asian countries (Amsden 1985; Evans 1985).

The role of interest groups in the organisation of economic policy

The Weberian perspective

The most important features of Weber's model of ideal bureaucracy (presented in his treatise *Economy and Society*) include its democratic character and decision-making without regard for persons. An exception to the rule of impartiality and primacy of administration is the engagement of certain social partners in determining important parameters of economic policy. Without their expert knowledge, the implemented solutions would be less efficient, since 'expertise is surpassed only by the bureaucracy, in the sphere of the economy, by the expertise of people engaged in private business' (Weber 2002, p. 987).

An in-depth knowledge of the various aspects of industry in which entrepreneurs operate is a prerequisite for their survival – successful businesspeople are the winners in the natural selection process. In this way, the bureaucratic apparatus gains an opportunity to find out about the specific parameters of important fragments of the economic reality in which it intends to pursue its policy. This, in turn, facilitates an efficient use of resources and helps to appropriately target support to domestic players competing in international markets.

However, one should not allow particularistic interests to prevail over the common good. Economic policy should not serve 'the current policy of rulers and ruling classes at a given time, but permanent, world power political interests of the nation' (1998a, p. 163).

In his essay 'The Nation-state and National Economic Policy', Weber refers to the widespread practice pursued by the Prussian Junkers of employing Polish agricultural workers from the Congress Poland, which led to unfavourable changes in the ethnic structure of Germany's eastern provinces. He argues that particularistic interests – those of individual social classes or rulers – must be regarded as secondary to the common national interest. An efficient bureaucracy can equalise the interests of various social groups in the name of *raison d'état*, while engaging the representatives of business in cooperation over the setting of objectives and parameters of economic policy.

The perspective of public choice theory

From the perspective of public choice theory, such a vision was considered to be too optimistic. M. Olson (1965) analyses the issues of pressure groups and demonstrates that, as a rule, large communities are incapable of organising themselves for collective action. Tightly knit groups are much more effective in pursuing their interests, since in small communities the incentives to act together are much stronger and the free-rider problem is much less noticeable. In *The Rise and Decline of Nations* (1982), Olson explains the reasons for different growth rates in various developed countries. Interest groups or their coalitions intent on changing the distribution of goods in society do their utmost to block the access of new members. This increases the complexity of reality and emphasises the importance of government, and hence bureaucratic forms of governance, leading ultimately to slower economic growth. In his work of 1967, G. Tullock compares the phenomenon of rent-seeking to a monopoly, where the net social loss is compounded by the cost corresponding to the monopolistic profit. Since the profit (from closing the market to newcomers) can be achieved through lobbying, doing so makes eminent sense. When the distribution of income is influenced by regulations rather than by market mechanisms, a significant proportion of resources is wasted. G. Stigler in his article of 1971 argues that in the 1930s, the truck weight control regulations in individual US states resulted from the relative strength of the agricultural lobby, the interests of the railway companies, and the public opinion. He goes on to prove that regulation arises primarily from a game of interests, not from concern for the public interest. In 1976, Sam Peltzman formalised Stigler's theory by demonstrating that the inclination of politicians to regulate (e.g. in the area of customs duties) results from a simple calculation: the anticipated number of consumer votes lost vs. the number of votes gained thanks to the funds obtained from the manufacturers favoured by the new regulations.

The representatives of public choice theory focus primarily on reducing the number of tasks performed by public administration (Tullock 1965). All the areas regulated by the state are open to the risk of regulatory capture: agencies originally established with a view to protecting the public interest begin to defend the interests of entities whose operation they were supposed to oversee. This phenomenon is more dangerous than no regulation at all, since it promotes private interests using state authority and resources. On the other hand, Olson favours a strong state, because only such an entity is capable of resisting the lobbying power of organised interest groups. M. and R. Friedman (1980) strongly argue in favour of the deregulation of social dialogue and the position of individual parties in it. In the chapter titled 'Who Protects the Worker?', they discuss the negative consequences of trade union activities, which as organised interest groups try to limit access to a number of professions and negotiate benefits for their members at the expense of other workers.

The reasons for and manifestations of departure from market-based public management models

The distinctly critical attitude towards the role of interest groups in the process of economic development appears to be changing, even though S. Lash and J. Urry in their book (1987) announced the end of an era of organised capitalism and asserted that the practices typical of corporatist systems would be disappearing in the coming decades. In retrospect, seeing the inaccuracy of those predictions, J. Grote and P. Schmitter (1999) reviewed selected trilateral agreements made by the EU15. The authors proved that in the 1900s, all those countries (apart from the UK and France) increasingly engaged interest groups in the process of coordinating public policies. The pressure of globalisation and structural changes in economies resulted in broader cooperation under the aegis of the state and within it (ibid.).

The British exception may be significant. The Anglo-Saxon countries have no developed traditions of corporatist organisations in the economy, which prompted P. Hall and D. Soskice (2004) to identify two types of capitalism. In their view, *liberal market economies* (LMEs), in which firms coordinate their activities primarily via hierarchies and competitive market arrangements, prevailed in the Anglo-Saxon countries, whereas in *coordinated market economies* (CMEs), firms depend more heavily on non-market relationships to coordinate their activities with other actors, more extensive relational contracting and more reliance on collaborative, as opposed to competitive, relationships in continental European countries. Yet in the last two decades, American economists have done a lot to discover the positive aspects of the inclusion of groups of interest in economic planning.

In his article written in 1995, R. Ball reminds us that interest groups may serve as a conduit of information to the sphere of policy and legislation. He argues that to the extent that such information allows governments to choose better policies, lobbying contributes to prosperity. Appropriately organised cooperation with representatives of industry, well-versed in running their businesses, may not only ensure the incorporation of the state's economic objectives in their policies, but even inspire such actions on the part of businesses that make long-term plans (Ashford 1993; Porter 2001; Morrissey, Lopez, Sharma 2015). D. Rodrik argues that the best results can be obtained thanks to social dialogue, and cooperation between the state and the business sector, which means that industrial policy is triggered by

> the *process* whereby the state and the private sector jointly arrive at diagnoses about the sources of blockage in new economic activities and propose solutions to them. . . . It simply requires it to build the public-private institutional arrangements whereby information on profitable activities and useful instruments of intervention can be elicited.
>
> (Rodrik 2006, p. 24)

In conclusion, the support of interest groups is increasingly appreciated since it assists the state and its administration in facing global challenges, including the challenge of international competitiveness (Halpin 2010).

After the fall of communism, the Central and Eastern European countries, which joined the EU after 2004, adopted certain solutions typical of LMEs. These included voluntary membership in business self-governing bodies (especially in those countries which initially sought to rebuild their pre-war system of interest representation; Duvanova 2015) and the relatively weak employee voice in order to remain competitive in terms of wages and worker protection schemes (Nölke, Vliegenthart 2009).

D. Ost (2010), who studied the social dialogue systems in Bulgaria, Czech Republic, Hungary, Slovakia, and Poland, argues that tripartism in CEE countries is only a mock symbol of corporatism – in fact, it is a fig-leaf for neo-liberally inclined governments cooperating with corporations. In this system, negotiations are specious, the parties do not comply with the agreements made and most private sector firms have no representation. This is due to the lack of willingness on the part of entrepreneurs to organise and the lack of class consciousness; as a result, tripartism helps secure labour's acceptance of its own marginalisation.

However, after the outbreak of the 2007/2008 crisis, in Central and Eastern European countries the first signs of change in the approach to the organisation of the interest representation system became apparent. B. Thorhallson and R. Kattel (2013) argue that the crisis affected the economies of Estonia and Iceland particularly hard due to the non-corporatist and neo-liberal features of their political systems. On the other hand, smaller economies with corporatist features appear to demonstrate a greater flexibility and resilience to fluctuations. Organised representations of interests also contribute to maintaining political stability built on consensus between the pressure for economic efficiency and the desire to foster equality among different social groups.

In recent years, other countries in the region have undertaken reforms aimed at strengthening social dialogue, including Hungary (Kren 2014) and Poland (SOR).

Incentives in the public sector

The Weberian perspective

In his *Economy and Society*, Weber (2002) identifies certain types of domination and discusses several of its varieties that occur with a greater or lesser intensity in various political communities throughout history. He considers the bureaucratic model of administration to be the crowning achievement of a rational and efficient way of domination. The modern bureaucratic apparatus is conducive to the formation of a unique kind of loyalty related 'to the material purpose supported by such ideas as the state, church, village, party, firm, but does not refer to any particular person' (Weber 2002, p. 938).

Accordingly, giving the administration a wide range of 'creative' freedom (p. 710) results from the recognition that 'the ultimate and highest lodestar for his [the official's] behaviour in public administration, the specifically modern and strictly "objective" idea of "raison d'état"'. Its implementation requires technical and economic efficiency: 'in principle a system of rationally debatable "reasons" stands behind every act of bureaucratic administration, namely, either subsumption under norms, or a weighing of ends and means' (p. 942), which promotes an effective and efficient implementation of public tasks. The issue of bureaucratic inefficiency is absent from the Weberian perspective, hence certain forms of national control over individual segments of the economy are considered to be legitimate and justified.

> Our descendants shall hold us responsible before history primarily for how much freedom of action we secured for them in the world and shall leave to them as legacy, and not for what kind of organisation of the economy that we pass on to them.
>
> (Weber, Fowkes 1980, p. 440)

The public choice theory perspective

The opposite view is held by the representatives of public choice theory. A. Downs in his *Economic Theory of Democracy* (1957) criticises the traditional models of the state and its administration, pointing to the fact that they all take for granted the existence of an altruistic homogeneous entity which, as soon as it finds out about the society's preferences and needs, will do everything to meet them. In fact, politicians tend to subordinate their political agendas to their objective of obtaining power, not vice versa. Owing to the possibility of winning the support of important social groups associated with specific industries, democratic governments tend to favour producers over consumers, since the latter cannot become an organised interest group.

The motives behind the operation of the administrative apparatus in a bureaucracy were analysed by W. Niskanen (1971). Its inefficiency is due to the asymmetry of information in the principal–agent relationships (agency problem). Such an organisation, unaffected by competition or market incentives, will likely set the number of services at such a level that their price will maximise the institution's budget. It offers the bureaucrats both a pretext to increase the non-cash portion of their salaries and an opportunity to raise their prestige and position (cf. also Tłaczała 2005). Thus, the administration's objectives are not identical with the objectives of its principal (society), which wants to obtain a large number of services at a low price (cf. Stiglitz 2004). The latter's political representatives have no effective tool with which to control public managers due to the asymmetry of information. The office manager always has an information advantage, and hence a stronger bargaining position in his/her dealings with the supervising body.

Given the administration's insufficient attention to the public interest, it was proposed that the number of tasks discharged by the public sector tasks should be limited. The provision of services should be entrusted to private entities, and power should be devolved, with a greater role of local governments, which was supposed to encourage tax competition and reduce public spending (Tullock 1965, pp. 221–224).

A summary of the key assumptions of public choice theory can be found in a manifesto of new public management compiled in 1992 by D. Osborne and T. Gaebler in their book *Reinventing Government*. It lists a number of recommendations regarding how administration should operate, as well as reasons why a large proportion its previously public tasks should be subjected to market coordination mechanisms. The titles of individual chapters of the book may serve as the main points of the programme of 'managerialisation' of public administration. Thus, in accordance with Osborne and Gaebler's recommendations, the authorities should:

* assign public service provision to entities other than the administration (p. 53);
* introduce the principle of competition into the system of service provision (p. 117);
* focus on the good of the citizens rather than strictly adhere to laws (p. 159);

- finance public services on the basis of performance instead of effort (p. 199);
- democratise the relations with internal and external stakeholders (p. 341);
- implement changes through markets instead of replacing them (p. 379).

Reforms in the spirit of NPM should result in the establishment of an administrative system which will curb the use of public resources for private purposes by improving management efficiency.

The reasons for and manifestations of departure from market-based public management models

Market-oriented reforms in the neo-liberal spirit characteristic of the 1990s met a growing public resistance in the subsequent decade. Market mechanisms in the provision of public services did not always yield the desired results; moreover, a deeper look at how the administration actually operated no longer warranted such one-sided criticism as that levelled by the proponents of public choice theory.

In view of the strengthening role of corporations and the privatisation of public services, the provision of such services has become the subject of a game of interests. Public administration abandoned a number of its important functions (e.g. health care, retirement security, public utilities), which has led to the questioning of its (democratic) legitimacy (Lynn, 2008; Pollitt, Bouckaert 2011; Kostakis 2011). Bringing it back (Seabrooke 2002, *Bringing Legitimacy Back*) requires restoring the administration's responsiveness to social needs, which sometimes entails its taking over the provision of certain public services. Activities to that end have been implemented, for example, in Canada (Chrabąszcz 2015) and in the United States, where it was observed that private partners contracted to provide services must be competently controlled by the administration, which either increases transaction costs or reduces the responsiveness of the public sector to social needs (Gluc 2015; Warner, Herfetz 2012). The increased professionalisation of public service provision at the local level was also observed in Germany (Kuhlman 2009), but without a clear impact on the dominant local administrative culture and at the cost of reducing the democratic control of administration.

A more positive attitude to the traditional public administration also results from in-depth studies of the public policy process in the spirit of new institutional economics. The findings show that the neoclassical models of bureaucratic action are too simplistic, especially if we take into account the heterogeneity of objectives pursued by the public sector, which makes it significantly different from corporations (i.e. in the latter, shareholder interests can be easily identified and parameterised). A. Dixit (2002), using the achievements of transaction cost economics, analyses the factors that may prevent the application of managerial methods in the public sector. The numerous and varied demands placed upon the public sector affect a wider range of stakeholders, often with conflicting interests, which means that the effectiveness of public policy should be assessed with greater caution (Dixit 1996, pp. 146–148).

A more significant retreat appears to be occurring in the area of recognising public administration's competencies in regulating economic processes in national economies. The scale of public intervention in the functioning of markets after the outbreak of the 2007/2008 crisis revealed the obvious need to regulate certain spheres of activity by the administration, until then believed to be effectively coordinated by market mechanisms. Moreover, transnational institutions showed greater empathy towards the activities of economic administration in the post-crisis years, when developed countries began to pursue large-scale interventions (Sharp, Loungani, Furceri 2016, *Neo-liberalism Oversold*, a very telling title in itself).

The European Union also began to notice the negative consequences of divorcing markets from political and administrative interventions, which, as was noted by L. Hooghe and G. Marks (1997), was built into the architecture of European governance through institutional impediments to market regulation. The elimination of national barriers to trade and capital flows has led to a rivalry both among companies and among governments in attracting capital through the so-called tax competition in line with the demands of market reformers. This, apart from the most important factor – the differences in wages – further encouraged businesses to move production to countries which reduce taxes and deregulate their labour markets. The consequences, however, involved the de-industrialisation of industrialised countries, lower pay and restricted workers' rights in less developed countries, and, as a result, the weakening of the bargaining position of labour in previously prosperous societies (Reinert, Kattel 2013; Milberg, Winkler 2013).

The fears of bureaucratic inefficiency and selfish motives have thus led to a reliance on the self-interest of entrepreneurs in the hope that the Smithian invisible hand of the market would deliver optimal outcomes for society. The current attempts to reverse the effects of the relocation of industry (re-industrialisation) require a committed and long-term-oriented public administration. It is needed especially in building an innovation-based economy, which entails tolerance for errors and a distant horizon of action – certainly not listed among the characteristic features of NPM. Therefore, the period of history in which we found ourselves after 2008 (expected to last for 20–30 years) is likely to be more friendly towards the state than the period of market-driven reforms at the turn of the century. This observation applies especially to the Central European countries, where, as Drechsler and Kattel (2008) note, several of the NPM-inspired reforms succeed only in systems based on a traditional, solid, stable and neutral Weberian bureaucracy. T. Randma-Liiv (2008) argues that this group of countries was particularly involved in the latter, which resulted in the unwarranted elimination of the state from important spheres of social and economic life, an emphasis on flexibility and cost-effectiveness at the expense of market stability (which is also needed), focus on deregulation, and ultimately, decentralisation without ensuring inter-agency coordination. Hence the challenge for the countries situated on the peripheries of Europe (including Central and Southern European ones) is not so much to implement reforms in the managerial spirit, which has happened all too often (Randma-Liiv 2008), but to rebuild their Weberian administration structures in order to make it possible to implement NPM reforms.

Conclusion

In response to the global economic crisis, which broke out in 2007/2008, and the slowing growth in developing countries, the legitimacy of active policy-making in the field of building and maintaining the competitiveness of the national economy is becoming increasingly recognised. This attitude stands in opposition to the demands of public choice theory with its attendant market-based and managerial model of public sector characterised by limited state intervention. These developments are accompanied by a discussion about the inclusion of entrepreneurs and interest groups in setting industrial policy objectives. The idea of a strict separation of business from administration is not as orthodoxly observed, because the benefits that accrue from access to information available only to entrepreneurs operating in a given market are quite clear. At the same time, it is becoming increasingly clear that analogies between the functioning of public administration and the business world are limited – for example, in the latter, it is much easier to define the interest of the principal. This fact marks a retreat from the employment of managerial methods in the public sector. In response to the first question posed in the introduction to this chapter, we may conclude that the administration's involvement in the economic reality via economic policy indeed means moving away from managerial models in favour of a less market-based public management model.

By way of summarising our considerations and in order to answer the second question, whether these trends actually reflect the neo-Weberian approach, it is worth recalling the findings of a study conducted by P. Evans and J. Rauch (1999). Analysing the impact of institutions on economic growth, they noticed that the existence of fairly well-developed forms of bureaucratic public administration facilitates the monitoring of state activity and the implementation of policies aimed at promoting economic development. Such a model of administration stands in opposition to the popular vision of the 'predatory hand of the state' (in opposition to Smith's invisible [and charitable] hand of the market). The hand belongs to the bureaucrat driven by the desire to maximise his narrowly understood economic benefits, who wants to capture public resources, in other words, behaves in accordance with rational choice theory. In the Weberian perspective, it is possible to appropriately set the parameters of the administration's operation, which should constitute one of the most important aspects of the state's institutional policy. Consequently, administration as a modern ruler becomes oriented towards reforms which raise public revenue through economic growth, not through plunder (Nee, Swedberg 2005, p. 807). In this spirit, Evans and Rauch analyse the relationship between the administrative apparatus organised in accordance with the principles of the Weberian bureaucracy and growth rates in developing countries in America, Asia, Africa, and Southern Europe in 1970–1990. They note a positive and statistically significant correlation between these variables (taking into account their GDP and human capital). They understand the Weberian bureaucracy as a kind of organisation of state agencies dealing with economic matters, whose attributes include an active involvement in the formulation of economic policy objectives and an appropriate combination of institutional solutions aimed at maintaining its loyalty to the state and detachment from individual interest groups, such as professional recruitment, employment stability, rate of overlap of work for the state with employment in the private sector, comparability of compensation in administration and in business, prevalence and the amount of bribing, as well as the attractiveness of employment in administration.

Thus, the neo-Weberian state reflects the rising social acceptance not only of the growing role of the state in the era of globalisation, but also of the reforms which appear to reaffirm the administration's commitment to achieving economic objectives.

Bibliography

Amsden, A. (1985). The state and Taiwan's economic development, in: P. Evans, D. Rueschemeyer, T. Skocpol (eds), *Bringing the State Back In,* Cambridge: Cambridge University Press.

Ashford, N. A. (1993). Understanding technological responses of industrial firms to environmental problems: implications for government policy, in: K. Fischer, J. Schot (eds) *Environmental Strategies for Industry*, Washington, DC: Island Press, pp. 277–307.

Ball, R. (1995). Interests groups, influence and welfare, *Economics and Politics*, 7 (2), July, pp. 119–146.

Becker, G (1985). The best industrial policy is none at all, *Business Week*, 26 August.

Bevir, M. (2009). Decentryczna teoria rządzenia [A decentral theory of governance], *Zarządzanie Publiczne*, 3 (9).

Białynicki, P., Ćwiklicki, M., Głowacki, J., Klich, J. (2016). The conceptualisation of the neo-Weberian state in the literature, in: S. Mazur (ed.) *The Neo-Weberian State; Towards a New Paradigm of Public Management?* Warsaw: Scholar Publishing House.

Chang, H. -J. (2002). *Kicking Away the Ladder: Development Strategy in Historical Perspective*, London: Anthem Press.

Chrabąszcz, R. (2015). Samorząd lokalny w Kanadzie [Local government in Canada], in: S. Mazur (ed.). *Sprawne państwo; Reformy samorządu lokalnego w wybranych krajach* [An Efficient State: Local Government Reforms in Selected Countries], Cracow: Cracow University of Economics.

Commission (2012). *Guide to Research and Innovation Strategies for Smart Specialisations* (RIS 3), Luxembourg: Publications Office of the European Union.

Dixit, A. (1996). *The Making of Economic Policy: A Transaction-Cost Politics Perspective*, Cambridge MA: MIT Press.

Dixit, A. (2002). Incentives and organizations in the public sector: An interpretative survey, *Journal of Human Resources*, no. 4.

Downs, A. (1957). *An Economic Theory of Democracy*, New York: Harper & Row.

Drechsler, W., Kattel, R. (2008). Towards the Neo-Weberian State? Perhaps, but Certainly Adieu, NPM! *NISPAcee Journal of Public Administration and Policy*.

Duvanova, D. (2015). *Building Business in Post-Communist Russia, Eastern Europe, and Eurasia: Collective Goods, Selective Incentives, and Predatory States*, Cambridge: Cambridge University Press.

Economist (2012). The middle-income trap, *The Economist*, 27 March.

Evans, P. (1985). Transnational linkages and the economic role of the state: An analysis of developing and industrialized nations in the post-World War II period, in: P. Evans,

D. Rueschemeyer, T. Skocpol (eds) *Bringing the State Back In*, Cambridge: Cambridge University Press.

Evans, P., Rauch, J. E. (1999). Bureaucracy and growth: a cross-national analysis of the effects of 'Weberian' state structures on economic growth, *American Sociological Review*, no. 64, pp. 748–765.

Fagerberg, J. (1988). International competitiveness, *The Economic Journal* 98 (June), pp. 355–374.

Foray, D., David, P., Hall, B. (2009). Smart specialisation – the concept, *Knowledge Economists Policy Brief*, no. 9.

Friedman, M., Friedman, R. D. (1980). *Free to Choose: A Personal Statement*. New York: Harcourt Brace Jovanovich.

Gawlikowska-Hueckel, K. (2014). Polityka przemysłowa i spójności wobec planów rein-dustrializacji Unii Europejskiej. Wnioski dla Polski [Industrial policy and cohesion policy in the context of the European Union's re-industrialisation plans. Conclusions for Poland], *Gospodarka narodowa*, no. 5, pp. 53–80.

Głuc, K. (2015), Samorząd lokalny w USA [Local government in the USA], in: S. Mazur (ed.). *Sprawne państwo; Reformy samorządu lokalnego w wybranych krajach* [An Efficient State: Local Government Reforms in Selected Countries]. Cracow: Cracow University of Economics.

Grote, J., Schmitter, P. C. (1999). The renaissance of national corporatism: unintended side-effect of Economic and Monetary Union or calculated response to the absence of European Social Policy? *Transfer*, 5 (1, 2), pp. 34–63.

Hall, P. A., Soskice, D. (2004). *Varieties of Capitalism: The Institutional Foundations of Comparative Advantage*. Oxford: Oxford University Press.

Halpin, D. (2010). *Groups, Representation and Democracy; Between Promise and Practice*. Manchester and New York: Manchester University Press.

Hausner, J. (2008). *Zarządzanie publiczne* [Public Management]. Warsaw: Wydawnictwo Naukowe Scholar.

Hooghe, L., Marks, G. (1997). The making of a polity: The struggle over European integration, *European Integration online Papers (EIoP)*, 1 (4). http://eiop.or.at/eiop/texte/1997–004a.htm [accessed 1 March 2015].

Kostakis, V. (2011). Commons-based peer production and the neo-Weberian state: synergies and interdependencies, *Halduskultuur – Administrative Culture*, 12 (2), pp. 146–161.

Krén, I. (2014). *Hungary – Labour Relations and Social Dialogue*, Annual Report. Friedrich Ebert Stiftung.

Krueger, A. O. (1974). The political economy of the rent-seeking society, *American Economic Review*, 64 (3), pp. 291–303.

Krugman, P. (1996). Making sense of the competitiveness debate, *Oxford Review of Economic Policy*, 12 (3).

Kuhlmann, S. (2009). Reforming local government in Germany: institutional changes and performance impacts, *German Politics*, 18 (2).

Lash, S., Urry, J. (1987). *The End of Organised Capitalism*. Cambridge: Polity Press.

Lynn, L. (2008). What is a neo-Weberian state? Reflections on a concept and its impli-cations, *NISPAcee Journal of Public Administration and Policy*, Special issue: 'A distinctive European model? The Neo-Weberian State.

Mazur, S. (2011). *Władza dyskrecjonalna wysokich urzędników publicznych. Perspektywa nowego instytucjonalizmu* [Discretionary Authority of High-Ranking Public Officials: The Perspective of New Institutionalism], Cracow: Cracow University of Economics Publisher.

Mazur, S. (2016). The neo-Weberian approach – its origins, understanding of the term, and trends, in: S. Mazur (ed.) *The Neo-Weberian State; Towards a New Paradigm of Public Management?* Warsaw: Scholar Publishing House.

Milberg, W., Winkler, D. (2013). *Outsourcing Economics. Global Value Chains in Capitalist Development*, New York: Cambridge University Press.

Morrissey, O., Lopez, R., Sharma, K. (eds) (2015). *Handbook on Trade and Development*, Cheltenham: Edward Elgar Publishing.

Myrdal, G. (1958). *Teoria ekonomii a kraje gospodarczo nierozwinięte* [Economic Theory and Economically Undeveloped Countries], Warsaw: Polskie Wydawnictwo Gospodarcze.

Nee, V., Swedberg, R. (2005). Economic sociology and new institutional economics, in: C. Menard, M. M. Shirley (eds) *Handbook of New Institutional Economics*, New York, Dordrecht, Berlin, Heidelberg: Springer, pp. 789–818.

Niskanen, W. A. (1971). *Bureaucracy and Representative Government*, New York: Aldine-Atherton.

Nölke, A., Vliegenthart, A. (2009). Enlarging the varieties of Capitalism: the emergence of dependent market economies in East Central Europe, *World Politics*, 61 (4).

OECD (2015). *Going for Growth*, Paris.

Olson, M. (1965 (2002)). *The Logic of Collective Action; Public Goods and the Theory of Groups*, Cambridge, MA: Harvard University Press.

Olson, M. (1982). *The Rise and Decline of Nations: Economic Growth, Stagflation, and Social Rigidities*, New Haven, CT: Yale University Press,.

Osborne, D., Gaebler, T. (1992). *Reinventing Government: How the Entrepreneurial Spirit is Transforming the Public Sector*, New York: Plume Books.

Ost, D. (2010). Illusory corporatism in Eastern Europe: neoliberal tripartism and post-communist class identities, *Warsaw Forum of Economic Sociology* 2 (2), pp. 91–122.

Ostry, J., Loungani, P., Furceri, D. (2016). Neoliberalism: Oversold? *Finance & Development*, June.

Peltzman, S. (1976). Towards a more general theory of regulation, *Journal of Law and Economics*, 19 (2), pp. 211–240.

Pollitt, C., Bouckaert, G. (2011). *Public Management Reform, a Comparative Analysis – New Public Management, Governance, and the Neo-Weberian State*, Oxford: Oxford University Press.

Porter, M. (2001). *Porter o konkurencji* [Porter on Competition], Warsaw: Polskie Wydawnictwo Ekonomiczne.

Randma-Liiv, T. (2008). New public management versus the neo-Weberian state in Central and Eastern Europe, *NISPAcee Journal of Public Administration and Policy*, 1 (2), pp. 49–71.

Reinert, E. (2007). *How the Rich Countries Got Rich ... and Why Poor Countries Remain Poor*, New York: Carroll and Graf.

Reinert, E., Kattel, R. (2013). Failed and asymmetrical integration: Eastern Europe and the non-financial origins of the European crisis, *Working Papers in Technology Governance and Economic Dynamics*, no. 49.

Rodrik, D. (2004). *Industrial Policy for the Twenty-First Century*, Harvard University Faculty Research Working Papers Series, RWP04–047.

Rodrik, D. (2006). Goodbye Washington consensus, hello Washington confusion? Review of the World Bank's economic growth in the 1990s: Learning from a decade of reform, *Journal of Economic Literature*, XLIV (December).

Rodrik, D. (2015). *Premature Deindustrialization*, NBER Working Paper, no. 20935.

Schumpeter, J. A. (1942). *Capitalism, Socialism and Democracy*. New York: Harper & Row.

Seabrooke, L. (2002). *Bringing Legitimacy Back In To Neo-Weberian State Theory And International Relations*, Canberra: Australian national Univ. Dept. of International Relations, Research School of Pacific and Asian Studies.

Skocpol, T. (1985). Bringing the state back in: Strategies of analysis in current research, in: P. Evans, D. Rueschemeyer, T. Skocpol (eds) *Bringing the State Back In*, Cambridge University Press, Cambridge.

SOR (2016). Strategia Odpowiedzialnego Rozwoju [The Strategy of Responsible Development], manuscript, version November 2016, Ministry of Development, Republic of Poland.

Stigler, G. J. (1971). The theory of economic regulation, *Bell Journal of Economics and Management Science*, 2 (1), pp. 3–21.

Stiglitz, J. E. (2004). *Ekonomia sektora publicznego* [Public Sector Economics], Warsaw: Wydawnictwo Naukowe PWN.

Stiglitz J. E., Lin J. Y., Monga, C. (2013). *The Rejuvenation of Industrial Policy*. Policy Research Working Paper, No. 6628. World Bank.

Thorhallsson, B., Kattel R. (2013). Neo-liberal small states and economic crisis: lessons for democratic corporatism, *Journal of Baltic Studies,* 44 (1).

Tłaczała, P. (2005). Podstawy ekonomicznej teorii biurokracji [Fundamentals of the economic theory of bureaucracy], in: J. Wilkin (ed.). *Teoria wyboru publicznego; Wstęp do ekonomicznej analizy polityki i funkcjonowania sfery publicznej* [Public Choice Theory: An Introduction to Economic Analysis of Politics and the Functioning of the Public Sphere], Warsaw: Wydawnictwo Naukowe Scholar, pp. 9–29.

Tollison, R. D. (1982). Rent-seeking: a survey, *Kyklos*, 35.

Tullock, G. (1965). *The Politics of Bureaucracy*, Washington, DC: Public Affairs Press.

Tullock, G. (1967). The welfare costs of tariffs, monopolies and theft, *Western Economic Journal*, 5.

Wade, R. (2012). Return of industrial policy, *International Review of Applied Economics*, 26 (2), pp. 223–239.

Wade, R. (2015). The role of industrial policy in developing countries, in: A. Calcagno, A. S. Dullien, A. Márquez-Velázquez, N. Maystre, J. Priewe (eds) *Rethinking Development Strategies after the Financial Crisis*, New York and Geneva: United Nations.

Warner, M., Herfetz, A. (2012). *Insourcing and Outsourcing, Journal of American Planning Association*, 78 (3).

Weber, M. (1998a). *Polityka jako zawód i powołanie* [Politics as a Vocation], Cracow: Znak.

Weber, M. (1998b). *Politics as a Vocation*, http://anthropos-lab.net/wp/wp-content/uploads/2011/12/Weber-Politics-as-a-Vocation.pdf.

Weber, M. (2002). *Gospodarka i Społeczeństwo; zarys socjologii rozumiejącej* [Economy and Society: An Outline of Interpretive Sociology], Warsaw: Wydawnictwo Naukowe PWN.

Weber, M. (2010). *Etyka protestancka a duch kapitalizmu* [The Protestant Ethic and the Spirit of Capitalism], Warsaw: Aletheia.

Weber, M., Fowkes, B. (1980). The national state and economic policy (Freiburg address) (Inaugural lecture, Freiburg, May 1895), *Economy and Society*, 9 (4), November, pp. 428–449.

5 The neo-Weberian approach in innovation policy

Piotr Kopyciński

Introduction

Recent years have seen a change in the approach to innovation policy. It is no longer consigned only to supporting such areas as science, technology or innovation, but has become a multi-level intervention of a multi- and interdisciplinary nature, including the quality of life, with the participation of public authorities and other stakeholders. The perception of innovation has also become broader – today it is not just about technological changes (product and process innovations) and non-technological ones (organisation and marketing), but also about treating change in social terms, with demands for open access, and the involvement of future users in developing new solutions. Innovation is thus treated in terms of systems, but intervention in the form of innovation policy, not least because of the limited resources and aspects of efficiency, cannot address all the elements of such a system. It is therefore necessary to prioritise activities, which is reflected e.g. in the smart specialisation strategies. Regrettably, changes in the perception of innovation and innovation policy are not accompanied by a broader discussion on the relevant coordination mechanisms, even though the question whether multi-level governance is still the best method for coordination or new solutions should be sought (those that emphasise the importance of public administration) is justified in this context. Such solutions may be provided by the neo-Weberian concept of state (NWS).

The modern understanding of innovation policy and its components

Any discussion about innovation policy should begin with the way innovation and innovation systems are understood. It is, however, difficult to find a coherent theory explaining the issues at hand (cf. Lundvall 2007). Rather, it is more appropriate to talk about certain approaches. The same is true of innovation policy perceived from the research perspective. As was noted by S. Radosevic (2012, pp. 6–8), in this case there are no consistent paradigms or even research plans. B. Martin (2012, p. 1220) states in no uncertain terms that in the context of stimulating innovation, the word *policy* seems to be too narrow and may be misunderstood.

In his opinion, in the case of innovation we can talk about a combination of policy, management and economics, which suggests *innovation studies* or *science policy and innovation studies*. However, despite these reservations, both in scientific debates and in the context of state activities, the term *innovation policy* embraces interventions covering various issues regarding the introduction of new solutions. Therefore, the following three issues are worth taking under consideration:

1   the evolution of the concept of innovation;
2   the systemic approach to innovation processes;
3   the change in the perception of innovation policy.

The evolution of the concept of innovation

In recent years, the concept of innovation has been expanding. Its perception exclusively in terms of technological change is a thing of the past. Currently, apart from the product, process, organisational and marketing innovations mentioned in the *Oslo Manual* (after J. Schumpeter, OECD/Eurostat 2005, p. 17), there are also social innovations (e.g. Murray, Caulier-Grice, Mulgan 2010, BEPA 2011). Innovations are produced in the process of cooperation with a wide spectrum of actors (open innovation, cf. Chesbrough, Vanhaverbeke, West 2006), or even with the participation of future users in the development of solutions that meet their expectations (user innovation, democratising innovation, cf. E. von Hippel 2005; living labs, e.g. World Bank 2014; collaborative innovation, e.g. J. Torfing (2016).

The systemic approach to innovation processes

The transition from science policy (supporting research by public authorities) to technological policy, and from technological policy (supporting the application of knowledge in business practice) to innovation policy was characterised by the framing of policies related to the impact on innovation processes, the associated changes in the range of instruments used and the extent of intervention. These issues are widely discussed in the literature (e.g. Lundvall, Borras 2005; Metcalfe 2000), and for this reason shall not be addressed in this chapter. What is noteworthy, however, is the reference to contemporary innovation policy understood as a systematic approach to a number of factors, institutions and relationships which affect innovation. Such a comprehensive approach was deemed necessary, because the study of complex processes related to innovation requires much more than the observation of a single company or a single technological area (Kuhlmann, Shapira, Smits, 2010, p. 2). Ch. Edquist (2005, p. 182) identifies the innovation system with determinants of the innovation processes, defining it as a collection of all the relevant economic, social, political, organisational, institutional and other factors which influence the development, dissemination and widespread use of innovations. Edquist states that the basic components of such a system are organisations and institutions. Kuhlmann *et al.* (2010, p. 3) add to these all the entities involved in the regulatory sphere (standards, legal norms) and public investment in infrastructure such as schools, universities, research institutes, and enterprises (the economic system), as well as public authorities with all the formal and informal networks linking these actors.

Questions are also raised about the boundaries of innovation systems. There are numerous works devoted to this topic, but here we shall take up the suggestions of Edquist (2005, pp. 199–200), who proposed the following three criteria:

1   the spatial aspect (e.g. national and regional innovation systems – NIS and RIS, respectively);
2   the sector of operation (e.g. a group of companies producing specific technologies as part of NIS/RIS);
3   the elements of the socio-economic system that can be subsumed under a specific innovation system.

The change in the perception of innovation policy

M. Balzat (2006, p. 9) notes that innovation policy becomes a compilation of various interventions, including elements of research and development, technology, infrastructure, regional and educational policies. At the same time, innovation policy constitutes part of the so-called industrial policy (Balzat 2006, p. 9). It draws on the current trends and economic theories, political science and sociology. Debates on innovation policy also emphasise the importance of institutions and path dependence. One may thus say that it is becoming multi- and interdisciplinary in nature (B. R. Martin 2012, p. 1137). As was noted by P. Shapira, R. Smits and S. Kuhlmann (2010, p. 449), it is not enough to support R&D activities in order to strengthen the innovative capacity of economies and societies. It is also necessary to influence the environment that triggers innovation. S. Kuhlmann, P. Shapira and R. Smits (2010, p. 7) use the metaphor of dance. They argue that ideas, rationales and instruments of innovation policy emerge as a result of interactions amongst the actors involved in innovation practice, innovation-related public intervention strategies, as well as innovation research and theory. The interactive learning space for these entities is the dance floor. According to some researchers, the group of dancers would be incomplete without citizens (*quadruple helix*; Carayannis, Campbell 2009, which follows up on the idea of the *triple helix* originated by Etzkowitz and Leydesdorff 2000), and intermediaries in accordance with the concept of *working regions* (Clark 2013).

Systemic problems as an essential justification for intervention in innovation policy

In the context of systemic innovation policy, which also includes evolutionary theory (Nelson, Winter 1982), the fundamental reason for intervention in the field of innovation it is not so much the neoclassical paradigm of market failure, but primarily systemic problems (Chaminade, Edquist 2010). E. Arnold (2004, p. 7) argues that integrated measures with a view to ensuring the smooth operation of innovation systems must be taken due to the following failures:

1   capability failures (obstacles preventing enterprises from utilising their inherent potential), which may include mismanagement or underestimation of the future role of new technologies;
2   failures in institutions (e.g. a rigid framework for the functioning of institutions of higher education leads to difficulties in implementing changes in scientific approaches due to the emergence of new knowledge);
3   network failures (problems related to the relationships among the stakeholders in innovation systems);
4   framework failures (e.g. problems with ensuring adequate health care or safety level).

Innovation policy – a multi-sectoral and multi-level approach

The systemic approach to innovation policy means that it should be considered in multi-level categories: public authorities intervene at national, sub-national, and supra-national levels (e.g. the European Union) in collaboration with other entities. Referring again to Shapira *et al.* (2010), the group of dancers includes mainly public authorities, enterprises, research institutions and other stakeholders. Innovation policy thus conceived recognises the importance of institutions, path dependence and tacit knowledge (Smits, Kuhlmann, Shapira, 2010). At the same time, if innovation policy is to eliminate systemic problems, it must be perceived as a broader phenomenon. In line with the approach taken by the OECD experts (2005, p. 22), innovation policy in the context of the multi-sectoral approach integrates science, technology and innovation policies, including, apart from efforts to stimulate economic growth, also the issues of quality of life (more on this subject in OECD 2005; Smits *et al.* 2010).

Smart specialisation

It is also worth paying attention to yet another issue related to the perception of systemic innovation from the perspective of the European Union. The concept in question is *smart specialisation*, which dates back to 2009, when the European Commission published its *Knowledge for Growth* report submitted by the EU expert advisory group. At the core of the concept was the search for more effective methods of disseminating the effects of public interventions undertaken in the field of innovation. D. Foray writes at length about this issue and defines it as

> the capacity of an economic system (e.g. region) to generate new specialties through the discovery of new domains of opportunity and the local concentration and agglomeration of resources and competences in these domains. Such a capacity is needed to initiate structural changes in the form of diversification, transition, modernisation or the radical foundation of industries and/or services.
>
> (Foray 2015, p. 1)

Under this approach, especially in the regional innovation systems, but also in the national ones, smart specialisation strategies are developed (with the participation of different stakeholders, notably companies in the process of entrepreneurial discovery), in which interventions in the field of innovation policy are focused on selected most promising areas. In the 2014–2020 programming period, such strategies must be implemented in all the EU regions as the so-called ex-ante conditionality for regional policy. More importantly, smart specialisation strategies support the implementation of the call for re-industrialisation present in industrial policy (Mamica 2016).

The mechanisms for coordinating innovation policy

New public management

The mechanisms typical of new public management (NPM) are being gradually phased out of innovation policy. As Drechsler (2009b) points out, the first critical remarks concerning NPM appeared around 1995, and in 2000, when the Lisbon Strategy came into force, NPM had already been in retreat. In recent years, particularly at regional and local levels, we can even see a strong opposition to reforms in that spirit. After 2005, analysts began to emphasise the role of public administration, especially in the context of innovation policy, e-government and public procurement (Drechsler 2009a).

Multi-level governance

Supranational organisations, such as the European Union, the OECD or the World Bank, recommended governance and its derivatives, including multi-level governance (MLG), as the optimal method for coordinating public policies. This approach emphasises the interactivity and interdependence of governance processes (Hausner 2008) which occur at numerous levels (national, regional, local and transnational). From the perspective of the European Union, the concept of MLG was sanctioned in 1993 by the Treaty of Maastricht as the most appropriate method of public policy coordination (including innovation policy). MLG appears in numerous Community documents, including the *White Paper on Multi-level Governance* (Committee of the Regions 2009), or the fifth *Cohesion Report* (European Commission 2010). MLG is also a method selected to support the achievement of the objectives laid down in the *Europe 2020 Strategy*, which determines the implementation of innovation policy at the EU, national and regional levels. Governance as a method of coordination is also recognised by other international organisations, including the World Bank, which is currently implementing a project comparing different aspects of governance in over 200 countries and territories – The Worldwide Governance Indicators (Kaufmann *et al.* 2010). Finally, public governance and MLG are mentioned in a number of OECD publications dealing with various public policies, issues and different levels of government (e.g. OECD 2013).

The criticism of multi-level governance and the neo-Weberian state

However, the focus on MLG as the only appropriate method for coordinating innovation policy has attracted strong criticism in the context of such processes as globalisation or the failure to implement the initial objectives of the Lisbon Strategy (Drechsler 2009a). W. Drechsler (2009a) notes that until 2005, the role of public administration in the implementation of the Lisbon Strategy had been completely ignored. In his opinion, the implementation of the strategy was unsuccessful due to the lack of public administration reform in the spirit of the neo-Weberian state (NWS). Such a modernisation is particularly important in the context of building an innovation-based economy. According to Drechsler (2009a), the EU administration is already showing certain signs of a return to the Weberian concepts (e.g. defining clear objectives to be achieved, with less importance attached to the tools used for that purpose). Individual EU member states may, however, need more time to return to the Weberian tradition, since it may be mistakenly perceived by their public opinions not as a transition from NPM to the NWS, but as a return to the dominance of an all-powerful bureaucracy.

It is also worth noting that MLG as a method of coordination can be associated with the blurring of responsibilities among the different levels of government. In this context, it is worth remembering the proposals for a more clear-cut division of tasks in the field of innovation policy between the national and regional levels (OECD 2009, pp. 14–15).

Another problem is the discrepancy between the recommended and the actually employed coordination methods. M. Potůček (2008) shows that attempts to introduce multi-level decision-making mechanisms in the Czech Republic met with reluctance and lack of understanding at both national and regional levels. Although these mechanisms were supposed to include market institutions, citizens and the state, it was the state that took the actual decisions, which points to the prevalence of the Weberian tradition in certain European countries (cf. Drechsler, Kattel 2008). Moreover, it should be noted that although MLG is the preferred mechanism for coordinating innovation policy, in practice, the policy design stage shows characteristic features of the neo-Weberian approach (Kopyciński 2016, p. 190).

To sum up, it can be said that tools proposed by NPM and MLG as used in innovation policy have proven to be partly ineffective (reforms in the spirit of MLG ostensibly implemented by adherents to the Weberian tradition are another issue). However, the new reality that emerged after the outbreak of the 2007/2008 crisis, coupled with the inability to achieve the objectives laid down in the original Lisbon Strategy, and the increasing expectations for government intervention in the field of innovative activity, mean that these tools require verification. Additionally, an innovation-driven economy requires competent public authorities focused on the implementation of long-term tasks with responsibilities clearly assigned to each level. Max Weber's tried and tested concepts may offer one of the ways of doing so.

Innovation policy and the neo-Weberian concept of state

Although it is difficult to find the operationalisation of the neo-Weberian approach in terms of innovation policy in the literature, several authors have found the reasons and justifications for its employment in interventions in the field of innovation. Analysing innovation policy from the perspective of the NWS, two perspectives should be taken into account:

1   implementation of innovations in the operation of public administration bodies;
2   implementation of innovations by companies and other entities (e.g. research institutions).

In both cases an important role is played by public authorities whose activities are key for the successful implementation of the new solutions.

Innovations in the operation of public administration bodies and the coordination methods

An efficient bureaucracy is important for the implementation of organisational innovations in the functioning of the state. Such a perspective was adopted by Pollitt and Bouckaert (2011, pp. 193–195). They point to the fact that civil servants play a crucial role in reconciling the need for innovation with building the citizens' trust in the state and governmental legitimacy. They cite the example of the closing down of unprofitable post offices in small towns throughout Finland and the UK, and the subsequent transfer of postal services to the local shops. The move was strongly opposed by local residents who trusted postal workers, but were unable to trust shop assistants to the same extent. According to Pollitt and Bouckaert, the sense of exclusion and loss of trust in the state may also occur in other situations, e.g. in the case of transition to digital services (which may be difficult especially for senior citizens), or rapid changes in the pension system. They indicate that while the NWS emphasises trust and legitimacy, NPM focuses on the efficiency aspect of public services. Plans to introduce such changes should benefit from the achievements of MLG, where the involvement of a broad range of stakeholders fosters confidence-building and facilitates the implementation of innovations. As we can see, the adoption of the neo-Weberian principles is not tantamount to rejecting the achievements of other coordination methods; the point is rather to underscore the importance of the recently underrated status of public administration in the process of implementing change, as well as drawing our attention to the consequences for the functioning of the state of hasty changes made without consultation with citizens.

Innovations implemented by companies and other entities in the context of the neo-Weberian approach

Considerations in this area should begin with a discussion of the general conditions conducive to effective public intervention. According to P. B. Evans *et al.* (1985, p. 68), the state that intervenes too far in some societal relationships reduces its own capacity to influence the economic growth and redistribution of income. In order to make public intervention effective, first 'the state must constitute a bureaucratic apparatus with sufficient corporate coherence' (1985, p. 68), and second, the bureaucratic apparatus in the decision-making process should be given 'a certain degree of autonomy from the dominant interests in a capitalist society' (Evans, Rueschemeyer, Skocpol 1985, p. 68).

This way of thinking is appreciated by certain authors who deal with the issues of influencing innovation processes. They believe (e.g. Drechsler, Kattel 2008; Drechsler 2009a) that innovative activity should constitute a particular concern of the state and find the theoretical grounds for intervention in the neo-Weberian approach. Drechsler (2009a) considers the neo-Weberian approach to be ideally suited to building a knowledge-based (innovation-based) economy. Drechsler and Kattel (2008) believe that the process requires the existence of a competent, long-term oriented civil service. It is particularly important in various kinds of advanced research in the biotechnology fields, which require a long-term perspective given the uncertainty of results and the potential for short-term failure. They also show that a modern and efficient public administration has a positive effect on productivity and economic growth. Moreover, they emphasise that innovation should be seen in terms of general public interest, not only that of individual companies. Therefore, the successful implementation of innovation policy depends on the existence of an efficient administration.

In the context of implementation of smart specialisation strategies, D. Foray (2015) does not refer directly to the neo-Weberian approach. He notes, however (2015, p. 86), that sometimes the execution of such strategies is difficult because of poor administrative and governance capacities at the regional level. These strategies can be implemented successfully only if a given region has a long-term development vision put into operation by the new generation of competent and committed civil servants. Such a situation can already be observed in certain regions (Foray 2015, pp. 88–89).

Until quite recently, interventions in the framework of innovation policy and its predecessors included significantly fewer categories than currently, hence the reliance on MLG mechanisms seemed to be sufficient. Now, however, it makes sense to look for new coordination tools due to the increasing multi- and inter-disciplinarity of innovation policy (which includes elements of different public policies, trends and research disciplines) and to the systemic approach that requires taking into account the different institutional conditions, path dependence and the involvement of various entities. A successful implementation of such a complex, multi-dimensional and finally, multi-level (national, sub-national, supranational) innovation policy depends on a strongly legitimised decision-maker that makes final decisions in the case of public interventions in the field of innovation. These functions can only be performed by the state or, to be more specific, by appropriate public authorities at all its organisational levels. It can be embodied in an independent, competent and long-term-thinking civil service. The existence of a strong regulator is also desirable in the context of the evolving perception of innovation towards open solutions with their important implications related to intellectual property rights.

In summary, both the theory and practice of innovation policy show clear signs of thinking in terms of the NWS. The need to strengthen the position of public authorities may be justified by the following:

1   the new challenges facing innovation policy resulting, among other things, from the 2007/2008 crisis, the failed implementation of the original objectives of the Lisbon Strategy and the implementation of smart specialisations strategies across the EU member states;
2   the need to implement innovations in the operation of public administration in a way that does not undermine trust in the state or in governmental legitimacy;
3   the risky and fraught-with-errors process of developing advanced solutions (e.g. in the bio-fields), which would not be undertaken without a competent civil service;
4   the increasing complexity of decision-making processes related to innovation policy in the context of its multi- and interdisciplinarity, the involvement of many actors and the need to implement a systemic approach taking into account the institutional background and path dependence;
5   the evolution of the approach to innovation, which has its consequences for intellectual property rights.

Innovation policy – multi-level governance or the neo-Weberian approach?

The attributes of the two coordination mechanisms – MLG and the NWS – are compared below based on the foregoing discussion in this chapter as well as on the literature review (Hausner 2008, p. 401; Matei, Flogaitis 2011, p. 305; Pollitt, Bouckaert 2011, p. 22). Since it is presented in universal terms, the comparison may also apply to innovation policy. MLG is a network-based coordination model. The NWS refers to the Weberian hierarchical approach, but endowed with certain features of NPM and MLG, such as taking into account the needs and expectations of citizens participating in the exercise of power through various consultation mechanisms (cf. Politt, Bouckaert 2011). In the case of MLG, the primary actors in the governance processes are political authorities keeping in touch with stakeholders, whereas the NWS underscores a precise division of powers among the various bodies and levels of governance, which may, of course, invite others to participate. Public action based on the principles of MLG is undertaken on the strength of the consensus among various stakeholders achieved under the aegis of public authorities, whereas the NWS underscores the role of administrative law, which does not preclude the use of different stakeholder consultation mechanisms. MLG makes use of communication tools, whereas the NWS emphasises the administrative ones, including integrated strategies (in the current era of overlapping interventions). In the case of public policy implementation, the key tools include negotiations (MLG) or actions by public authorities based on legal regulations (NWS).

Multi-level governance or the neo-Weberian approach in the implementation of smart specialisation strategies – case studies of Scotland and Małopolska Region (Southern Poland, capital city Cracow)

In this section, we shall focus on specific examples of innovation policy implementation (Table 5.1) at the sub-national level and on the issue of smart specialisation strategies. We shall review the coordination mechanisms used in the implementation of such strategies in Scotland (*Scotland's Digital Future*) and in Małopolska Region (*Regional Innovation Strategy for Małopolska Region 2014–2020*).

Scotland's Digital Future[1]

The strategy *Scotland's Digital Future* (SDF) was announced by the Scottish Government in 2011 and updated in 2017. According to its provisions, each sector has its own strategy, aligned with national strategy, and a governance board. The responsibility for preparing SDF was entrusted to a ministerial subcommittee. The implementation of the strategy is a task of the Programme Board, chaired by

Table 5.1 Multi-level governance and the neo-Weberian state – features of innovation policy coordination mechanisms

Features of coordination mechanism	Multi-level governance	Neo-Weberian state
Coordination method	Network	Hierarchical, but some market elements (NPM) and network (MLG) present
Entities	Political authorities in collaborative relationships with stakeholders	Clear separation of political authorities and public administrations at various levels, consideration of opinions of other actors (cooperation in the diagnosis, planning, implementation and monitoring)
Basis for intervention	Consensus among various stakeholders approved by public authorities	Provisions of administrative law
Basic tools	Communication among various stakeholders	Administrative: integrated strategies affecting various public policies at the same time
Implementation method	Negotiations	Integrated, joint activities of public administration at various levels with a clear division of tasks and responsibilities

Source: Own study based on Hausner (2008); Matei, Flogaitis (2011); Pollitt, Bouckaert (2011).

a senior civil servant at director level. The strategy is integrated with other public policies, since they entail ICT interventions in different areas. The approach to developing the strategy included engagement with all parts of the public sector in Scotland, including health, local government, universities and colleges, public agencies and the ICT industry, and including them in the governance boards to deliver the strategy and the actions contained therein. The strategy was not just endorsed by government, but also by political leadership at the local level, and all parties signed up to deliver on the ambitions and actions. The actions specified in the strategy were coordinated with the plans of the UK Government Digital Service for the development of ICT in the United Kingdom.

Regional Innovation Strategy for Małopolska Region 2014–2020 (RIS 2020)

The *Regional Innovation Strategy for Małopolska Region 2014–2020* (Geodecki *et al.* 2014) is one of the ten strategic programmes of the Development Strategy for Małopolska Region 2011–2020 and refers to the area of innovative economy. It was adopted by the Board of Małopolskie Voivodeship (the executive body of the regional government). RIS 2020 specifies the tasks to be implemented both at the national and regional levels of strategies to support innovative activities. Actions in one of the priorities of the RIS 2020 regarding ICT can be considered partly integrated with other public policies. The implementation of the tasks was entrusted to the staff of the Department of Economic Development of the Małopolska Marshal Office (an auxiliary executive body of the regional government). These actions are supported by the Małopolska Innovation Council and working groups bringing together the stakeholders in accordance with the quadruple helix idea, namely entrepreneurs, the R&D sector, representatives of administration, and citizens. Care was taken to ensure that the emergence of smart specialisation strategies corresponds with the key programme documents which define priorities in the areas of investment in research infrastructure, support to enterprises in their efforts to innovate, and in smart specialisation at the level of the national economy.

Scotland's Digital Future and Regional Innovation Strategy for Małopolska Region 2014–2020: multi-level governance or the neo-Weberian approach?

The implementation processes of both strategies are summarised in Table 5.2 with a special focus on the features of the dominant coordination mechanisms (MLG, NWS or elements of both).

In both cases under review, the coordination mechanism applied combines the features of NWS and MLG, with the former being predominant. However, it cannot be interpreted as a rejection of the achievements of MLG by the regions concerned. It must be remembered that NWS draws on the achievements of the previous governance paradigms, therefore its characteristics also comprise certain attributes of MLG.

Table 5.2 Characteristics of coordination mechanisms in the implementation of smart specialisation strategies – Scotland and Małopolska Region

Features of coordination mechanism	Scotland	Małopolska Region
Coordination method	*NWS:* Hierarchical coordination, but elements of MLG taken into account	*NWS:* Hierarchical coordination, but elements of MLG taken into account
Entities	*NWS:* 1 Preparation and adoption in the political sphere: a ministerial subcommittee and the Scottish Government, respectively 2 Implementation: programme board chaired by a senior civil servant at director level	*NWS:* 1 Adoption: the executive body of the regional government 2 Implementation: designated regional government office
Basis for intervention	*MLG:* Consensus: strategy developed in cooperation with all parts of the public sector and ICT industry	*MLG:* Consensus: with stakeholders focused around the quadruple helix
Basic tools	*MLG:* Communication among various stakeholder groups in governance boards	*MLG:* Communication among various stakeholder groups in the Małopolska Innovation Council and working groups
Implementation method	*NWS:* Integrated actions of Scottish authorities in consultation with the local level and taking into account the ICT development plan at the level of the entire UK	*NWS:* Partly integrated (in the area of ICT) actions of regional (RIS 2020) and national authorities (other innovation strategies)

Source: Own study.

Conclusion

The inherent features of innovative activities, including advanced research and uncertainty about its results, mean that public intervention in this area should be long-term oriented and allow for failure. Therefore, when building a knowledge-based (innovation-based) economy, we should be aware that the intervening side must have a well-functioning, competent public administration unafraid of undertaking long-term and risky ventures.

The sources of failure of certain assumptions adopted for innovation policy (e.g. the original Lisbon Strategy) should be partly sought in the diminished role of public administration (lack of explicit legal provisions, overlapping responsibilities at different levels of government); hence the idea to implement innovation policy using the attributes of the neo-Weberian state. The problem, however, is that the neo-Weberian approach is yet to be operationalised. Unless it is equipped with appropriate tools, it will be difficult both to evaluate its practicality and to formulate relevant recommendations for decision-makers. It may also prove to be problematic to differentiate such a future neo-Weberian approach from other methods of coordination due to the presence in it of the characteristic features of the original Weber's model, NPM, or MLG.

Another issue concerns the apparent discrepancies between the recommended and the actually used coordination methods. Some countries, despite the declarations made by their governments, are reluctant to implement policies in the spirit of MLG (Potůček 2008) due to the continuing dominance of the Weberian model in their tradition.

The innovative smart specialisation strategies provide a good illustration of innovation policy interventions. They reflect a relatively new approach, in which, as evidenced by the case studies, one may notice certain features of the neo-Weberian approach employed as a management mechanism. However, regardless of whether the implementation of smart specialisation strategies occurs through MLG or the NWS, managing such complex strategies requires a greater involvement of public authorities, both at the intervention design stage, including the selection of regional specialisations (coordination of the process of entrepreneurial discovery) and at the strategy implementation stage (selection of projects that meet the appropriate requirements for 'smartness').

In the light of the above considerations, it is worth taking up the challenge of operationalising the neo-Weberian approach in innovation policy, which would strengthen the position of public administration in the decision-making and coordination processes. These processes should be governed by law and clearly define the responsibilities and powers of public authorities. However, this is not tantamount to rejecting the achievements of other coordination methods, such as NPM or MLG, especially their respective focus on the effectiveness of state administration and consultations.

Note

1 The study is based on the following materials: The Scottish Government, *Scotland's Digital Future: A Strategy for Scotland*, Edinburgh 2011; Jane Morgan, *A Digital Growth Strategy: The Scottish Approach*; minutes of the peer review meeting in Seville, 3–4 December 2013. The author gives special thanks to Julie Kane (Head of Digital Public Services Policy, Scottish Government) for supplying the materials and useful information.

Bibliography

Arnold, E. (2004). Evaluating research and innovation policy: a systems world needs systems evaluations. *Research Evaluation*, vol. 13, no 1, April, pp. 3–17.
Balzat, M. (2006). *An Economic Analysis of Innovation. Extending the Concept of National Innovation Systems*. Cheltenham/Northampton, MA: Edward Elgar.

BEPA (2011). *Empowering People, Driving Change. Social Innovation in the European Union*. Luxembourg: Publications Office of the European Union.

Carayannis E.G., Campbell D.F.J. (2009)."Mode 3" and "Quadruple Helix": toward a 21st century fractal innovation ecosystem. *International Journal of Technology Management,* vol. 46, nos 3/4, pp. 201–234.

Chaminade, C., Edquist, Ch. (2010). Rationales for public policy intervention in the innovation process: systems of innovation approach. In: R. E. Smits, S. Kuhlmann, P. Shapira, *The Theory and Practice of Innovation Policy. An international research handbook.* Cheltenham/Northampton, MA: Edward Elgar.

Chesbrough, H., Vanhaverbeke, W., West, J. (2006). *Open Innovation: Researching a New Paradigm*. Oxford: Oxford University Press.

Clark, J. (2013). *Working Regions: Reconnecting Innovation and Production in the Knowledge Economy*, London/New York: Routledge.

The Committee of the Regions (2009). *White Paper on Multilevel Governance.* Brussels.

Drechsler, W. (2009a). Towards a Neo-Weberian European Union? Lisbon agenda and public administration. *Halduskultuur*, vol. 10, pp. 6–21.

Drechsler, W. (2009b). The rise and demise of the New Public Management: Lessons and opportunities for South East Europe. *Uprava*, vol. 7, no. 3, pp. 7–27.

Drechsler, W., Kattel, R. (2008). Towards the neo-Weberian State? Perhaps, but certainly adieu, NPM! *The NISPAcee Journal of Public Administration and Policy*, Special Issue: A Distinctive European Model? The Neo-Weberian State, vol. I, no. 2 (Winter).

Edquist, Ch. (2005). Systems of innovation. perspectives and challenges. In: J. Fegerberg, D. C. Mowery, R. R. Nelson (eds), *The Oxford Handbook of Innovation.* New York: Oxford University Press.

Etzkowitz, H., Leydesdorff, L. (2000). The dynamics of innovation: From national systems and "Mode 2" to a triple helix of university-industry-government relations. *Research Policy*, vol. 29, pp. 109–123.

European Commission (2010). *Fifth Report on Economic, Social and Territorial Cohesion – Investing in Europe's Future.* Luxembourg: Publications Office of the European Union.

Evans, P. B., Rueschemeyer, D., Skocpol, T. (1985, reprinted 2002). *Bringing the State Back In.* Cambridge/New York: Cambridge University Press.

Foray, D. (2015). *Smart Specialisation: Opportunities and Challenges for Regional Innovation Policy.* London/New York: Routledge.

Geodecki, T., Kopyciński, P., Mamica, Ł., Zawicki, M. (eds) (2014). *Strategic Programme: Regional Innovation Strategy of the Małopolska Region 2020.* Cracow: Department for Economic Development at the Marshal's Office of the Małopolska Region.

Hausner, J. (2008). *Zarządzanie publiczne* [Public Management].Warsaw: Wydawnictwo Naukowe Scholar [Scholar Publishing House].

von Hippel, E. (2005). *Democratizing Innovation.* Cambridge, MA/London: The MIT Press.

Kaufmann, D., Kraay. A., Mastruzzi, M. (2010). *The Worldwide Governance Indicators Methodology and Analytical Issues*, Policy Research Working Paper 5430, The World Bank Development Research Group Macroeconomics and Growth Team, September.

Kopyciński, P. (2016). The neo-Weberian approach to public management and innovation policy. In: S. Mazur (ed.) *The Neo-Weberian State. Towards a new paradigm of public management.* Warsaw: Scholar Publishing House.

Kuhlmann, S., Shapira, P., Smits, R. E. (2010). Introduction. A systemic perspective: the innovation policy dance. In: R. E. Smits, S. Kuhlmann, P. Shapira, *The theory and practice of innovation policy. An international research handbook.* Cheltenham/Northampton, MA: Edward Elgar.

Lundvall, B-Å. (2007). Post script: innovation systems research. Where it came from and where it might go. In: Lundvall, B.-Å. (ed.) *National Systems of Innovation: Toward a Theory of Innovation and Interactive Learning*. Aalborg University.

Lundvall, B. A., Borras, S. (2005). Science, technology and innovation policy. In: J. Fegerberg, D. C. Mowery, R. R. Nelson, *The Oxford Handbook of Innovation*. New York: Oxford University Press.

Mamica, Ł. (2016). An analysis of Poland's industrial policy in the context of Neo-Weberian principles. In: S. Mazur (ed.) *The Neo-Weberian State: Towards a New Paradigm of Public Management*. Warsaw: Scholar Publishing House.

Martin, B. R. (2012). The evolution of science policy and innovation studies. *Research Policy*, vol. 41, pp. 1219–1239.

Matei, L., Flogaitis S. (2011). Public administration in the Balcans: From Weberian bureaucracy to new public management. *Editura Economică*.

Metcalfe, J. S. (2000). Science, technology and innovation policy in developing economies. Paper prepared for the Workshop on Enterprise Competitiveness and Public Policies, Barbados, 22–25 November 1999.

Morgan, J. (2013). *A Digital Growth Strategy: The Scottish Approach*, peer review materials. Seville, 3–4 December.

Murray, R., Caulier-Grice, J., Mulgan, G. (2010). *The Open Book of Social Innovation*. NESTA.

Nelson, R. R., Winter, S. G. (1982). *An Evolutionary Theory of Economic Change*. Cambridge, MA/London: The Belknap Press of Harvard University Press.

OECD (2005). *Governance of Innovation Systems, volume 1: Synthesis Report*. Paris: OECD Publishing.

OECD (2009). *Regions Matter: Economic Recovery, Innovation and Sustainable Growth*. Paris: OECD Publishing.

OECD (2013). *Investing Together: Working Effectively across Levels of Government*. OECD Publishing.

OECD/Eurostat (2005). *Oslo Manual: Guidelines for Collecting and Interpreting Innovation Data*, 3rd edition. Paris: OECD Publishing.

Pollitt, C., Bouckaert, G. (2011). *Public Management Reform a Comparative Analysis-New Public Management, Governance, and the Neo-Weberian State*. Oxford: Oxford University Press.

Potůček, M. (2008). The concept of the neo-Weberian state confronted by the multidimensional concept of governance. *The NISPAcee Journal of Public Administration and Policy*, Special Issue: A Distinctive European Model? The Neo-Weberian State, vol. I, no. 2 (Winter).

Radosevic, S. (2012). Innovation policy studies between theory and practice: a literature review based analysis. *STI Policy Review*, vol. 3, no. 1, 1–45.

The Scottish Government (2011). *Scotland's Digital Future: A Strategy for Scotland*. Edinburgh.

Shapira, P., Smits, R. E., Kuhlmann, S. (2010). An outlook on innovation policy, theory and practice. in: R. E. Smits, S. Kuhlmann, P. Shapira., *The Theory and Practice of Innovation Policy. An International Research Handbook*. Cheltenham/Northampton, MA: Edward Elgar.

Smits, R. E., Kuhlmann, S., Shapira, P. (2010). *The Theory and Practice of Innovation Policy. An International Research Handbook*. Cheltenham/Northampton, MA: Edward Elgar.

Torfing, J. (2016). *Collaborative Innovation in the Public Sector*. Washington, DC: Georgetown University Press.

World Bank & European Network of Living Labs (2014). *Citizen-Driven Innovation: A Guidebook for City Mayors and Public Administrators*. Brussels: World Bank & European Network of Living Labs.

6 The neo-Weberian public management model in the context of labour market policy in Poland

Maciej Frączek

Introduction

Poland's public policy in the labour market faces the challenge of finding an optimal model for managing processes and activities which involve a number of actors from the public, social and private spheres. One such model proposal is the neo-Weberian approach in public management.

The main aim of this chapter is to describe LMP as pursued in Poland using the categories characteristic of the neo-Weberian public management model. The author uses a model set of key features of LMP pursued according to the neo-Weberian approach developed for one of his previous studies.

The author reviews Polish literature in the field of LMP and relevant legal regulations applicable to it. The inspirations and conclusions also come from the author's experience and research cooperation with the representatives of public employment services (PES).

LMP in the light of the neo-Weberian approach

In the literature on managing LMP in Poland, it is hard to find works dealing with the neo-Weberian approach in public management as a reference plane for its implementation. The existing texts tend to mention the traditional Weberian administration, NPM and public governance, all of which to a greater or lesser extent contribute to the neo-Weberian approach.

Throughout this chapter, references will be made to LMP implemented according to the following models: (1) bureaucratic; (2) NPM; (3) public governance; and (4) neo-Weberian. Box 6.1 presents the most important characteristics of the policy in question associated with the last type of public management. The analysis below is based on a list of model features of LMP implemented according to the neo-Weberian principles, which was compiled by the author for the purpose of another study (Frączek 2016) and slightly modified.

Box 6.1   Characteristic features of LMP in the neo-Weberian model

- Fairly high level of centralisation of the policy programming process (EU solutions transposed to the national, then regional, and finally, local level);
- extensive system of agencies and public organisations which implement policy measures (but in cooperation with private and social entities);
- use of network- and market-based mechanisms for policy programming and implementation with the dominant position of public actors preserved;
- decentralisation of powers from the central level to regional and local ones (while maintaining central government influence);
- relatively high level of LMP financing with an emphasis on passive LMP (PLMP);
- goal-oriented and efficiency-oriented performance measures to evaluate the quality of actions;
- consideration of the concept of the 'doing' state via intensive interactions between PES staff and service users (customers) – activation involves not only the customers, but also the employees responsible for direct contact with customers;
- professional PES staff considered to be one of the most important policy success factors;
- use of evidence-based policy mechanisms thanks to elaborate public analytical institutions (including labour market observatories), better communication among experts, decision makers and street-level officials.

Source: Own study based on Frączek (2016, pp. 205–206).

The key features of LMP according to the neo-Weberian public management model and its practical implementation in Poland

Fairly high level of centralisation of the policy programming process

The LMP programming process in Poland is fairly highly centralised in terms of the development and contents of the basic operational documents – the National Action Plan for Employment (NAPE) and regional plans for employment (regional plans).

Poland as an EU member state is obliged to implement the European Employment Strategy (EES). This implies the need to take into account EES principles in the NAPE (as stipulated by the Employment Promotion and Labour Market Institutions Act, EPLMIA), which means in practice that policy priorities and lines of action defined in the EU guidelines must apply to Poland's employment policy. Since the regional plans must correspond with the NAPE provisions, the former also show numerous features of the EES. At the poviat (county) level, there are employment promotion programmes and local labour market activation initiatives, which are implemented as part of the strategies to solve social problems at this level. At the poviat level, there are no legal guidelines that require the EU, national, or regional priorities to be taken into consideration. However, according to existing studies (Tyrowicz 2010), approximately one-third of poviats in Poland have no strategy applicable to the labour market sphere.

In the sphere of LMP programming, one may thus see a fairly wide transposition of EU priorities and solutions (under the EES) especially at the national level, a little less of it at the regional level, while the individual poviats mostly deal with their own specific challenges resulting from the condition of their labour markets. Hence, although one cannot deny that Poland's LMP is to a significant extent dominated by EU-proposed solutions (cf. e.g. Kopyciński 2015, p. 117), it should also be remembered that the EU employment guidelines, which apply to all its member states, are hardly the only or the main institutional source of LMP content and implementation in Poland.

The centralisation of LMP programming is reflected by the allocation of resources from operational programmes for the development of the labour market (human resources). For example, in the case of the Human Capital Operational Programme (2007–2013), the central component accounted for as much as 34% of the total funds (the regional component 62%). In the author's view, increased funding for the regions would be more conducive to solving the problems faced by the Polish labour market.

Extensive system of agencies and public organisations that implement policy measures (but in cooperation with private and social entities)

Poland's institutions responsible for the implementation of LMP are diverse in nature and represent all the sectors – public, private and social. Public labour market institutions include Public Employment Services (PES) and the Voluntary Labour Corps (VLC). The term PES subsumes the so-called employment authorities – the minister in charge of labour, voivodes (governors of regions), marshals, and poviat (county) governors – which are assigned appropriate competencies regarding LMP under the EPLMIA. It should be emphasised, however, that the responsibility for the actual implementation of the activities rests with institutions subordinated to the said employment authorities: the office of the minister in charge of labour (currently, the Ministry of Family, Labour and Social Policy), regional offices, regional labour offices (RLOs) and poviat labour offices (PLOs). They are also part of PES.

RLOs and PLOs play a key role in the implementation of LMP in terms of specific measures aimed at the unemployed and job seekers. RLOs have separate Centres for Information and Career Planning, while PLOs act through their Professional Activation Centres which perform tasks in the area of labour market instruments and services. Since the Polish legislative framework does not provide for any poviat government involvement in LMP, it is worth noting the presence of Local Information and Consultation Points (within PLOs, but in cooperation with the local government at the commune level). They provide employers and job seekers with information on the available opportunities and assistance offered by PLOs.

Another important public labour market institution is the VLC – a state-run organisation specialising in activities aimed at young people at risk of social exclusion. The VLC not only offers young people career counselling and job placement, but also helps them to complete their education (primary and secondary), as well as to acquire skills useful in the labour market (Culepa, Rotkiewicz, Wołoszyn-Kądziołka 2015, p. 53).

As part of LMP, the above-mentioned public labour market institutions cooperate with private entities. The latter include employment agencies which assist the unemployed in finding jobs (including placements abroad), career counselling, personal counselling and temporary work. Since the amendment of the EPLMIA in 2014, the importance of employment agencies as partners of PLOs has markedly increased. The agencies are responsible for job placements of unemployed people disfavoured on the labour market. This form of cooperation is known as 'small contracting.' By comparison, 'big contracting' takes place at the regional level and involves hiring employment agencies to find jobs for unemployed people (or to help them start their own business) and make sure that they keep those jobs (or stay in business). These activities cover the long-term unemployed, including those with special needs. Employment agencies also participate in LMP by providing labour market services to workers as part of the monitored redundancy programme.

PES also work together with labour market institutions representing different sectors, including public and non-public training institutions. There are responsible for the provision of extramural (lifelong) education. The training institutions cooperate with the PLOs in retraining the unemployed and job seekers, as well as in providing vocational training to unemployed adults.

Local partnership institutions, a group of institutions contracted to carry out projects in the labour market, have a similar multi-sectoral nature. As Culepa, Rotkiewicz and Wołoszyn-Kądziołka (2015, p. 55) observe, these partnerships are usually established by local government units together with trade unions and employers' organisations in the form of agreements, programmes, or distinct legal entities.

Last, the EPLMIA provides for the establishment of social dialogue institutions, including actors from the social sector (trade unions, employers' organisations, the unemployed and non-governmental organisations). The cooperation of public labour market institutions with social dialogue institutions primarily takes the form of participation in labour market councils functioning at the national, regional and county levels. These councils are consultative and advisory bodies to the minister in charge of labour, voivodeship marshals and poviat governors, respectively.

The LMP carried out by Poland's public authorities is based on dialogue and cooperation with social partners. The manifestations of this philosophy include labour market councils, local partnerships and auxiliary PES services offered by social partners and employment agencies (European Commission 2013). Additionally, marshals and poviat governors pursuing regional and local policies can outsource certain tasks to other entities as part of public procurement procedures.

Despite the existence of various institutional cooperation mechanisms between the public and non-public entities within Poland's LMP, it should be made clear that in practice, at all the LMP stages (1 – analysis and design, 2 – implementation and monitoring, 3 – evaluation; Chrabąszcz, Zawicki 2014) cooperation – if it occurs at all – is not that close (quite often, it is limited to information exchange) and is mostly dictated by public actors. It is the case at the national, regional and local levels, although it is worth noting that local and regional governments tend to be more open to labour-market measures that combine the potential of representatives of different sectors.

Use of network- and market-based mechanisms for programming and implementing policies with the dominant position of public actors preserved

Looking at the recent changes to Poland's LMP (such as profiling the unemployed, activation of the unemployed by non-public entities, cooperation of PES with social welfare institutions, replacement of employment councils with labour market councils, increasing pressure on the effectiveness of PES), we may conclude that some of them are rooted in the logic of NPM, while others take advantage of the principles of public governance. Despite the use of the network- and market-based mechanisms in LMP programming and implementation, it is quite easy to spot the institutional 'catches' which allow the state and its agencies to preserve their dominant role in influencing the contents and way of implementation of individual measures under this policy, which appears to reflect the assumptions of the NWS.

The dominant role of public actors in the management of LMP is confirmed by research (Sztandar-Sztanderska 2013; Męcina 2013; Kozak 2014; Frączek 2014, 2015b; Zybała 2015). The last author detects in the Polish model, among other things, unilateral decisions and low stakeholder empowerment. Frączek (2015c) recognises the openness of public authorities to mechanisms of shaping LMP other than the bureaucratic ones, but emphasises the crucial importance of actors representing the public sphere. This is evidenced, among other things, by the labour market councils, the way key operational documents (NAPE and regional plans) are drawn up, and the operation of the Tripartite Commission, which is a key collegial body that influences the shape of LMP (or more broadly, employment policy). In 2015, the Tripartite Commission was replaced by the Social Dialogue Council. The Social Dialogue Council and Other Social Dialogue Institutions Act provides for a greater contribution of non-public actors in the process (e.g. rotary presidency of the Council, powers reserved to autonomous dialogue between representatives of workers and entrepreneurs), but it has not operated for a sufficiently long time to be reliably evaluated.

Decentralisation of powers from to the regional and local levels (while maintaining central government influence)

Since the 1990s, a number of changes have been introduced in the institutional sphere of LMP implementation in Poland. Initially (1990–1992), labour administration was purely governmental and included the Ministry of Labour and Social Policy, regional employment office (operating within regional offices) and poviat labour offices (operating within poviat offices). In 1993–1998, there were separate, special administration units operating within a centralised system of labour offices, which included the Ministry of Labour and Social Policy, the National Labour Office, regional and poviat labour offices (Nagel, Smandek 2010, pp. 102–108).

The foundations of the current system of LMP's institutional management were established in 1999 as part of the administrative system reform. The system became fully operational in 2005. The current model of PES has a mixed nature – both central and local government units are responsible for it. The central government segment comprises the minister in charge of labour aided by his department and regional governors supported by regional offices. The local government segment comprises RLOs (local government organisational units subordinated to the marshal) and at the poviat level PLOs (subordinated to the poviat executive). Thanks to the very far-reaching decentralisation of powers from the central level to the regional one, and especially to the poviat level, local government units have been equipped with instruments that enable them to respond to the specific challenges of their labour markets. It should be emphasised that in Poland, PLOs are responsible for the provision of direct assistance to the unemployed/the job seekers, and a major institutional as well as public actor influencing the situation in its local labour market. They can deploy appropriate instruments and programmes in order to reduce the existing mismatch between the demand and supply of labour (Kukulak-Dolata, Pichla 2007, pp. 80–81).

Central government institutions, therefore, determine the broad guidelines for LMP in Poland, but have no direct impact on independent policies pursued at the regional or poviat levels. However, one may note several mechanisms of interaction with the national level. First, regional governments must take NAPE into consideration when preparing their action plans for employment, specifically, the LMP directions set by the central level. Second, as noted by Sztandar-Sztanderska (2013, p. 10), the regulations on the standardisation of services influence the activities of PES at regional and local levels. The third kind of impact is non-institutionalised and is rooted in the lingering perception of the ministry in charge of labour by the RLO and PLO staff as a superior unit (Frączek 2015c, p. 35).

Relatively high level of LMP financing with an emphasis on PLMP

Analysing the OECD data on the share of spending on LMP in GDP, it can be noted that in 1993–2013, in Poland, it constituted on average 1.29% of GDP, while in countries representing the neo-Weberian model (France, Germany, the Netherlands and Sweden) it was 2.49%, 2.85%, 3.04% and 2.81% of GDP, respectively (i.e. at least twice as much). It must be emphasised that for the last several years, the rate in Poland has been lower than average and rarely exceeded 1% of GDP (Figure 6.1).

The breakdown of spending on LMP in Poland shows that in the analysed period, the average weighted share of spending on PLMP in total LMP spending equalled almost 62%, i.e. more was spent on passive policies than on active ones, though in 2008–2013 the situation was reversed. Meanwhile, in France, Germany and the Netherlands the spending on passive policies clearly dominated in 1993–2013 (59%, 62% and 60% of total spending, respectively), whereas Sweden spends distinctly more on active policies (approx. 56% of total spending in the period studied).

Thus, the funding of Poland's LMP differs in terms of spending patterns from the majority of countries in which the neo-Weberian approach is considered to be most strongly rooted, due to both the much lower relative volume of funding and the increased proportion of funds spent on active policy in recent years.

Goal-oriented and efficiency-oriented performance measures to evaluate the quality of actions

The mechanisms and instruments aimed at achieving specific results and at improving the efficiency of public spending (especially in the field of ALMP) are becoming increasingly common in Poland's LMP (they are mainly used by PES).

The practice of evaluating LMP allows for the use of a very wide range of instruments to assess the effectiveness of these policy programmes. Among the methods of measuring performance, gross measures far outweigh the net ones. In Poland, PES use two main kinds of data obtained from PLOs: employment effectiveness (re-employment rate), and cost effectiveness (re-employment cost) (Ministry of Labour 2013, p. 4). The measurements are widely criticised in the literature for their controversial construction both in terms of methodology and in relation to LMP objectives (cf. Góra, Sztanderska 2006; Sztandar-Sztanderska 2013).

More importantly, goal-oriented and performance-oriented measures apply not only to PES and their activities, but also to the social and private actors contracted by public authorities to implement elements of this policy (also providing feedback on the results achieved by non-public entities). For example, private employment agencies can be remunerated for finding jobs or other kinds of gainful employment ('small contracting'). Employment agencies are paid in instalments, with the largest, final payment made only if a previously unemployed person has

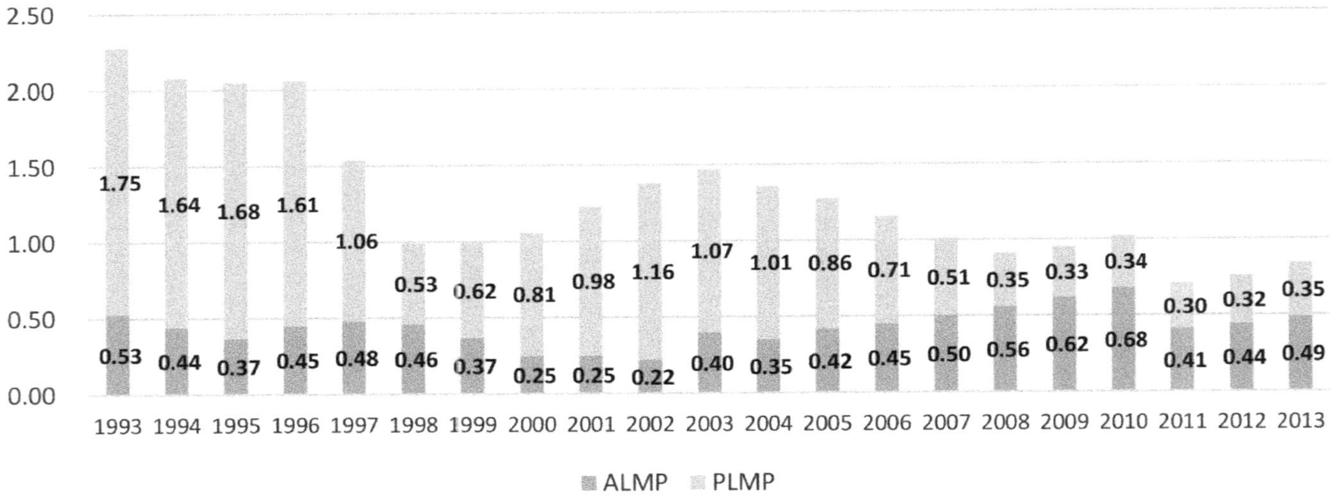

Figure 6.1 Spending on active (ALMP) and passive (PLMP) labour market policies in Poland (as percentage of GDP).

Source: Own calculations based on OECD data (*Public Expenditure and Participant Stocks on LMP*), http://stats.oecd.org/# (accessed 19 November 2016).

kept his/her job for at least 6 months. Moreover, the payments already made must be refunded in proportion to the period for which the condition was not met.

A similar payment mechanism applies to contracting for specific activation measures ('big contracting'). Employment agencies are obliged to perform certain actions or to achieve expected employment outcomes. The compensation due also depends on their meeting specified targets (job placement and retention effectiveness) set in the contract.

Extensive use of goal-oriented and performance measures can also be seen at the stages of development, implementation and evaluation of key operational documents in LMP, namely NAPE and regional plans.

The last two NAPEs differ with respect to the application of both kinds of measures. NAPE/2012–2014 contained one overall objective: to increase the employment rate of persons aged 20–64 to 66.5% as at the end of 2014. The document also set additional targets to be achieved as at the end of 2012: (1) to reduce the registered unemployment rate at least to 12.3%; (2) to achieve the employment rate of persons aged 20–64 of 65.4% (NAPE 2012, p. 19). By comparison, NAPE/2015–2017 set one general objective – to increase the total employment rate of persons aged 20–64 to 68.1% in 2017. The plan also set the following targets: (1) to reduce the total unemployment rate; (2) to increase the economic activity rate (NAPE 2015, p. 17). In the latest plan, the general objective was formulated correctly, unlike its specific targets. First of all, they lack a timeframe, and second, it is not clear whether the stipulated targets refer to the registered unemployment rate or to that computed on the basis on the Labour Force Survey (LFS). Finally, no target values were actually specified.

NAPE/2012–2014 contained five main indicators for the monitoring and evaluation of the national plan and regional plans (two of them with a total of additional ten sections) reflecting the situation in the Polish labour market and the extent to which the objectives of the EU 2020 Strategy had been achieved. Thirty-four auxiliary indicators were also provided to assess the progress made in the individual directions of action (NAPE 2012, pp. 78–81). NAPE/2015–2017 contains six main indicators (two of them with a total of additional ten sections) and 34 auxiliary indicators (NAPE 2015, pp. 62–65).

It should also be emphasised that the annual reports on NAPE implementation must contain information on the quantitative and qualitative results achieved, which is a positive development.

Consideration of the concept of the 'doing' state via intensive interactions between PES staff and service users

Labour administration (PES) gradually departs from its 'egocentric' mode of operation (where customers are treated en bloc using the same schematic rules) in favour of the 'allocentric' approach (focus on their individual needs). For example, it involves individual action plans (IAP) – individualised consultancy services provided to the unemployed/job seekers, which require the involvement of both sides in finding employment.

According to EPLMIA, IAPs are action plans which comprise basic labour market services supported by labour market instruments in order to offer job placements to unemployed persons or to those seeking employment. The plan includes actions on the part of PLOs, activities to be pursued individually by unemployed people (i.e. looking for work), and specifies the timeframes of these activities. It is worth mentioning that the IAPs are mandatory for all the registered unemployed persons and must be jointly drawn up by the consultant and the unemployed person involved.

Polish PLOs activate not only the unemployed, but also their own staff responsible for direct contact with the former. This is reflected in profiling the unemployed (profile I – active job seekers; profile II – unemployed persons requiring support; profile III – unemployed persons alienated from the labour market), which allows the PLOs to offer services and labour market instruments better tailored to the individual needs of the customers (Męcina 2013, p. 169). It also strengthens the responsibility of PES staff for identifying customer needs and for finding the most effective route to employment. However, the rigidly pre-defined range of interventions within specific profiles deserves criticism, since it may significantly reduce the possibilities of activating persons assigned to profile III (Culepa, Rotkiewicz, Wołoszyn-Kądziołka 2015, p. 198).

Professional PES staff considered to be one of the most important policy success factors

In recent years, Polish PES have placed increasing emphasis on improving the professional skills of their staff. Particularly intensive training activities involve the so-called key employees (employment agents, career counsellors, professional development specialists, programmes specialists, consultants and EURES assistants) and are often financed by the EU funds.

The above-mentioned PES staff members are obliged to improve their professional qualifications by participating in module-based training workshops available in special databases maintained by the minister responsible for labour. Labour offices are required to provide their staff with information about training, to cover part of training costs, and to enable their staff to participate in such workshops (Culepa, Rotkiewicz, Wołoszyn-Kądziołka 2015, p. 542).

Another solution meant to improve the quality of services provided under LMP is performance-related remuneration. RLO, PLO and VLC staff may receive bonuses (financed by the Labour Fund) depending on their position, performance and professional qualifications. The bonus may not exceed PLN600 per month (approx. €150), which is not a particularly large amount.

Under the neo-Weberian approach, highly qualified, professional officials play the most important role in the provision of high-quality public services. Unfortunately, Poland's PES are predominantly criticised for employing insufficient numbers of competent staff (which translates into a very high number of unemployed persons per a single key PES employee), cumbersome administrative duties (including issues related to health insurance for the unemployed), and insufficient funds available for PES staffing policy (Drabek 2007, p. 8; Sztandar-Sztanderska 2013, p. 8). The shortage of funding makes it impossible to maintain the current level of human resources (not to mention improve their quality). Central funds are inadequate, whereas poviat authorities remain unwilling to spend their money on either quantitative or qualitative training-up of PES staff due to their economic and financial difficulties.

Use of evidence-based policy mechanisms thanks to elaborate public analytical institutions (including labour market observatories) and better communication among experts, decision makers and street-level officials

The institutions which implement LMP in Poland have access to numerous sources of information and knowledge generated by public, private and social sector entities. They include a system of public statistics, data generated by public labour market institutions (the minister in charge of labour, RLOs, PLOs and VLC), and studies conducted by government research institutions (e.g. labour market observatories).

These observatories are also associated with non-governmental organisations, universities or the business environment. A very important complement to the knowledge in the area of LMP is the information sourced from private and public think-tanks (links with employers' organisations, trade unions and the third sector). Equally important is academic research, which provides empirical and theoretical basis for defining and solving LMP-related problems.

Poland lacks a central-level strategic thinking centre dealing with the broader labour market issues (including LMP), which could raise the decision makers' awareness of long-term projections and development scenarios, and support them in making ad-hoc political decisions (by providing reliable evidence). In the author's opinion, drawing on the experience of the now defunct Government Centre for Strategic Studies, such an institution should definitely be created. Its remit should include not only the issues related to a narrowly understood LMP, but also other key topics related to the development of the labour market in Poland. Using Guzikowski's typology (2016, p. 16) related to the national institutional system of the labour market, these topics may comprise: (1) minimum wage legislation; (2) working time legislation; (3) legal protection of employment; (4) PLMP system; (5) ALMP system; (6) pensions; (7) trade union system; and (8) labour taxation system.

Poland's membership in the EU provided a very positive development stimulus in the field of monitoring and evaluation of labour market activities. Public institutions at various levels responsible for managing this policy began to create and use mechanisms as well as instruments to extend the decision makers' knowledge of the labour market. Moreover, especially in the case of activities financed by the EU funds, studies, reports and analyses prepared by think tanks and research centres (academic, social and, above all, commercial entities specialising in evaluation projects) external to public administration have become valuable sources of information. However, the multitude of existing evaluations and analyses, the huge information load that they contain, and the often hermetic language used by experts and researchers prevent the authorities from tapping this potential. Using this knowledge to design and implement effective actions requires, among other things, vastly improved communication among experts, decision makers, and street-level officials. This should be done through intensive PES staff training in the area of analysing public policies, statistics, knowledge management, developing PES own research units, and a greater involvement of PES staff in the preparation of analyses conducted by external entities.

Challenges to the implementation of LMP in Poland in accordance with the neo-Weberian model

The findings discussed above and the author's own observations regarding Poland's LMP can be summarised as challenges. Addressing them may help the parties responsible to achieve the objectives of the policy using the model assumptions of the neo-Weberian approach.

A serious problem facing LMP in Poland is due to the fact that its systemic rationality is not sufficiently rooted in law. It must be emphasised that the most important normative act for the executors of LMP, namely the EPLMIA, has been amended seventy times since its passage in 2004. Despite (but also because of) the significant changes made to it in 2014, the act is widely criticised by academics, experts, policy makers and experienced officials. It reveals the operational weakness of the neo-Weberian public management model in Poland, since it is hard to expect PES staff (or other labour market institutions) to act effectively in a system whose fundamental logic is impaired.

Unfortunately, neither labour matters nor LMP have been recognised as priorities by most governments of the Third Polish Republic. This is evidenced, among others, by the relatively weak position of the minister in charge of labour in the hierarchy of the Council of Ministers. Among the 14 heads of the Ministry of Labour so far, only J. Hausner and L. Komołowski were at the same time deputy prime ministers. Further, in 2011 and in 2012, the then Minister of Finance blocked part of the Labour Fund (administered by the minister in charge of labour) citing 'the need to reduce public expenditure due to the fact that Poland is subjected to the excessive deficit procedure' (Odpowiedź 2012).

Another important flaw of Poland's LMP is the avoidance of responsibility. Regrettably, examples of this phenomenon abound: insufficient funding of ALMP by the state (the available funds are occasionally frozen due to the pressure of the public finance sphere), shifting responsibility between the central government and PLOs for linking health insurance entitlements to the unemployed person status, or the lack of involvement of regional and poviat-level decision makers in managing LMP (despite their statutory responsibility to do so).

Next, a large proportion of measures implemented under Poland's LMP is funded by the European Social Fund (ESF). Central, regional and poviat authorities, instead of earmarking sufficient funds for the implementation of the policy, rely on external resources as if unaware of the fact that soon these may be significantly limited.

In the author's view, the most important challenge facing Poland's LMP implemented according to the neo-Weberian management model is how to endow it with a systemic rationality given the decentralised and autonomised institutional system of PES. Despite the numerous group of public, private and social institutions with which public administration cooperates, the latter still remains – especially in the context of the neo-Weberian model – the key player responsible for the success (or failure) of the policy.

Conclusion

LMP as implemented in Poland shows a lot of similarities with the neo-Weberian public management model. However, the presence of mechanisms and instruments typical of other public management models point to the hybrid nature of this policy with a tendency to evolve towards the neo-Weberian approach.

From the point of view of LMP, the changes and political processes which have led to the radical systemic transformation, Poland can be seen as a country particularly open to the neo-Weberian approach. The reasons include the absence of fully developed mechanisms typical of the classical Weberian model of administration and the sometimes premature (or even unthinking) adoption of solutions from other models. Therefore it makes sense to return to the 'fundamental' Weberian features, at the same time taking into consideration those elements of NPM and public governance that have stood the test of time, i.e. turned out to be more efficient in meeting collective needs in the area of LMP.

Poland's LMP implemented in accordance with certain elements of the neo-Weberian model may provide an impulse for positive change in the labour market sphere, because it offers a different perspective on the processes taking place within the policy without rejecting the positive experiences and well-functioning mechanisms typical of other public management models. In order for this to happen, the most important problems and challenges of the LMP must be addressed, namely its limited law-based rationality, the weak position of the minister in charge of labour, avoidance of responsibility, overdependence on EU funds, and the likelihood of introducing systemic rationality into the decentralised and autonomised world of PES.

Bibliography

Chrabąszcz, R., Zawicki, M. (2014). Nauki o polityce publicznej [Public policy sciences], in: M. Zawicki (ed.), *Wprowadzenie do nauk o polityce publicznej* [An Introduction to Public Policy Sciences] (pp. 17–40). Warsaw: Polskie Wydawnictwo Ekonomiczne.

Considine, M., Lewis, J. M. (2003). Bureaucracy, network, or enterprise? Comparing models of governance in Australia, Britain, the Netherlands, and New Zealand. *Public Administration Review*, 2 (63), pp. 131–140.

Culepa, M., Rotkiewicz, M., Wołoszyn-Kądziołka, D. (2015). *Ustawa o promocji zatrudnienia i instytucjach rynku pracy. Komentarz* [The Employment Promotion and Labour Market Institutions Act: A Commentary]. Warsaw: Wydawnictwo C. H. Beck.

Drabek, A. (2007). Pracownicy Publicznych Służb Zatrudnienia [The staff of public employment services], *Polityka Społeczna*, 2, pp. 6–9.

European Commission (2013). *Peer Review on Performance Management in Public Employment Services (PES)*. Copenhagen: DG Employment, Social Affairs and Inclusion, The European Commission.

Frączek, M. (2014). Polityka rynku pracy [Labour market policy], in: M. Zawicki (ed.), *Wprowadzenie do nauk o polityce publicznej* [An Introduction to Public Policy Studies] (pp. 117–147). Warsaw: Polskie Wydawnictwo Ekonomiczne.

Frączek, M. (2015a). Współzarządzanie a polityka rynku pracy [Governance in the context of labour market policy], in: S. Mazur (ed.), *Współzarządzanie publiczne* [Public Governance] (pp. 151–177). Warsaw: Wydawnictwo Naukowe Scholar.

Frączek, M. (2015b). Układ prawno-instytucjonalny polityki rynku pracy w Polsce [The legal and institutional framework of labour market policy in Poland], in: M. Frączek (ed.), *Polityka rynku pracy: teoria i praktyka* [Labour Market Policy: Theory and Practice] (pp. 101–107). Warsaw: Polskie Wydawnictwo Ekonomiczne.

Frączek, M. (2015c). Praktyka realizacji polityki rynku pracy w Polsce a współzarządzanie publiczne [The practical implementation of labour market policy in Poland vs public governance]. *Zarządzanie Publiczne*, 2 (32).

Frączek, M. (2016). Polityka rynku pracy w neoweberowskim modelu zarządzania publicznego [Labour market policy in the neo-Weberian governance model], in: S. Mazur (ed.), *Neoweberyzm w zarządzaniu publicznym. Od modelu do paradygmatu?* [The Neo-Weberian State in Public Management. From a Model to a Paradigm?] (pp. 192–209). Warsaw: Wydawnictwo Naukowe Scholar.

Góra, M., Sztanderska, U. (2006). *Wprowadzenie do analizy lokalnego rynku pracy. Przewodnik* [An Introduction to Local Labour Market Analysis. A Guide]. Warsaw: Ministerstwo Pracy i Polityki Społecznej.

Guzikowski, M. (2016). *Instytucje rynku pracy w krajach transformacyjnych: dynamika, interakcje, prawidłowości empiryczne* [Labour Market Institutions in Transition Countries: Dynamics, Interactions, and Empirical Observations]. Warsaw: Oficyna Wydawnicza Szkoła Główna Handlowa w Warszawie.

Kopyciński, P. (2015). Strategie i plany na rzecz zatrudnienie w Polsce [Employment promotion strategies and plans in Poland], in: M. Frączek (ed.), *Polityka rynku pracy: teoria i praktyka* [Labour Market Policy: Theory and Practice] (pp. 108–118). Warsaw: Polskie Wydawnictwo Ekonomiczne.

Kozak, W. (2014). *Rynek pracy. Perspektywa instytucjonalna* [Labour Market: An Institutional Perspective]. Warsaw: Wydawnictwa Uniwersytetu Warszawskiego.

Kukulak-Dolata, I., Pichla, J. (2007). *Rola publicznych służb zatrudnienia i agencji zatrudnienia na rynku pracy* [The Role of Public Employment Services and Employment Agencies in the Labour Market]. Warsaw: Instytut Pracy i Spraw Socjalnych.

Mazur, S. (2015). Modele zarządzania publicznego a typy polityk publicznych rynku pracy [Public management models and types of public labour market policies], in: M. Frączek (ed.), *Polityka rynku pracy: teoria i praktyka* [Labour Market Policy: Theory and Practice] (pp. 19–30). Warsaw: Polskie Wydawnictwo Ekonomiczne.

Męcina, J. (2013). *Niewykorzystane zasoby. Nowa polityka rynku pracy* [Untapped Resources: A New Labour Market Policy]. Warsaw: ASPRA-JR.

Ministry of Labour (2013). *Efektywność podstawowych form aktywizacji zawodowej realizowanych w ramach programów na rzecz promocji zatrudnienia, łagodzenia skutków bezrobocia i aktywizacji zawodowej w 2012 roku* [The Effectiveness of Basic Forms of Vocational Activation Implemented within the Framework of Employment

Promotion, Unemployment Mitigation and Vocational Activation Programmes in 2012]. Warsaw: Ministerstwo Pracy i Polityki Społecznej, Departament Funduszy.

Nagel, K., Smandek, I. M. (2010). *Polityka rynku pracy i źródła jej finansowania* [Labour Market Policy and Sources of Its Funding]. Katowice: Wydawnictwo Uniwersytetu Ekonomicznego.

NAPE (KPDZ) (2012). *Krajowy Plan Działań na rzecz Zatrudnienia na lata 2012–2014. Załącznik do uchwały nr 138/2012 Rady Ministrów z dnia 21 sierpnia 2012 r* [National Action Plan for Employment 2015–2017. Annexe to Resolution No. 28/2015 of the Council of Ministers of 10 March 2015]. Warsaw: Rada Ministrów.

NAPE (KPDZ) (2015). *Krajowy Plan Działań na rzecz Zatrudnienia na lata 2015–2017. Załącznik do uchwały nr 28/2015 Rady Ministrów z dnia 10 marca 2015 r* [National Action Plan for Employment 2015–2017. Annexe to Resolution No. 28/2015 of the Council of Ministers of 10 March 2015]. Warsaw: Rada Ministrów.

Odpowiedź (2012). Odpowiedź podsekretarza stanu w Ministerstwie Pracy i Polityki Społecznej – z upoważnienia ministra – na interpelację nr 2180 w sprawie ograniczania środków finansowych na aktywną walkę z bezrobociem [The response of the Undersecretary of State in the Ministry of Labour and Social Policy – as authorised by the Minister – to parliamentary question no 2180 concerning the limitations on funding active unemployment measures], www.sejm.gov.pl/sejm7.nsf/InterpelacjaTresc.xsp?key=167F4621 (accessed 23 May 2016).

Sztandar-Sztanderska, K. (2013). *Nie zrzucajmy całej winy na nieefektywne urzędy pracy i fikcyjnych bezrobotnych* [Let Us Not Blame Ineffective Labour Offices and the Fictitious Unemployed for Everything]. Warsaw: Wrzos EAPN Polska.

Tyrowicz, J. (2010). Powiatowe strategie rynku pracy – gdzie jesteśmy i dokąd warto byłoby zmierzać? [Labour Market Strategies at Poviat [County] Level: Where We Are and Where We Should Go?] Warsaw: FISE.

Zybała, A. (2015). Struktura ryzyk w reformie wybranych elementów polityki rynku pracy [The structure of risks in the reform of selected labour market policy measures]. *Zarządzanie Publiczne*, 3 (33), pp. 41–55.

7 The neo-Weberian approach in industrial policy

Łukasz Mamica

Introduction

Industrial policy in the second half of the 20th century was marked by numerous turnabouts both in the free-market economies and in the socialist ones. Not only did the share of public ownership in the structure of enterprises change over the years, but also the extent of state influence on the industrial sphere evolved. In Poland, the evolution of industrial policy proceeded from a centrally planned socialist economy, in which statism permitted sectoral industrial policy, to its total absence in the transition period, which started in 1989. However, the 2007/2008 crisis sparked a renewed interest in the regulatory role of the state and in the development opportunities associated with taking sectoral action. The analysis of Polish industrial policy presented below is based on a verification of the neo-Weberian approach in public management. Max Weber saw the state as the only entity equipped with sufficient powers to implement regulations that affect the interests of the various actors of socio-economic life. His message appears to be gaining more and more currency. In the context of globalisation, society increases its expectations of the state as the only entity capable of effectively opposing the interests of multinational corporations. One of the manifestations of these expectations is the result of the US presidential election in 2016. The state is expected to generate resources to protect its citizens against the negative effects of globalisation. Although the present study focuses on the neo-Weberian concepts in public management, it should be borne in mind that this approach is also employed in managing organisations (Brock, Saks 2016; Taylor 1997).

The fundamental determinants of evolution of industrial policy

In *The Wealth of Nations*, Adam Smith argued that without appropriate interventions on the part of the state, the efforts of monopolies will not only lead to increased social inequalities, but also to an inefficient allocation of resources. Attempts to minimise the negative effects of monopolistic activities included the Sherman Antitrust Act (adopted by the US Congress in 1890) and the Clayton Antitrust Act (1914), which expanded the list of practices considered harmful to consumers. These regulations have had a direct impact on the balance of power in the industrial sphere. Managers of large companies, fearing antitrust action in the United States, decided to move into international markets, which resulted in the emergence of powerful transnational corporations.

Important reasons which determine the need for industrial policy include market failures involving public goods, limited competition, incomplete markets and externalities (Stiglitz 1988). Externalities provide an especially important impetus for active state intervention. A good example of this phenomenon is the reorientation of German energy industry towards renewable sources motivated by the need to halt climate change. The unprecedented scale of intervention and public subsidies to stimulate structural changes in this area gave rise to the term *Energiewende* (Renn, Marshall 2016).

Industrial policy in the first half of the 20th century was used by two totalitarian regimes in order to enter the fast track of development. In the 1930s, the totalitarian Soviet Russia collectivised agriculture, forcing farm workers to create quasi co-operative enterprises (collective farms), and pursued a vigorous and effective industrialisation organised under five-year plans (Mertelsmann 2016). Another example of growth through accelerated industrialisation at the expense of villagers was the communist China after Mao Zedong came to power in 1949. Direct government interventions targeted at selected industries took place in China again in 2003 (Chen and Naughton 2016).

In the 1960s and 1970s, post-colonial countries facing limits to external development impulses attempted to accelerate industrialisation. Due to the shortage of capital, only the state possessed sufficient financial resources to build large industrial plants. These efforts, however, did not bring about clearly positive results in all the countries concerned. For example, South American countries began to develop fast, but public spending focused on central investment encouraged the emergence of monopolies, and regulated commodity prices weakened the competitive position of their economies in international markets.

Evans (1985) associates the increasing role of public authorities in developing countries with the intensification of transnational economic linkages and the fact that they have become exporters of capital. At the same time, he points out that this kind of intervention may be ineffective, contribute to corruption, and encourage takeover attempts by other social actors. While in Evans' opinion the state's capacity increases in organisational terms and in terms of power relative to local actors, influencing international markets remains beyond the reach of a single country.

The 1980s saw the reduction of state involvement in the economy, especially through the denationalisation of public assets. F. von Hayek's liberal approach was revived and led to the privatisation of numerous industries (including coal mining, metallurgy, energy and telecommunications). Deregulation and privatisation were the economic hallmarks of the decade, especially of the United Kingdom under Margaret Thatcher and the United States during the tenure of President Ronald Reagan. But in the dynamically developing Asian economies, it was the state with its interventionism and active industrial policy that strengthened the competitive position of local economies. According to an OECD survey, industrial policy in its member countries is at a turning point . . . during the 1980s; it gradually moved away from an approach principally defined by policies aimed at sheltering declining industries or 'picking winners.' . . . Emphasis was instead put on reforming tax systems to make them more efficient and more neutral with respect to industrial investment choices, and on the need to enlarge as much as possible the scope for market forces by large scale privatisation and deregulation in many countries.

(OECD 1992, p. 11)

In the early 1990s, owing to the publication of the Bangemann Report (European Commission 1990), European industrial policy began to evolve from a focus on declining industries towards those based on R&D. The importance of research and innovation in European industrial policy further increased with the adoption of the Maastricht Treaty in 1993, which accentuated the need to speed up the adjustment of industry to structural change. The role of innovation in industrial development was also highlighted in the Lisbon Strategy adopted by the European Council in 2000. In 2004, the European Commission decided to modify the role of public administration in the context of challenges faced by industrial policy. The proposed solutions were exclusively horizontal and included the simplification of legal provisions and the EU regulation system in the EU, and the strengthening of administrative cooperation between the European Commission and the EU member states (EU Commission 1994).

Weber also addressed the issues concerning the relationships between state authorities and economic policy in his lecture 'The Nation State and Economic Policy' delivered in 1895, in which he treated state actions as the ultimate criterion for economic policy (1895/2008). Weber considered himself a political economist, and in his fundamental work *Economy and Society* published in 1922 he analysed the role of the state in shaping the so-called industrial capitalism. In industrial capitalism, the key roles are played by industrial enterprises capable of making correct calculations, which organise labour to supply products to mass markets. According to the German sociologist, in order to make it possible, 'industrial capitalism must be able to count on the continuity, trustworthiness and objectivity of the legal order, and on the rational, predictable functioning of legal and administrative agencies' (1922/1978, p. 1095). These expectations come down mainly to the provision of a stable business environment, which is guaranteed by the state administration. According to Weber, the stability of external conditions is particularly important for large economic entities, moreover, only the state is in a position to introduce regulations that affect the interests of the big players. A. Anter argues that Weber regarded the state as an instrument for setting certain standards (2014, p. 106). The activities of transnational corporations, whose resources are often comparable to those at the disposal of small nation states, show that only the state can effectively oppose their interests. However, the relationships between the business world and politicians responsible for decisions in the area of industrial policy are ultimately based on the expectations of both sides concerning the preservation of their interests (Magee 1994).

The former group sees it as an opportunity to obtain above-average profits, whereas politicians expect to stay in power and secure extra income or future employment after leaving the world of politics. In some cases, a clear conflict of the public and private interests arises. (A particularly striking example: in his last weeks in office, the German Chancellor Gerhard Schröder signed an agreement with Russia to build a gas pipeline under the Baltic seabed, bypassing the Baltic countries, Ukraine, and Poland, and then took a senior position on the board of the Nord Stream consortium controlled by Russia.)

The changing approach to industrial policy as a result of the 2007/2008 economic crisis

The EU industrial policy is implemented both at the level of the European Commission and by national governments. Pelkmans (2006) analysed the stimu-latory role of the EU institutions in terms of a better environment in a number of sectors, but without considering protectionist measures, distortive subsidies or permissive competition policy. Several years before the outbreak of the crisis, the belief that industrial policy should only be horizontal prevailed. It was neatly summed up by Bianchi and Labory (2006, p. 22):

> Policy making is no longer an action decided by a central government to limit or subsidize individual behaviour but rather a programme that involves all the institutions of a territory and that is aimed at consolidating an environment able to increase the collective competitiveness and therefore to stimulate the latent innovation capacity.

In 2002, industrial policy in the documents promulgated by the European Commission was defined as 'horizontal in nature and aiming to secure framework conditions favourable to industrial competitiveness' (EC 2002, p. 3). The neces-sity to carry out of sectoral activities was mentioned, however, in the *Strategy for Smart, Sustainable and Inclusive Europe 2020* (European Commission 2010a). As shown by the OECD surveys, certain interventions originally thought to be horizontal and not intended to favour any sectors of the economy have an unbal-anced impact on various categories of industry (Bravo-Biosca *et al.* 2013). For example, activities meant to improve investment opportunities in a given area attract the interest of representatives of different industries to varying degrees.

The turning point in setting the directions for industrial policy was the global crisis which broke out in 2008. Although not everyone agrees that there was a clear qualitative change in this respect (Szalavetz 2015), the scope of state inter-vention in the economy and the associated budget costs were exceptionally high. Only the state was capable of undertaking such large-scale interventions. The crisis also led to a renewed interest in sectoral activities. The Commission's documents highlight the areas of industry which deserve special support, such as motor vehicles and transportation equipment, energy supply and chemicals (European Commission 2010b). On the other hand, the Communication from the Commission *Action Plan for a Competitive and Sustainable Steel Industry in Europe* of June 2013 recognised the importance of its impact on value chains including automotive, construction, electronics, and mechanical and electrical engineering (EC 2013). After 2008, state intervention in the economy ceased to be seen mainly as interference with free-market mechanisms. The increasing public deficit caused by the declining banking sector strengthened public pressure for a greater degree of state involvement in the economy. These actions were consistent with the neo-Weberian approach, which, according to Pollitt and Bouckaert, emphasises 'the modernisation of financial control systems so that they are able to more forcefully express the general political and strategic priorities in the process of resource allocation' (2011, p. 82).

The 2007/2008 crisis undermined the existing beliefs about market efficiency characteristic of the period of new public management. Likewise, the network-based solutions proposed by public governance proved to be insufficient to maintain economic growth. It was generally accepted that the state may play the role of the ultimate lender that saves the banking system from collapse, but the view that a strong public authority can oppose the interests of multinational corporations also gained popularity. The election of Donald Trump was certainly influenced by his views on strengthening the role of the state in dealing with large corporations, including persuading them to transfer their manufacturing operations back to the USA. The crisis thus triggered a revival of the drive to consolidate the powers of the state in the area of economic and industrial policy in line with the model of neo-Weberian state characterised by W. Drechsler and R. Kattel (2008) as a distinctive actor which operates according to its own principles, methods and culture. Pollitt notes that the neo-Weberian approach does not mean minimal state involvement in the sphere of regulation, but treats it as 'the guarantor of social order and partner for markets and society' (2008/09, p. 14). It remains an open question whether and if so, how the new protectionist US policy will lead to economic growth, or alternatively, result in increased global tensions.

It needs to be borne in mind, however, that there are a number of reservations regarding the legitimacy of industrial policy. Even Rodrik, who, for the most part, is in favour of it, notes the following risks: industrial policy is conducive to corruption and allows for the adoption of preferential solutions which raise the income of groups politically associated with those in power; governments face a significant number of important issues, such as fiscal policy and combating corruption, and hence should not be burdened with additional tasks; it is by no means certain that industrial policy delivers the expected results; market failures in practice rarely hinder economic growth; and even if we consider it reasonable to conduct industrial policy, governments rarely have adequately detailed data to help them accurately target their interventions (2008, p. 31).

It can be concluded that state-led industrial policy began to reflect the neo-Weberian approach in public management, which, according to C. Pollitt and G. Bouckaert consists in in a 'reaffirmation of the role of the state as the main facilitator of solutions to the new problems of globalisation and technological change' (2011, p. 118).

In the *Strategy for Smart, Sustainable and Inclusive Europe 2020* (European Commission 2010a), which to some extent constitutes a response to the crisis, all three of these priorities – including smart growth (developing an economy based on knowledge and innovation), sustainable growth (promoting a more resource efficient, greener, and more competitive economy), and inclusive growth (fostering a high level of employment, ensuring social and territorial cohesion) – are directly related to the challenges posed by industrial policy. Out of the seven flagship projects proposed by the European Commission, two ('An industrial policy for the globalisation era' and 'Innovation Union') are directly related to industrial policy. The mounting pressure on the part of such countries as China and India associated with their growing expenditure on research and technology forces European businesses to focus on qualitative growth.

In its Communication of January 2014 *For a European Industrial Renaissance*, the European Commission 'calls on Member States to recognise the central importance of industry for boosting competitiveness and sustainable growth in Europe and for a systematic consideration of competitiveness concerns across all policy areas' (European Commission 2014, p. 24). Industrial policy is thus treated as a direct determinant of success in other policy areas, particularly in the area of innovation policy (Kopyciński 2016).

The evolution of Poland's industrial policy in the context of the neo-Weberian approach

In Poland's socialist economy, heavy industry (nearly 80%) dominated over the consumer goods industry (20%). The political transformation, which involved the departure from a centrally planned economy, began in 1989 and brought about disastrous consequences. At least one-third of all the large and medium-sized industrial enterprises (employing over 100 workers) ceased to exist. Nearly two million jobs disappeared, and the decline in Poland's production potential was estimated at about 40% (Polskie Lobby Przemysłowe 2012). By comparison, the decreasing share of industry in the economic structure of Western European countries, although evident since the 1970s, was much more evolutionary in nature. For example, in 1975–1991, the share of industry in GDP in France fell from 36.1% to 21.2%, while in the UK it fell from 26.5% to 21.4% (Klamut 1996, p. 169).

In the early years of market economy in Poland, in September 1993, the Council of Ministers adopted a document *Industrial Policy. Assumptions. Implementation Programme 1993–1995*. The programme was intended to respond to the problems of restructuring and proposed sectoral action. In the 1990s, sectoral studies were also undertaken. However, the concept of undifferentiated industrial policy (Gorynia 1994) was winning more and more supporters, as evidenced e.g. by the *Industrial Policy Programme for 1995–1997* aimed at strengthening the competitiveness of the Polish industry in an open market. Simultaneously, Polish exports steadily grew. A year before the outbreak of the 2007/2008 crisis, the belief in the superiority of horizontal policy had already been widespread. The dominant attitude was reflected in the title of the document prepared in 2007 by the Ministry of Economy *The Concept of a Horizontal Industrial Policy*. It provided that

> industrial policy will focus on making the most out of horizontal measures to support long-term growth and development of the Polish industry . . . , whereas the policies that affect the Polish industry should rely on the sustained improvement of the quality of industrial activity framework through actions aimed at increasing the competitiveness of industrial enterprises in all the sectors.
>
> (Ministry of Economy 2007, p. 3)

The main coordinator of Poland's industrial policy is the Ministry of Development (formed from the merger of the Ministry of Development and the Ministry of Infrastructure and Development). The attempt to coordinate central government activities in the area of economic policy is also reflected by the delegation of functions of the Minister of Finance to the Minister of Development in 2016. One of the purposes of the merger was to strengthen the effective range of state influence on socio-economic development, which fits in with the most important aspects of the neo-Weberian approach in public management. In 2010, the strategic plan formulated by the Ministry of Economy shows a clear preference for the horizontal approach manifested in the choice of the adopted strategic priorities including national economic security, supporting innovation and competitiveness, better regulation, and activity in the international market (Ministry of Economy 2009). It should be remembered that the public sphere is an important, but not the only factor affecting industrial policy. The neo-Weberian model emphasises the importance of stakeholders apart from the political sphere and public administration. According to V. Pryce, the 'fourth-generation' industrial policy, which is currently pursued, is based on a partnership between the state and the private sector as part of a holistic approach (2012).

Apart from the measures aimed at increasing the competitiveness of existing industries, industrial policy is also responsible for the selection of new industries for support. The latter process is aided by technological foresight. In Poland, crucial activities in this area began in 2007, when the National Foresight Programme – Poland 2020 was launched. The technologies with a high growth potential were identified under 20 specific topics covering three broad fields of research (sustainable development of Poland, information and telecommunications technologies, and security). Foresight analyses also included individual industries, such as scenarios for the technological development of the mining industry and the processing of brown coal, modern metallic, ceramic and composite materials, and the system of monitoring and scenarios of development of medical technologies. An example of foresight programme devoted to the choice of leading technologies is the Industry Technology Foresight InSight 2030 completed in 2011. It assisted in the selection of 99 technologies and 10 research areas with above-average growth prospects.

Industrial policy is increasingly perceived through its qualitative dimension of innovation. *The Strategy for Innovation and Efficiency of the Economy 'Dynamic*

Poland 2020' published in 2013 set out to achieve a highly competitive (innovative and efficient) economy based on knowledge and cooperation. This strategy focuses in particular on fostering innovation, improving the business environment, and the internationalisation of the Polish economy.

A fundamental change in the perception of the state's role in industrial policy is linked with the adoption by the Polish Council of Ministers in February 2016 of the *Action Plan for Responsible Development*, which gives the state the main role in stimulating structural change and development in the economy. The programme is based on five pillars – reindustrialisation, development of innovative firms, development capital, international expansion, and social and regional development – and clearly overcomes the limitation of interventions to the horizontal dimension. The Polish Development Fund will aid in the implementation of special programmes involving such industries as aviation, armaments, shipbuilding, chemicals, food, transport and IT. This kind of thinking in terms of sector-focused activities fits in directly with the assumptions of the neo-Weberian model as applied to public management.

Financing investment from public funds is one of the consequences of the state assuming responsibility for economic and industrial policy in line with the neo-Weberian assumptions. This can be carried out through state-run investment banks (Mazzucato, Penna 2016) or through the structural funds. Apart from the EU structural and investment funds (which amounted to 454 billion euros in 2014–2020), similar solutions are applied by individual countries. For example, in 2008, France established its Strategic Investment Fund with an attached loan fund worth 35 billion euros in order to stimulate, among others, such areas as the digital economy, renewable energy, nano- and biotechnologies. Ensuring adequate funding for investment in the economy is also an important area of interest to Polish decision makers. In Poland, in June 2015, Bank Gospodarstwa Krajowego signed an agreement with other entities establishing four investment funds with a target capitalisation of 6.5 billion zlotys (ca. 1.5 billion euros), through which it plans to run the Polish Investments programme. From the point of view of industrial policy objectives, the most important one appears to be the Polish Enterprise Investment Fund. Initially, it will be worth 1.5 billion zlotys and will focus on highly innovative projects capable of delivering ground-breaking products.

Conclusion

The increasing uncertainty in the financial markets, slowing economic growth, and the rising income disparities lead to a greater interest in the role of the state in the economy. The free market is no longer universally considered to be the only system capable of allocating resources efficiently, as was the case in the NPM era. The need to increase budget deficits due to the recapitalisation of banks on the verge of bankruptcy clearly revealed the cost of the state's withdrawal from exercising effective control of the financial markets, where the desire for short-term profit turned out to be more important than long-term socio-economic growth. Under the neo-Weberian approach, the state begins to be seen as the only entity strong enough to resist the global interests of transnational corporations. Industrial policy can also be seen to depart from the dominant horizontal policy in favour of sectoral interventions. This is especially evident in Poland's industrial policy, where the call for re-industrialisation is accompanied by the identification of promising sectors and sources of financial support for their development.

Bibliography

Anter, A. (2014). *Max Weber's Theory of the Modern State: Origins, Structure and Significance*, Basingstoke: Palgrave Macmillan.

Bianchi, P., Labory, S. (2006). 'Old' industrial policy to 'new' industrial development policies, in: P. Bianchi, S. Labory, *International Handbook on Industrial Policy*, Cheltenham, Northampton, MA: Edward Elgar.

Bravo-Biosca, A., Criscuolo, C., Menon, C. (2013). *What Drives the Dynamics of Business Growth?*, OECD Science, Technology and Industry Policy Papers, no. 1, OECD Publishing, Paris.

Brock, D. M., Saks, M. (2016). Professions and organizations: A European perspective. *European Management Journal*, 34 (1), pp. 1–6. ISSN: 02632373.

Chen, L; Naughton, B. (2016). An institutionalised policy-making mechanism: China's return to techno-industrial policy. *Research Policy,* 45 (10), pp. 2138–2152.

Drechsler W., Kattel, R. (2008). Towards the neo-Weberian state? Perhaps, but certainly, adieu, NPM, *NISPAcee Journal of Public Administration and Policy*, Special issue: A Distinctive European Model? The Neo-Weberian State, 1 (2).

European Commission (1990).'Industrial policy in an open and competitive environment', (Bangemann Memorandum), Working paper, 14 December, Brussels.

European Commission (1994). *An industrial competitiveness policy for the European Union. Communication from the Commission to the Council, the European Parliament, the Economic and Social Committee and the Committee of the Regions*. COM (94) 319 final, 14 September.

European Commission (2002). *Industrial Policy in an Enlarged Europe*, COM (2002) 714.

European Commission (EC) (2010a). *Europe 2020. A European Strategy for Smart, Sustainable and Inclusive Growth*, Brussels.

European Commission (EC) (2010b). *Communication from the Commission to the European Parliament, the Council, the European Economic and Social Committee, and the Committee for Regions: An Integrated Industrial Policy for the Globalisation Era – Putting Competitiveness and Sustainability at Centre Stage*, SEC (2010), pp. 1272–1276, Brussels, COM (2010) 614.

European Commission (EC) (2014). *Communication from the Commission to the European Parliament, the Council, the European Economic and Social Committee and the Committee of the Regions for a European Industrial Renaissance*, Brussels, COM/2014/014 final.

Evans, P. B. (1985). Transnational linkages and the economic role of the state: an analysis of developing and industrialized nations in the post-World War II period, in: P. Evans, D. Rueschemeyer, T. Skocpol (eds), *Bringing the State Back In*, Cambridge: Cambridge University Press.

Gorynia, M. (1994). Polska polityka przystosowawcza 1990–1993 [Poland's Adaptive Policy 1990–1993], *Gospodarka Narodowa*, 01.

Klamut, M. (1996). *Ewolucja struktury gospodarczej w krajach wysoko rozwiniętych* [The Evolution of the Economic Structure in Highly Developed Countries], Wrocław: Wydawnictwo Akademii Ekonomicznej.

Komisja Europejska (KE) (2013). *Communication from the Commission to the European Parliament, the Council, the European Economic and Social Committee and the Committee of the Regions: Plan for a Competitive and Sustainable Steel Industry in Europe*, Strasburg, 11. 6. 2013 COM (2013) 407 final.

Kopyciński, P. (2016). Neoweberyzm (neo-Weberian state) jako sposób zarządzania w polityce innowacyjnej [The neo-Weberian state as a way of managing innovation policy]. *Zarządzanie Publiczne, 37* (3), pp. 26–37.

Magee, S. (1994). The political economy of trade policy, in: D. Greenaway, L. A. Winters (eds) *Surveys in International Trade*, pp. 139–176. Oxford: Blackwell.

Mazzucato, M., Penna, C. (2016). Beyond market failures: the market creating and shaping roles of state investment banks. *Journal of Economic Policy Reform, 19* (4), pp. 305–326.

Mertelsmann, O. (2016). The industrialisation of Soviet Russia 6. The years of progress. The Soviet economy, 1934–1936. *Europe-Asia Studies, 68* (3), pp. 529–530.

Ministry of Economy [Ministerstwo Gospodarki] (2007). *Koncepcja horyzontalnej polityki przemysłowej w Polsce* [The Concept of Horizontal Industrial Policies in Poland], Warsaw, February.

Ministry of Economy (2009). *Plan Strategiczny Ministerstwa Gospodarki* [The Strategic Plan of the Ministry of Economy], Warsaw, December.

OECD (1992). Industrial Policy in OECD Countries. *Annual Review* 1992, Paris.

Pelkmans J. (2006). European industrial policy, in: P. Bianchi, S. Labory. *International Handbook on Industrial Policy*, Cheltenham and Northampton, MA: Edward Elgar.

Pollitt, C. (2008/2009). An overview of the papers and propositions of the first Trans-European Dialogue (TED1). *The NISPAcee Journal of Public Administration and Policy*, I (2).

Pollitt, C., Bouckaert, G. (2011). *Public Management Reform A Comparative Analysis. New Public Management, Governance, and the Neo-Weberian State*, Oxford, New York: Oxford University Press.

Polskie Lobby Przemysłowe (2012). *Straty w potencjale polskiego przemysłu i jego ułomna transformacja po 1989 roku. Wizja nowoczesnej reindustrializacji Polski* [The Lost Potential of the Polish Industry and its Flawed Transformation after 1989. A Vision of Modern Re-industrialisation of Poland], Warsaw, March.

Pryce, V. (2012). *Britain Needs a Fourth Generation Industrial Policy*, Centre Forum, June.

Renn, O., Marshall, J. P. (2016). Coal, nuclear and renewable energy policies in Germany: From the 1950s to the 'Energiewende.' *Energy Policy, 99*, pp. 224–232.

Rodrik, D. (2008). *Normalizing industrial policy*, Commission on Growth and Development Working Paper, no. 3, Washington, DC: World Bank.

Stiglitz, J. (1988). *Economics of the Public Sector*, New York: W. W. Norton.

Szalavetz, A. (2015). Post-crisis approaches to state intervention: New developmentalism or industrial policy as usual? *Competition & Change, 19* (1), pp. 70–83.

Taylor, C. (1997). Charles Perrow and business history: A neo-Weberian approach to business bureaucratization. *Business & Economic History*, 26 (1), p. 138.

Weber, M. (1895/2008). *The Nation State and Economic Policy* (1895) in his *Political Writings*, ed. P. Lassman, R. Speirs, 6th ed., Cambridge: Cambridge University Press.

Weber, M. (1922/1978). *Economy and Society, an Outline of Interpretive Sociology*, G. Roth, C. Wittich (ed.), Los Angeles, London: University of California Press.

8 The neo-Weberian approach in health policy in selected countries

Jacek Klich

Introduction

The aim of this chapter is to compare the health policies pursued in Germany, Great Britain, France, Denmark and the Netherlands from the perspective of the neo-Weberian public management model.

The comparison will be based on two ways of understanding of the term *neo-Weberian approach*, namely as a public management model and as a type of health sector reform (Mazur 2016). The adoption of this perspective dictated the selection of countries for analysis. A brief presentation of health care systems in individual countries with a vast experience of public management reform will be followed by a discussion of their performance. Then, selected elements of their respective health policies will be evaluated.

Health care systems in the analysed countries

For the purposes of this analysis, the health care system is understood as all the organisations and institutions whose primary purpose is to preserve, improve or restore health, and all the resources used for that purpose.

The key elements of any health care system include: the sources of funding, legal regulations governing the cooperation of the public and private sectors in the system, the governance/management system, health insurance, logistics, fees for services, incentives and motivators, information system, well-trained staff, basic infrastructure, and providers (Weber *et al.* 2010, p. 4).

In narrow terms, the health system can be reduced to five elements: financing, payment for services, organisation, regulation and behaviours/motivation of the entities involved (Roberts *et al.* 2008).

The basic functions of the health care system comprise organisation and management, provision of health services, and their financing (Chernichovsky 1995). Table 8.1 presents the key qualitative and quantitative features of health care systems in the analysed countries. Clearly, the analysed health care systems significantly differ in terms of management and financing.

Table 8.1 Key characteristics of the analysed health systems (based on data from 2013)

Item	France	Germany	United Kingdom	Denmark	Netherlands
Mandatory health insurance	Yes	Yes	n/a	n/a	Yes (public or/and private)
Upfront payments	Yes	No	No	No	Depends on policy
Cost-sharing	Yes	Yes	Yes	Yes	Yes
Predominant source of financing	Job-holders' income	Job-holders' income	State budget	State budget	Job-holders' income
Role of the central government/ministry of health	Strong	Medium	Medium	Low	Medium/ low
Health care spending as percentage of GDP (%)	11.6	11.2	8.8	11.1[a]	11.1
Health care spending: real average annual growth rate per capita 2009–2013 (%)	1.35	1.95	-0.88	-0.17	8.73[b]
Current private, out-of-pocket health care spending per capita (in $)	277	649	321	625	270
Practising physicians per thousand population	3.1	4.1	n/a	3.6	n/a
Annual physician visits per capita	6.4	9.9	n/a	4.6	6.2
Acute care hospital beds per thousand population	3.4	5.3	2.3	2.5	3.3
Hospital discharges per thousand population	166	252	129	172	119
MRI machines per million population	9.4	n/a	6.1	n/a	11.5
CT scanners per million population	14.5	n/a	7.9	37.8	11.5
Average number of prescription drugs taken regularly by patients aged 18 or older	1.5	1.6	1.3	n/a	1.2

Notes:
a Current spending only.
b Current spending only: excludes spending on capital formation of health care providers.

Source: US Health Care from a Global Perspective; Obermann et al. (2013).

The performance of the analysed health systems: selected issues

The performance of individual health care systems can be assessed using a variety of measures and indicators, including the patients' opinions on the subject. Typically, in-depth evaluations of national health care systems employ a dozen or several dozen parameters, but due to the considerations of space Table 8.2 includes only the most important ones. Data contained in Table 8.2 warrant the conclusion that the performance of the health care systems in the analysed countries varies, especially as regards such indicators as mortality rate due to coronary heart disease or the number of limb amputations (or their parts) as a result of diabetes complications.

An important complementary criterion in the evaluation of health care systems is their place in international rankings. In a methodologically well-prepared WHO ranking of 2000 (which included 190 countries), France topped the list of the best-performing health care systems, followed by the Netherlands (17), United Kingdom (18), Germany (25) and Denmark (34) (WHO 2000, p. 200). In the European Health Care Index of 2006, which uses patient-focused indicators, France also came first, but in the same ranking published in 2015 (35 countries) France slipped to 11th place, behind the Netherlands (1), Germany (7) and Denmark (9),

Table 8.2 Selected aspects of performance of health care systems (based on data from 2013)

Item	France	Germany	United Kingdom	Denmark	Netherlands
Life expectancy at birth (years)	82.3	80.9	81.1	80.4	81.4
Infant mortality per 1000 live births	3.6	3.3	3.8	3.5	3.8
Mortality as a result of cancer, 1995/2007 (Deaths per 100,000 population, adjusted)[a]	210/179	202/175	221/179	249/220	221/196
Mortality as a result of ischemic heart disease, 1995/2013 (Deaths per 100,000 population)	78/43	223/115	255/98	242/71	157/50
Lower extremity amputations as a result of diabetes (Amputations per 100,000 population)	7.1	18.4	5.1	19.2	13.5

Note:
a Mortality rate adjusted for likelihood of death from other causes.

Source: *US Health Care from a Global Perspective*; Davis *et al.* (2014).

but ahead of the United Kingdom (14) (Björnberg 2016, p. 24). In another ranking list covering only 11 countries (excluding Denmark), which compared the performance of the US health care system with other selected systems, the British system was judged to be the best. Germany came 5th, the Netherlands 6th and France 9th (Davis *et al.* 2014).

Selected health policy features in the analysed countries

The neo-Weberian approach may be interpreted as a public management model and as a type of health sector reform. Hence the term 'health policies' in this section will refer to these two areas.

The presentation of the specific solutions adopted by the countries studied will be based on selected features (i.e. those that can refer to the health care system) of the neo-Weberian public management model as presented by Oramus (2016, p. 147). Such a neo-Weberian public management model in relation to the health care system includes the following six factors:

- role and function of public administration;
- mechanisms and instruments for managing health care issues;
- ways of implementing health policy;
- forms of health service provision;
- relationships with social actors;
- mechanisms of organisational and systemic learning.

The key features of the neo-Weberian management model as applied in health care systems with regard to these six factors are listed in Table 8.3.

Health care system reforms in the analysed countries

France

The main objectives of health care system reforms implemented since 2010 have been to improve governance, to increase the transparency of the system, to contain statutory health insurance expenditure without damaging equity in financial access, to increase geographical equity in access to care and to meet the needs of vulnerable populations, particularly by ensuring access to care for frail elderly individuals and by decreasing social health inequities (Chevreul *et al.* 2015, p. XXV).

Due to the limited involvement of patients in the operation of the French health sector (in comparative terms), the 2015 reform introduced measures to increase their participation by e.g. putting patient representatives on the boards of health agencies and expanding hospital patients' commissions, which must be consulted on hospital quality and safety policies, and informed of adverse events.

It is worth noting that some of the recently adopted solutions resulted in limiting central government powers in the area of health care.

Table 8.3 Key elements of the neo-Weberian management model in health care systems in the analysed countries

Feature	France	Germany	United Kingdom	Denmark	Netherlands
The role and function of public administration	The state has a dominant position in the health care system in terms of organisation and management, and an important one in the provision of health services. The state's share in financing health services is increasing. The health care system is based on the Bismarck model (insurance) with elements of the Beveridge model (increasing share of tax in health expenditure).	The state retains a dominant position in the health care system in terms of organisation and management, and an important one in the provision and financing of health services. Emphasis on functions of the state in terms of guaranteed access to services, their quality, safe use of medicines and medical equipment. The system is based on the Bismarck model (insurance).	The state has a dominant position in the health care system in terms of organisation, management and financing. The role of the state in the area of health services remains significant. An important factor is the process of decentralisation and delegation of relevant powers in the process of devolution. Health services are provided to all citizens by the National Health Service (NHS) and financed by taxes. The system is based on the Beveridge model (national health service).	The state has a dominant role in all three dimensions of health care system as identified by Chernichovsky. Denmark has a rich tradition of decentralisation of health care. The system is based on the Bismarck model, but uses elements of the Beveridge model (with a growing share of public funds in the financing of health care).	The state has a dominant role in the organisation of health care system. Its role in management and financing remains important. The system is based on the Bismarck model.

Mechanisms and instruments for managing health care issues	The minister in charge of health has substantial control over the health care system. Management of the health system is split between the state and the Statutory Health Insurance (SHI). The minister in charge of health operates on the basis of laws adopted by the parliament in accordance with the Public Health Act. Legal provisions are enacted in collaboration with the Ministry in charge of Finance and Public Accounts — Social Security Finance Act annually voted by parliament. The minister in charge of health prepares detailed analyses of budget expenditure on health, demand for services and health policy guidelines intended to ensure balance (sustainability) and equity (fairness) of the health care system.	The German system is based on three principles: subsidiarity, self-administration, and corporatism. Government delegates regulation to self-governing corporatist bodies of both Sickness Funds and medical providers' associations. Book V of the German Social Law (SGB V) defines and organises the self-regulating 'corporatist' structures and empowers them to determine the benefits, prices, and standards. At the federal level, health care is managed by Federal Assembly, Federal Council and Federal Ministry of Health. Ministry of Health is advised by a range of ad hoc committees, as well as by Advisory Council for the Assessment of Developments in Health Care System (SVR).	England, Scotland, Wales and Northern Ireland have individual planning mechanisms in place as well as their own advisory, planning and monitoring framework for their health care system. A key body is the National Institute for Health and Care Excellence (NICE), which advises on the cost-effectiveness of interventions, though its guidance does not automatically mean funding for a recommended treatment is available. Regulation: some regulators oversee all of the UK (such as health professional groups), and	At the state level, the Ministry of Health has a governing role over regional and municipal organisation and management of health care, as well as the supervision and partial financing of the municipalities and regions. Planning and regulation take place at both state and local levels. The state performs overall regulatory and supervisory functions as well as fiscal ones, but is also increasingly taking responsibility for more specific planning activities, such as quality monitoring and planning of distribution of medical specialties at hospital level. Regions are responsible	The government has ultimate responsibility for the health care sector. It sets the national health budget and the rules for risk adjustment among health insurers. Primary responsibilities for health and health care lie with the Ministry of Health, Welfare and Sport. The Ministry develops policies and measures to promote the health and well-being of the Dutch population and to safeguard access to a high-quality system of health care. These responsibilities are shared with local authorities. The operational role of the government in the delivery of services is very limited, as this is largely delegated to private initiative and non-governmental organisations. For the government, the introduction of market forces meant less central planning and a focus on regulatory frameworks, whereas specific decisions are made by local agencies, or via self-regulation. Exceptions: tight planning of medical professionals via admission

(Continued)

Table 8.3 Continued

Feature	France	Germany	United Kingdom	Denmark	Netherlands
	In discharging these tasks the minister works with a number of advisory committees.	The most important body is Federal Joint Committee (G-BA), created in 2004 to increase efficacy and compliance. G-BA is a forum of providers (physicians and hospitals) and insurers (payers). Planning, resource allocation, provisioning and financing are separate for the outpatient and inpatient sectors. Responsibility for ensuring availability of emergency services rests with the governments of individual Lands, which have delegated this task primarily to hospitals.	others are specific to a single system (such as quality of care providers). Several patient empowerment strategies are in place, including specific rights for patients.	for hospitals as well as for self-employed health care professionals. Municipalities are responsible for disease prevention and health promotion.	limits at the medical faculties. The Ministry of Health, Welfare and Sport cooperates with the Ministry of Finance, the Ministry of Social Affairs and Employment and with numerous government and civil society advisory bodies and agencies.
Ways of implementing health policy	The minister in charge of health is responsible for the preparation and implementation of government policy in relation to public health, organisation and financing of health care in accordance with the provisions of the Public Health Act.	Primary (systemic) principles of health policy are set at federal level. The shape of health policy results from the solutions adopted by negotiations with the representatives of professional bodies, providers and payers. Consultations with stakeholders are widely	Since devolution, England, Scotland, Wales and Northern Ireland have taken their own distinctive approaches to health care.	The Ministry of Health is responsible for defining the overall framework for the national health care system and health-related social services for the elderly.	Health policy is set by the Ministry of Health, Welfare and Sport. It is based on a system of standards developed at the central level in consultation with representatives of the key stakeholders of the health care system.

The minister controls expenditure in the health care system within the remit approved by the parliament (based on an overall framework).

Health policy employs standards and measures defined by the government in consultation with representatives of insurers, providers and patients.

applied in the system. Patients' rights are strongly institutionalised. In health policy, an important role is played by prices, costs of health services and medicines. As is the case in other countries, health policy is based on medical standards, including prices of hospital procedures and diagnosis-related groups (DRG).

Health policy is implemented using national and regional guidelines, licensing systems for health professionals and national quality monitoring systems.

The Danish DRG system and diagnosis-related costs were developed in the late 1990s and play a major role in financing health care.

In health policy, great importance is attached to strengthening patients' rights (including the right to choose their physician and hospital, and the right to information).

The complex and extensive field of regulation in health care in the Netherlands can be divided into regulations regarding public health, quality of health care services and health insurers, and health care providers (including self-regulation). A special category applies to legislation and regulation on rights, complaints, and participation of patients and users. 'Health-in-all-policies' is fragmented and not well developed, especially at the national level.

(Continued)

Table 8.3 Continued

Feature	France	Germany	United Kingdom	Denmark	Netherlands
Forms of health service provision	Primary and secondary outpatient care is provided by self-employed doctors, dentists and medical auxiliaries (including nurses and physiotherapists) working in their own practices, and, to a lesser extent, by salaried staff in hospitals and health centres. General practitioners (GPs) play an important role in coordinating health care services through a semi-gatekeeping system that provides incentives to people to visit their GP prior to consulting a specialist. At the regional level, Regional Health Agencies (ARSS) coordinate outpatient and inpatient care for the population as well as health and social care for the elderly and the disabled.	Primary and secondary (outpatient) health care is mainly provided by private for-profit providers, including physicians, dentists, pharmacists, physiotherapists, speech and language therapists, occupational therapists, podologists and technical professions. Acute care and long-term care are commonly provided by non-profit or profit-making providers employing nurses, assistant nurses, carers for the elderly, social workers and administrative staff. It is thus a mixed public-private delivery system with a significant for-profit component even among hospitals.	Primary care is mainly provided by self-employed general practitioners, with practices increasingly including other health care professionals such as nurses. Most secondary care is provided by salaried specialists and others who work in state-owned hospitals. Tertiary services offer more specialised care, and are often linked to medical schools or teaching hospitals. Tertiary care services often focus on the most complex cases, rarer diseases and treatments. Across the UK there has been a move to concentrate specialised care in	The primary care sector consists of private (self-employed) practitioners (GPs, specialists, physiotherapists, dentists, chiropractors and pharmacists) and municipal health services, such as nursing homes, home nurses, health visitors and municipal dentists. GPs act as gatekeepers, referring patients to hospital and specialist treatment. Most secondary and tertiary care takes place in general hospitals owned and operated by the regions. Doctors and other health professionals are employed in hospitals on a salaried basis.	The provision of health care services has a tradition of private initiative often rooted in charity. That is why most providers are still private and non-profit. Primary care is provided by independent non-profit entrepreneurs. GPs are at the core of primary care act as gatekeepers. Hospitals have both inpatient and outpatient units, as well as 24-hour emergency wards. Apart from typical hospitals, the group includes independent treatment centres, providing day care only, and trauma centres. Most hospitals are run by foundations. They are non-profit institutions since the for-profit motive is not allowed. Whether or not hospitals should be allowed to generate profit and to have shareholders is still a topic of political debate. In hospitals, approx. 60% of medical specialists are self-employed and used to be organised in partnerships by specialty.

Acute medical care is mainly provided by public hospitals which perform a much wider range of surgeries than profit-making hospitals, including the most complex procedures.

Private profit-making hospitals specialise in a small number of technical procedures with profit opportunities, such as invasive diagnostic procedures (e.g. endoscopy or coronary angiography), and surgical procedures that can be performed routinely within a short stay with a predictable length.

fewer centres in order to improve quality.

Private providers can also be contracted in to provide a wide range of services under NHS contracts in England. In Scotland, private providers are generally only used by the NHS to ease waiting-time pressures.

Hospitals have both inpatient and outpatient clinics as well as 24-hour emergency wards. Most public hospitals are general hospitals with different specialisation levels. Community pharmacies are privately organised but subject to comprehensive state regulation on price and location to ensure that everybody has reasonable access to a pharmacy, even in rural areas.

(Continued)

Table 8.3 Continued

Feature	France	Germany	United Kingdom	Denmark	Netherlands
Relationships with social actors	Cooperation with social actors takes place on several levels and several forums. At the national level, it occurs in the framework of the French National Health Authority (HAS), which works in such areas as the evaluation of drugs, medical devices and procedures, the publication of guidelines and accreditation of health care organisations and physician certification. It liaises with government health agencies, SHI funds, research organisations, unions of health care professionals and patients' representatives.	Key stakeholders include legislators (federal and individual lands), local authorities, representations of patients and associations of providers and hospitals. In this last group, important competencies are legally delegated self-regulated organisations of payers and providers. The basic mechanism used in relationships with stakeholders are negotiations. They are conducted at the federal level. There are also consultation mechanisms. The current strategy attaches great importance to qualitative change in the patient-physician relationship through modelling interaction: medical knowledge, medical standards, professional attitude (physicians) and health literacy, trust, needs (patients).	Cooperation with stakeholders is conducted at all levels using a variety of organisations and institutions, including Health and Wellbeing Boards established after 2012, operating at the local level. Great importance is attached to patient empowerment, including improving patient access to information and freedom of choice of physician and hospital (as is the case in England). Public participation is considered important across the UK in order to make the NHS a more responsive health system. Public participation is considered as a way of integrating health and social care.	A high level of decentralisation of the health care system and the tradition of involving local communities in organising health care make the relationships with stakeholders intense and multi-level; they involve numerous organisations and institutions. Emphasis and protection of patient's rights, especially the right to information (including the right to interpretation into minority languages).	The health sector consists of numerous associations representing health professionals, patients or employers in the sector. There are examples of inter-sectoral cooperation between the Ministry of Health, Welfare and Sport and other ministries. A wide range of public bodies are involved in the health field. Some oversee different aspects of the health system, such as content of the basic health insurance package and care quality (Care Institute Netherlands), and fair competition between insurers and providers (Dutch Health Care Authority). Others provide advice and evidence on different aspects of health, including several scientific research institutes such as the National Institute for Public Health and the Environment. Cooperation with stakeholders occurs on many levels. Broad involvement of local community and neighbours in providing informal care to ill or disabled people.

In NHS England, patients and carers are included in managing their own care and treatment in the services they commission.

On paper, public participation is sought through partnerships among Healthwatch, Health and Wellbeing Boards, clinical commissioning groups, local authorities, patient groups, patient leaders and the voluntary sector. In practice, it is hard to ensure public participation in decision-making.

(Continued)

Table 8.3 Continued

Feature	France	Germany	United Kingdom	Denmark	Netherlands
Mechanisms of organisational and systemic learning	No spectacular examples of organisational learning understood as acquisition, development and exploitation of knowledge and skills, adaptation, preparation and implementation of actions plans and changing organisational behaviour. The process of systemic learning is based on previous national experience. High level of research on health care system.	No spectacular examples of organisational learning. The process of systemic learning is mainly based on previous national experiences, e. g. the establishment in 2009 of Central Health Fund to compensate for financial flows between SF. International experience is also used, e. g. introduction of DRG, Disease Management Programmes (DMP), Selective Contracting, Home Care or the Ambient Assisted Living (AAL). High level of research on health care system.	Although there are no spectacular examples of either organisational or systemic learning, it should be emphasised that the British health system has proved open to new solutions (e.g. budget holding GPs) based on own knowledge and experience. Very high level of research on health care system, and knowledge thus gained is transferred to other countries.	No spectacular examples of organisational learning. It is worth noting an important step in systemic learning, which involves centralisation (reducing the number of regions) and concentration (merger of payers, hospitals and other health care providers). High level of research on health care system.	In the absence of clear evidence of organisational learning, the Dutch health care system has significant achievements in systemic learning introduced as part of the 2006 reform, such as: • introduction of uniform mandatory health insurance; • introduction of managed competition among actors as a new driving mechanism in health care. High level of research on health care system.
Comments	As of November 2017, physicians will no longer be able to charge patients a fee per visit (23 euros). This fee will be borne by the state and insurers (*mutuelle*).				Most health care providers use some form of electronic patient records. However, the national roll-out of an electronic patient record system to interconnect these practice-based systems failed, mainly for reasons of privacy.

Sources: Busse, Wasem (2013); Obermann *et al.* (2013); Busse, Blümel (2014); Chevreul *et al.* (2015); Cylus *et al.* (2015); Olejaz *et al.* (2012; Kroneman *et al.* (2016).

Germany

The most important objectives of the health care system reforms undertaken over the last several years are related to controlling and lowering the system's operating costs. Between 2001 and 2012, eleven laws concerning these issues were adopted (Obermann *et al.* 2013). One of them banned the sickness funds (as of January 2009) from setting the insurance premiums, and a federal law (SGB V) introduced a unified health insurance premium.

It is worth remembering that the process of reforming the German system employs an extensive public consultation mechanism (Busse, Blümel 2014, p. 38).

The United Kingdom

The policy of devolution mentioned in Table 8.3 and the associated diversity of reforms in England, Wales, Scotland and Northern Ireland, respectively (Cylus *et al.* 2015, p. xviii) make it difficult to identify the overall direction of change in the UK as a whole. England has opted for decentralisation, strengthened its internal market and transferred decision-making powers to the local level. Conversely, Scotland and Wales have been moving away from the internal market in favour of centralisation. The Scottish solutions differ from the English ones in that the former provide public health services to each resident in accordance with high quality standards, whereas the latter allow a greater private sector involvement and internal competition mechanisms with providers subject to exacting performance measures (Cylus *et al.*, 2015, p. 99).

Denmark

The administrative reform of 2007 reduced the number of regions (from 14 to 5) and municipalities (from 275 to 98), which had a significant impact on the operation of the Danish health system. In recent years, it has seen centralisation (e.g. of the planning process), concentration (e.g. combining hospitals) and the introduction of a system of financing the public sector which stimulates performance (activity-based financing).

Changes in inpatient care cover the restructuring of acute hospitals and the grouping of units into joint acute wards. Other initiatives include the introduction of national clinical pathways for cancer and heart disease, respectively, and national planning of the distribution of specialties across hospitals. The Danish Health care Quality Programme (DDKM), based on an accreditation system, has also been established and is to be implemented across the entire system.

The Netherlands

Over the years, the Dutch health care system has seen a number of reforms, both large and small, which affected all its levels. The 2006 reform replaced public and private insurance with a single universal social health insurance system and introduced managed competition as a driving mechanism.

The reforms also include the financing of health care, primarily hospitals and long term care facilities. As a result of the introduction of budgetary constraints and exacting performance indicators, in 2016, the fees paid by patients increased from 150 euros to 385 euros per year (Kroneman *et al.* 2016, p. 169).

Conclusion

The analysed health care systems, even though they are based on the same models, show significant differences both in terms of the organisation and financing of health services and the results obtained. The comparison of these systems from the perspective of the neo-Weberian public management model justifies the following conclusions:

- In all the countries under consideration, officials are regulators responsible for the smooth operation of the systems with the state acting as a coordinator. All the health care systems in question are institutionally complex.
- All the countries seek to make their legislation more transparent and increasingly oriented to the needs of the patients and to the results achieved by the service providers.
- Health policy is dominated by legalism, relationships among the stakeholders are regulated by law and standards are established in the process of negotiation and consultation. Although health policy is holistically defined in legal regulations, the harmonisation of activities of different ministries and stakeholders remains a challenge for all the analysed systems.
- The share of private for-profit and non-profit operators in the provision of health care services is large and still growing. The scope of application of market mechanisms is significant (it predominates in the Netherlands).
- The relationships with the stakeholders of the health sector in all the countries surveyed (except France) are broad and intense, with the position of the patient appreciated and strengthened. To a considerable (and increasing) extent, the central government delegates health care tasks to lower levels.
- The mechanisms of organisational and systemic learning in the analysed systems are barely visible.

In most analysed countries, decentralisation constitutes an important aspect of health policy. Only Denmark with its preference for centralisation and concentration provides an interesting counterpoint. This can be explained by the desire to take advantage of the economies of scale and thereby contain the costs of services, which remains one of the top health policy priorities in all the countries studied.

The drive to reduce health care costs is part of a wider problem, which is how to ensure adequate funding of health services in the context of growing demand and increasing costs. This, in turn, justifies the question whether the neo-Weberian public management model might actually contribute to solving the structural problem that affects all the health care systems, namely the incompatibility between the objectives set for them (ambitious) and the allocated resources at the disposal of the state (insufficient). Regrettably, at this stage, the neo-Weberian public management model is yet to be defined with sufficient precision. For this reason, its current application to the analysis of health policies produces only vague generalisations. It appears, however, that this model, which recognises the position of the state as a regulator, organiser, coordinator and monitor, has a large potential for health policy. Indeed, health service providers are usually dispersed and are confronted with oligopolistic or even monopolistic suppliers (e.g. the medical equipment, materials and medicinal products market is often dominated by powerful transnational corporations). In such a situation, only the state can (partly) offset this imbalance by appropriate legislation.

Bibliography

Björnberg, A. (2016). *Health Consumer Powerhouse. Euro Health Consumer Index 2015 Report*, Health Consumer Powerhouse Ltd. www.healthpowerhouse.com/en/news/euro-health-consumer-index-2015 (accessed 28 October 2016).

Busse, R., Blümel, M. (2014). Germany. Health system review. *Health Systems in Transition*, 16 (2). Copenhagen: European Observatory on Health Systems and Policies.

Busse, R., Wasem, J. (2013). *The German Health Care System – Organization, Financing, Reforms, Challenges ...*, www.mig.tu-berlin.de/fileadmin/a38331600/2013.lectures/Brussels_2013.02.13.rb_GermanyHealthCareSystem-FINAL. pdf (accessed 26 October 2016).

Chernichovsky, D. (1995). Health care reforms in industrialized democracies: an emerging paradigm, *The Millbank Quarterly*, 73 (3), pp. 339–372.

Chevreul, K., Brigham, K. B., Durand-Zaleski, I., Hernández-Quevedo, C. (2015). France. Health system review, *Health Systems in Transition,* 17 (2). Copenhagen: European Observatory on Health Systems and Policies.

Cylus, J., Richardson, E., Findley, L., Longley, M., O'Neill, C., Steel, D. (2015). United Kingdom. Health system review, *Health Systems in Transition*, 17 (5). Copenhagen: European Observatory on Health Systems and Policies.

Davis, K., Stremikis, K., Squires, D., Schoen, C. (2014). *Mirror, Mirror on the Wall. How the Performance of the U. S. Health Care System Compares Internationally. 2014 Update*, The Commonwealth Fund, June 2014, www.commonwealthfund.org/publications/fund-reports/2014/jun/mirror-mirror (accessed 3 November 2016).

Kroneman, M., Boerma, W., van den Berg, M., Groenewegen, P. de Jong, J., van Ginneken, E. (2016). Netherlands. Health system review, *Health Systems in Transition*, 18 (2). Copenhagen: European Observatory on Health Systems and Policies.

Mazur, S. (2016). Neoweberyzm – źródła, rozumienie, nurty [The neo-Weberian approach: Its sources, understanding and trends]. In: S. Mazur (ed.) *Neoweberyzm w zarządzaniu publicznym. od modelu do paradygmatu?* [The Neo-Weberian State in Public Management. From a Model to a Paradigm?] (pp. 15–27). Warsaw: Wydawnictwo Naukowe Scholar.

Obermann, K., Müller, P., Müller, H-H., Schmidt, B., Glazinski, B. (eds) (2013). *Understanding the German Health Care System*. Mannheim Institute of Public Health, www.goinginternational.eu/newsletter/2013/nl_03/SpecialDE_EN_Understanding_the_German.pdf (accessed 4 November 2016).

Olejaz, M., Nielsen, A. J., Rudkjøbing, A., Birk, H. O., Krasnik, A., Hernández-Quevedo, C. (2012). Denmark. Health system review, *Health Systems in Transition*, 14 (2). Copenhagen: European Observatory on Health Systems and Policies.

Oramus, M. (2016). Analiza neoweberowskiego paradygmatu zarządzania publicznego [An analysis of the neo-Weberian public management paradigm]. In: S. Mazur (ed.) *Neoweberyzm w zarządzaniu publicznym. od modelu do paradygmatu?* [The Neo-Weberian State in Public Management. From a Model to a Paradigm?] pp. 147–168. Warsaw: Wydawnictwo Naukowe Scholar.

Roberts, M., Hsiao, W., Berman, P., Reich, M. (2008). *Getting Health Reform Right.* Oxford: Oxford University Press.

U.S. Health Care from a Global Perspective. www.commonwealthfund.org/publications/issue-briefs/2015/oct/us-health-care-from-a-global-perspective (accessed 31 October 2016).

Weber, S., Brouhard, K., Berman, P. (2010). *Synopsis of Health Systems Research Across The World Bank Group from 2000 to 2010* (*Draft Report*). Washington, DC: The World Bank.

WHO (2000). *The World Health Report 2000. Health Systems: Improving Performance,* World Health Organization, www.who.int/whr/2000/en/whr00_en.pdf?ua=1 (accessed 26 October 2016).

9 The neo-Weberian approach in territorial policy

Piotr Kopyciński

Introduction

In this chapter, the theories and concepts of territorial (regional) development are applied to selected issues related to managing public affairs at the regional level. The author points out that the new integrated approach to territorial development, involving the departure from sectoral policies in favour of territorial policy, where interventions involve a combination of actions by public authorities at various levels, requires a reflection on the mechanisms of coordination. First of all, it is necessary to emphasise the importance of the state with a clear assignment of roles and responsibilities of public authorities at different levels. It involves altering the previously used tools offered by multi-level governance (MLG), or even the creation of a new paradigm based on the neo-Weberian idea of state (NWS).

The theories of regional development derived from or drawing on dominant mainstream economic science were used to structure the implementation of national and transnational policies. For example, neoclassical economics emphasised the operation of the invisible hand of the market, whereas (neo-) Keynesian economics accepted the need for intervention at the regional level. Recent years saw the emergence of new institutional economics, which, however, is not perceived as the third doctrine in economic theory, but is rather considered as a necessary institutional complement to neoclassical economics. In this case, analysts underscore the importance of institutions and path dependence (North 1990; Storper 1997). Methods for coordinating regional policies include the solutions proposed by the various public management models, namely the bureaucratic model, new public management (NPM), public governance and its derivatives (including MLG, and in recent years, in territory-specific cases, also territorial governance). Regional development theory reflects the influence of new institutional economics (e.g. the importance of institutions and path dependence), but the management method recommended, among others, in EU documents, is MLG. Given the contemporary challenges and problems facing regional policies, the question arises whether such a mechanism provides adequate tools to that end, or new and more efficient solutions should be sought e.g. in the neo-Weberian approach.

The evolution of the understanding of regional policy

The beginnings of regional policy

The beginnings of regional policy, at least from the perspective of the developed countries, date back to the 1950s and 1960s. In this period of intensive industrialisation, the main objective of such policy was to ensure sustainable growth by means of centrally distributed national resources and public investment. Next, in the 1970s and 1980s, the focus shifted to supporting businesses which created new jobs (OECD 2009a, pp. 50–51). These actions consisted in central interventions (top-down approach) associated with infrastructure investment and were uniform in nature, i.e. they did not take into account the specifics of a given territory. Such interventions were based on various theoretical concepts, which are widely discussed in the literature, so at this point we shall mention only several selected ones. The most important of them include the economic base theory (Hoyt 1954; North 1955; Tiebout 1956), which emphasises the importance of exports for regional development, the concept of growth poles (Perroux 1955), and geographical growth centres (Myrdal 1957; Hirschman 1958), which focus on the concentration of development in selected regions and targeting interventions at selected areas.

A new understanding of regional policy

While various centrally coordinated state actions to a certain extent prevented the development gap between regions from increasing, they did not reduce intra-regional disparities. Therefore, since the crisis of the 1970s, one may notice a gradual modification of the concept of regional policy, which was also associated with such processes as the decline of the state's financial capacity, decentralisation, and the recognition of the local environment as an important factor in the development of new technologies. The impact of globalisation, the development of networking, and accelerated technological progress was also noted (Pietrzyk 2000, pp. 16–18). An emphasis on the importance of endogenous conditions can be seen in the core and peripheries model (Friemann, Weaver 1979), which highlights the need to stimulate development by taking advantage of the potential of the most developed regions, where competitive companies tend to concentrate their operations. The new endogenous growth theory (Romer 1986; Lucas 1988) highlights the importance of internal factors and innovation. On the other hand, D. C. North (1990) and M. Storper (1997) emphasise the role played by institutions and path dependence in the development processes. In turn, new economic geography (Krugman 1991) and the core–periphery model examine the importance of a specific location for the development and concentration of selected industries (primarily in urban areas). Castells (2007) focuses on the development of the information society and a variety of formal and informal networks which influence economic growth. Lastly, R. Florida (2000) discusses the impact of innovation and advanced technologies on the level of economic development.

In general, it can be said that that the reorientation of regional policy involved the following issues (OECD 2009a, p. 51; Pietrzyk 2000, pp. 19, 25):

1   transition from exogenous central intervention, such as financial transfers and large infrastructure projects, to the recognition of the importance of endogenous regional resources contributing to development and integrated measures aimed at correcting market problems (e.g. by promoting locally rooted small and medium-sized firms) (a bottom-up approach instead of a top-down one);
2   decentralisation of management of regional affairs associated with the reduced role of national authorities in favour of a greater responsibility for regional/local authorities and other entities;
3   new methods for coordinating collective action, including public governance, which involves making decisions by a number of actors with a decisive (coordinating) role played by public authorities;
4   recognition of the importance of socio-cultural factors (institutions, path dependence) and innovation for development.

Finally, it was concluded that the formation of new values (innovation) is closely linked to territory understood as an area inhabited by a specific community, with a number of interacting institutions and entities (Pietrzyk 2000, pp. 20–29, 48–49).

The list above can be supplemented by new concepts, such as the working region or place-based policy. In the first case, regions are perceived through the prism of their specialised labour markets, business environment institutions, and research or strongly rooted authorities at various levels with the capacity to intervene in a flexible manner (Clark 2013, p. 8). Place-based policy is a concept proposed by F. Barca (2009) in the context of the EU cohesion policy reform. This approach

> refers both to the context-dependent nature of the efficiency and equity problems that the policy deals with, and to the fact that the design of integrated interventions must be tailored to places, since it largely depends on the knowledge and preferences of people living in it.
>
> (Barca 2009, pp. 5–6)

From regional to territorial policy – modern management of territorial development

'Territorial' rather than 'regional'

From the point of view of the modern theories of development, territory is considered to be a dynamic area whose boundaries rarely overlap with the division of a given country into administrative units. Thus, the boundaries of an area subjected to intervention are likely to be liquid and the interventions involve different actors (an integrated approach involving the cooperation of national, sub-national and other actors). The proposed reorientation of public action aimed at the region has become so profound that in recent years some scholars have come to treat as outdated the phrase 'local and regional development' in reference to the quantitative and qualitative changes in an area smaller than a single country, and 'regional policy' to describe interventions on a regional scale. Instead, new concepts emerge or old ones are redefined, such as territorial policy, territorial development, or territorial governance. In the context of ensuring cohesion of the European Union, territorial cohesion is mentioned quite frequently. One may say that the adjective 'territorial' tends to displace the qualifiers 'spatial', 'regional' and 'local'.

In the context of regional management, it is worth taking a closer look at this relatively new approach to territorial policy and territorial governance initiated by the OECD report *Territorial Outlook 2001* (OECD 2001) and now adopted both by scientists and by public authorities.

Territorial approach to local development and territorial policy

The European Commission (Directorate General for International Cooperation and Development) initiated a discussion on the operationalisation of the concept called *territorial approach to local development* (TALD). This approach assumes that the basic features of local development include the following (Bilbao 2015, p. 19):

1   endogeneity based on local resources, with a strong role of local authorities coordinating the efforts of local actors;
2   integrated nature which requires a departure from point-based public intervention in favour of a comprehensive approach;
3   multi-scalar nature which entails cooperation among different actors at different levels;
4   incremental value with an appropriate level of decentralisation, which allows local actors to develop their own ideas.

L. Romeo (2015, p. 17) concludes that in dealing with issues of development of territories on a different scale (usually sub-national), the term *territorial development* better captures the essence of the processes taking place in this area than *local development*. In this perspective, territorial development can be understood as 'development that is endogenous and spatially integrated, leverages the contribution of actors operating at multiple scales and brings incremental value to national development efforts' (Romeo 2015, p. 17). He goes on to argue (2015, p. 16) that in this perspective, it is not only the size of the territory in which development occurs that is important, but also who is responsible for the development activities and in what way. Such a new perception of development processes underscores the following principles: endogenous development, sustainable development, and more accountable governance (OECD 2001, p. 27).

How to manage territorial development?

At this point, the question arises how to manage territorial development thus conceived. Are the previously used methods and tools sufficient or is it necessary

to redefine them? B. Pecqueur (2013) points out that although in such development processes the relationships among numerous actors are important, a crucial
role is played by public authorities. In these new circumstances, it is necessary
to redefine public policies. In his opinion, interventions must adequately address
the needs of a given territory and combine the efforts of both local and national
authorities. Even if the former fulfil their functions properly, the success of territorially aimed policies depends on strong central authorities with their important
functions of redistribution, mediation, and coordination (Pecqueur 2013, p. 25).
The necessary, although by no means sufficient condition is the existence of a state
capable of effectively intervening in a given territory (Pecqueur 2013, p. 27). Such
a reasoning is part of a wider reflection on the perception of the role of the state
in socio-economic processes. The authors of *Bringing the State Back In* (Evans,
Rueschemeyer, Skocpol 1985) tried to build a bridge between modernity and the
achievements of such researchers as M. Weber and O. Hintze. They note the need

> to improve conceptualisations of the structures and capacities of states, to
> explain more adequately how states are formed and reorganised, and to explore
> in many settings how states affect societies through their interventions –
> or abstentions – and through their relationships with social groups.
>
> (1985, p. vii)

Territorial governance

More recently, in order to emphasise the importance of managing a territory and
in contrast to management in other areas, scholars have begun to use the term
territorial governance. Initially, it was seen as a mode of coordination, in which
'territories of a national state are administered and policies implemented, with
particular reference to the distribution of roles and responsibilities among the
different levels of government (supranational, national, and sub-national) and
the underlying processes of negotiation and consensus-building' (OECD 2001,
p. 142). The approach consists in the search for an optimum division of responsibilities among the various actors involved in the processes of governance (public
authorities and other entities) (OECD 2001, p. 142). Later, this formula was
adapted to the needs of the EU territorial cohesion policy.

An attempt to distinguish territorial governance from related concepts – public
governance and MLG – was made e.g. by Stead (2013, 2014). In his opinion,
territorial governance can be viewed from the following perspectives:

1 The vertical or horizontal coordination of policies and/or actors.
2 The promotion of participation and consensus-building among public
   and/or private actors.
3 The devolution of powers and/or resources to lower levels of decision-making.
4 The delivery of territorial cohesion.
5 The assessment of territorial impacts and development of territorial
   visions.

(Stead 2013, p. 142)

The first three approaches refer to the very essence of governance, while the other two have a clear territorial aspect. From the perspective of the European Union, of particular interest is, of course, cohesion policy and the need for its place-based implementation, which was emphasised by F. Barca (2009). The authors of the report *Towards Better Territorial Governance in Europe* argue that territorial governance thus understood can be applied at all levels of government (from the local ones to the European one), stressing that it is tantamount to augmenting MLG with aspects of knowledge and territory using the place-based approach, where an effective coordination of activities undertaken by different actors is crucial (ESPON 2014, pp. 5–6, 10).

One may wonder to what extent territorial governance actually adds value to MLG or constitutes a completely new approach to managing a territory. In the context of this chapter, however, it is more important to demonstrate that MLG does not offer a lot in terms of how public administration may conduct territorial policy. Let us take a look at a case study.

Territorial management problems – spatial planning in Poland

Box 9.1   Spatial planning system in Poland (as at 2017)

Between the World Wars, Poland's spatial planning was governed by modern regulations which provided for an active role of urban planners. On the local scale, it was manifested by successful residential projects. On the supralocal scale, it involved building from scratch an entirely new port city of Gdynia (in response to modest access to the sea) and the Central Industrial District (to stimulate industrial development). In the new political reality after 1945, land use was centrally planned with an active role of urban planners consistent with the Soviet ideology. The transformation of the political system after 1989 was characterised by a general and, to a certain extent, historically justified aversion to the command and control economy. This sentiment also applied to spatial planning. The Spatial Planning Act of 1994 abolished the central planning system and delegated the (optional) task of creating local spatial plans to the local level (municipalities). The new act of 2003 cancelled the existing plans drawn up under the previous system, which did not stipulate any compensation for reserving private land for public investment. As a result, municipalities had the opportunity (but not the obligation) to enact new plans.

Currently, Poland has a multi-level spatial planning system. The overall policy is shaped at the national level, whereas general spatial development plans are adopted at the regional level. Individual municipalities influence investment policy in their jurisdictions by enacting local zoning plans (as at the end of 2013, such plans covered 28.6% of the area of Poland). In the absence of such a plan, investment decisions can be issued by the executive authority at the municipal level (borough leader, mayor or president), i.e. they do not have to conform to any system of plans. There are no clear guidelines governing such decisions, as a result, investors often manage to obtain permits to build blocks of flats or even office buildings in the middle of housing estates. Another problem is the popularity of gated communities, especially new housing estates, which results in their ghettoisation.

Poland's MLG-based system of managing space provides for no single effective coordinator at the central level. To make matters worse, imprecise regulations pertaining to construction permits increase the chaos in spatial planning. The territory of Poland already covered by such plans (28.6%) could accommodate 60 million people (the current population is approx. 38 million). The system also entails substantial expenditure. For example, according to studies published in 2012–2015, only the costs associated with the legal obligation to repurchase land resulting from the plans adopted by municipalities amount to 90 billion zloty (ca. 22 billion euro) (Olbrysz, Zachariasz 2015). Uncontrolled spatial development can be checked by adopting an urban planning code (as at 2017 code on it was still in progess).

Problems related to spatial planning in Poland largely result from certain historically conditioned processes (Box 9.1). This does not alter the fact that the current solutions based on MLG are ineffective, contribute to confusion in the area of planning and generate substantial costs for the future. It is therefore necessary to enact clear legislation, which will allow public authorities to make decisions in accordance with land-use regulations (which also demand clarification). The operationalisation of territorial governance (e.g. ESPON 2014) is yet to contribute to solving this problem. It constitutes an interesting response to the territorialisation of public policies, but offers no clear-cut solutions which would strengthen the role of public administration or reform it.

Problems and challenges related to (managing) territorial policy

Towards increasing the role of the state

As shown by Zaucha *et al.* (2015, p. 375), in recent years, researchers have noted the importance of territory for development, thus introducing the topic of territoriality into mainstream economics. Theoretical considerations have found their practical application proposed by supranational institutions: the World Bank, the OECD and the European Union (e.g. OECD 2009b; Gill 2010). The EU's fifth Cohesion Report for the first time mentioned territorial cohesion apart from economic and social cohesion. Accordingly, territorial policy accentuates the use of endogenous potential for development, the importance of institutions, and path dependence. More and more attention is devoted to such issues as regional competitiveness, innovation or the use of ICT. Analysts suggest abandoning the top-down approach in favour of bottom-up policymaking in line with the principles of place-based policy.

The 2007/2008 financial crisis resulted in the emergence of a new approach to development problems. As the authors of the OECD report (2009a) *Regions Matter: Economic Recovery, Innovation and Sustainable Growth* point out, regions should participate in overcoming the crisis by strengthening the financial system, stimulating demand and employment growth. It is not enough to bring together the available resources; what is more important is how these resources are used, what interactions may occur and whether the synergy effects can be achieved (OECD 2009a, pp. 3, 11). The authors of the report emphasise the significance of MLG as a mechanism for the coordination of such activities, but, at the same time, they argue that the traditional division into top-down and bottom-up approaches has become less crucial. Currently, public authorities at various levels should participate in the design and implementation of public policies aimed at resolving the crisis. It is also necessary to divide the tasks and responsibilities clearly among the various levels of government (central authorities – national development strategies, sub-national levels – exploiting the endogenous potential of their territory and involving local actors). The tasks of this kind of regional policy include strengthening the coordination processes at the central level (OECD 2009a, pp. 12–13). The authors of the report claim that 'regional policy suffers from unclear management at national level' (OECD 2009a, p. 15). This policy should be coordinated centrally by a single entity. On the other hand, at the sub-national level, it is necessary to focus on the quality of governance (good governance principles) and on the cooperation with other levels and actors (European Commission 2013, pp. 3, 6). According to B. Pecqueur (2013), a strong central authority is needed to implement territorially oriented reforms, while L. Romeo (2015) focuses on assigning clear responsibility for individual development processes.

Some authors argue against the application of the open method of coordination in its present form, since it is not accompanied by adequate regulatory or redistributive action on the part of the EU (e.g. Grosse 2010, p. 20). Besides, it remains unclear to what extent the establishment of new coordinating institutions, the strengthening of the existing ones or increasing the EU budget would be realistic given the repeated demands to weaken the ties among the EU member states.

Criticism of multi-level governance and new public management

The main areas of criticism levelled at MLG include the following:

1   The risk of collision of competencies related to the multiplicity of decision-making bodies.
2   Difficult interventions in the context of protracted negotiations and low level of trust among stakeholders.

3   Inappropriate choice of intermediate organisational forms between market and enterprise (...).
4   Difficulties in ensuring socio-economic cohesion of a given country in the context of too far-reaching regionalisation.
5   Inappropriateness of interventions planned at the supranational level to the specific institutional circumstances of individual countries.

(Kopyciński 2015, p. 238)

Moreover, Zaucha *et al.* (2015, p. 376) argue that from the perspective of the European Union, where objectives are formulated at the pan-European level, but their implementation is left largely to individual countries and regions, the territorial policy management system based on MLG is inconsistent with the territorial approach to development, which takes grassroots needs and opinions as its starting point. Sometimes one may also notice the reluctance to implement the MLG concept, especially in countries whose public administrations are strongly rooted in the Weberian tradition. This criticism is sometimes combined with the demands to implement public policies in the spirit of the neo-Weberian state (Drechsler, Kattel 2008; Pollitt, Bouckaert 2011; Potůček 2008; Randma-Liiv 2008). Furthermore, it emphasises the strong empirical and normative position of the Weberian tradition in continental European countries, including Central and Eastern European ones (e.g. Drechsler, Kattel 2008). Occasionally, they have been reluctant to introduce MLG as a method of coordination at the national or sub-national level – despite appearances to the contrary, central authorities remained the actual decision-maker (cf. Potůček 2008 and his analysis of the situation in the Czech Republic).

Likewise, after a period of intensive implementation efforts, NPM attracted strong criticism and was abandoned in its 'pure' form (cf. e.g. Drechsler 2009). The reasons for the rejection of NPM can be sought not only in its core ideas (market-based attitude to public affairs), but also in the attempts by its proponents to develop a universal solution to fit every situation in every country (Pollitt, Bouckaert 2011), with a blatant disregard for the local institutional contexts.

Likewise, we should reflect on the extent to which MLG is actually used as coordination method, despite the ubiquitous guidelines and declarations. Pollitt and Bouckaert (2011) suggest that whereas in the past it was possible to identify the dominant trend in the discussion on how to manage the state, today one cannot find a single prevailing approach. Although since the Treaty of Maastricht the EU documents have promoted MLG, and more recently its variety – territorial governance – the question arises whether the latter is only consigned to the declarative sphere or its assumptions are actually implemented.

Contemporary challenges to managing territorial policy

The contemporary challenges and problems affecting every level of government, which translate directly or indirectly into territorial policy, include:

1   the global level – the consequences of the 2007/2008 crisis, ongoing changes in the global political and economic systems (e.g. President Trump's focus on domestic issues, the increasing importance of China, Russia's active international policy);

2   the EU level – the dominant economic and political role of one of the member states, the absence of a clear plan for the modernisation of the Community, the weakening of the European Union torn by internal problems, including the imminent withdrawal of one of the largest EU economies from the EU – the United Kingdom (Brexit), Greece's lingering socio-economic problems, unstable political situation in countries close to the EU (e.g. Syria, Ukraine), and the related problem of refugees/immigrants;

3   the national level – the growing popularity (or coming to power) of political parties which champion the role of the nation state and, in some cases, plan to redefine certain transnational organisations, including the EU (e.g. France, Poland, Hungary), the fact that diverse institutional environments (including administrative systems) of individual EU member states impede harmonisation efforts;

4   the regional level – the inability to deal with some of the increasingly complex territorial policy challenges: in the case of several EU member states, an emphasis on spending the available EU funds with less reflection on how to use them effectively.

Problems and dilemmas of territorial policy

In the light of the foregoing discussion, the problems and dilemmas related to managing territorial policy include the following:

1   difficulties in selecting appropriate coordination methods and tools (the proportion of bargaining and consultations, top-down decisions, the lack of tools for implementing the open method of coordination);

2   the declared/postulated vs. the actual coordination method (MLG in countries with deeply-rooted Weberian traditions);

3   the perceived importance of territorial (regional) policy for development vs. the shortage of recipes for managing territories effectively;

4   the multiplicity of actors and multi-level decision-making processes, blurred accountability, protracted negotiations prevent rapid response;

5   the lack of a strong actor at the national level (with clearly assigned responsibilities) to coordinate the implementation of national tasks in the field of territorial policy.

Clearly, given the mounting challenges and problems affecting every level of government with a direct or indirect impact on territorial policy, it is important to consider the actual coordination method applied and the reform of public administration. Such considerations usually emphasise the need to strengthen public authority through a clear division of powers and responsibilities, and the proposals tend to be subsumed under the name of the neo-Weberian state. Let us now examine their possible implications for territorial policy.

The neo-Weberian approach – the context of territorial policy

The neo-Weberian concept of state is widely discussed in the literature (e.g. Kattel, Drechsler 2008; Pollitt, Bouckaert 2011; Potůček 2008; Randma-Liiv 2008). Below, we consider the question whether and if so, how, the neo-Weberian approach can be applied in territorial policy.

Since the 1950s and the 1960s, when regional policy began, researchers and politicians began to show increased interest in approaches to the implementation of public policies which directly or indirectly affected regional policy. Their disputes were related to the following matters of principle:

1   the approach to economics (neo-Keynesian economics, neoclassical economics, new institutional economics) which was to constitute the basis for state intervention;
2   the methods of governance (traditional administration, new public management, public governance and its derivatives);
3   the theories of/approaches to regional policy (from exogenous top-down intervention to bottom-up approaches based on endogenous potential).

These debates led to the evolution of the approach to the implementation of public policies, including regional policy (described earlier). Depending on the methodology adopted, public authorities were assigned different roles. However, in the mainstream discussion insufficient attention was paid to the reform of public administration, which should operate efficiently and effectively in the face of new challenges and problems. Ch. Pollitt and A. G. Bouckaert (2011) put forward a proposal to that effect with the provision that it relates primarily to central government (2011, p. 3), not to the sub-national level. Nevertheless, their ideas also inform the considerations presented in this chapter, since the demand to clearly and unequivocally allocate the roles in territorial policy applies to all the levels of government.

Given the current state of knowledge and in view of the foregoing discussion, the NWS cannot yet be called a public management paradigm. However, the following aspects of the neo-Weberian approach appear to be relevant to managing territorial policy:

1   The evolution of regional policy towards territorial one requires a redefinition of the existing coordination methods, which are becoming inadequate for today's challenges and development problems.
2   Currently, MLG as the preferred mechanism for coordinating collective action in the context of territorial policy does not respond to the demands to strengthen the powers and to clarify the division of responsibilities among the different public authority levels.

3   The eight distinctive features of the neo-Weberian state identified by Pollitt and Bouckaert (2011, pp. 118–119) represent an effort to address these territorial policy problems (strengthening the role of public authorities which make the decisions related to modernisation based on the evolving and precise provisions of administrative law, while preserving the positive features of NPM and MLG as regards orientation to the needs and expectations of citizens participating in the exercise of power through various consultation mechanisms).

4   For this reason, it seems justified to apply their suggestions to the executive branch responsible for implementing territorial policy and thereby take advantage of the merits of the bureaucratic system, which, according to Pollitt and Bouckaert (2011, p. 23) include: clear accountability, probity, predictability, continuity and close attention to the law.

5   Such an approach does not mean that public authorities at other levels become weaker, on the contrary, the neo-Weberian principles also contribute to the strengthening of the sub-national and supra-national levels (e.g. by significantly modifying the open method of coordination with well-defined regulatory and redistributive actions across the EU). Public administration units at all the levels of governance and according to their remit should operate according to the characteristics of neo-Weberian administration (such an approach could be called the *multi-level neo-Weberian state*).

Table 9.1 outlines the features of the neo-Weberian approach applicable to managing territorial policy.

Table 9.1 Neo-Weberian state in territorial (regional) policy

Features of coordination mechanism	*Neo-Weberian state*
Method of coordination	Hierarchy with some market (NPM) and network (public governance) elements
Entities	• National authorities (legislation and national development strategies) • Sub-national authorities (endogenous potential of the territory and involvement of local actors) • Other actors – businesses, universities, residents, NGOs, intermediaries (cooperation in policy diagnosis, planning, implementation and monitoring)
Rationale for intervention	Administrative law
Basic tools	Integrated strategies
Method of implementation	Integrated action by public authorities at different levels with a clear division of tasks and responsibilities

Source: Own study.

Conclusion

At the moment, it is still too early to treat the neo-Weberian approach as a new method of managing territorial policy. However, it appears reasonable to incorporate the principles of this approach into territorial governance, which postulates, among other things, an effective coordination of activities among the various entities (minimum version). Of course, it is possible that a new paradigm of managing territorial policy based on this approach (maximum version) will be developed in the future.

The following list comprises the arguments in favour of the inclusion of certain elements of the neo-Weberian approach in territorial governance:

1   The observed departure from the sectoral approach in favour of an integrated implementation of territorial policy, where the interventions of various actors overlap, and the traditional distinction between top-down and bottom-up approaches loses its importance, requires a single coordinator, namely national authorities.
2   The effectiveness of public intervention in the face of contemporary challenges to territorial policy depends on the existence of a state capable of taking such action. Strong central authorities are thus necessary to perform the important functions of redistribution, mediation and coordination (Pecqueur 2013, pp. 25, 27). The lack of such a coordinator functioning according to clear legal provisions may result in a significant financial burden for the state, as shown by the example of spatial planning in Poland.
3   The individual EU member states have different administrative traditions with different roles assigned to the various tiers of government and other actors in the processes of governance. While respecting the principles of MLG, given the territorialisation of public policies (place-based policies), a strong integrator is needed to coordinate the efforts of different actors who would subsequently become partners in negotiations with other countries and supranational organisations. National authorities should take on this role.
4   In some cases, the call for a strong integrator at the national level actually confirms the existing state of affairs. The implementation of the principles of public governance turned out to be illusory, because, despite the protestations that the decision-making process involves the representatives of market institutions, citizens and the state, it was the state that had the casting vote (Potůček 2008). Moreover, the NWS may also be an attractive option for reforming countries with low levels of social trust (Matei, Flogaitis 2011).

Bibliography

Barca, F. (2009). *An Agenda for a Reformed Cohesion Policy. A Place-Based Approach to Meeting European Union Challenges and Expectation*. April. www.europarl.europa. eu/meetdocs/2009_2014/documents/regi/dv/barca_report_/barca_report_en.pdf

Bilbao, J. R. (2015). EU's new thinking on decentralisation and territorial development. *GREAT Insights,* 4 (4, June/July), pp. 18–20.

Castells, M. (2007). Communication, power and counter-power in the network society. *International Journal of Communication,* 1 (1), pp. 238–66.

Clark, J. (2013). *Working Region. Reconnecting Innovation and Production in the Knowledge Economy.* London and New York: Routledge.

Drechsler, W. (2009). Towards a Neo-Weberian European Union? Lisbon agenda and public administration. *Halduskultuur,* 10, pp. 6–21.

Drechsler, W., Kattel, R. (2008). Towards the neo-Weberian State? Perhaps, but certainly adieu, NPM!. *The NISPAcee Journal of Public Administration and Policy,* Special Issue: A Distinctive European Model? The Neo-Weberian State, I (2, Winter).

ESPON (2014). *Towards Better Territorial Governance in Europe.* ESPON & Politecnico di Torino.

European Commission (2013). *Empowering Local Authorities in Partner Countries for Enhanced Governance and More Effective Development Outcomes.* Brussels, 15 May.

Evans, P. B., Rueschemeyer, D., Skocpol, T. (1985, reprinted 2002). *Bringing the State Back In.* Cambridge/New York: Cambridge University Press.

Florida, R. (2000). The learning region. In: Z. J. Acs (ed.) *Regional Innovation, Knowledge and Global Change.* London: Pinter.

Friedmann, J., Weaver, C. (1979). *Territory and Function: The Evolution of Regional Planning.* Berkley: University of California Press; London: Edward Arnold.

Gill, I. (2010). *Regional Development Policies: Place-Based or People-Centred.* Washington, DC: The World Bank.

Grosse, T. G. (2010). Doświadczenia Strategii Lizbońskiej – perspektywy Strategii, Europa 2020": o kontynuacji i zmianach w polityce UE [Lisbon Strategy Legacy – Europe 2020 Outlook: Continuity and Change in UE Economic Policy]. *Zarządzanie Publiczne,* 1 (11).

Hirschman, A. (1958). *The Strategy of Economic Development.* Yale University Press.

Hoyt, H. (1954). Homer Hoyt on the development of economic base concept. *Land Economics,* May, pp. 182–7.

Kopyciński, P. (2015), Governance and innovation policy. In: S. Mazur (ed.), *Public Governance,* Warsaw: Scholar Publishing House.

Krugman, P. (1991). *Geography and Trade,* Cambridge MA: MIT Press

Lucas, R. E. (1988). On the mechanics of economic development. *Journal of Monetary Economics,* 22 (1), pp. 3–42.

Matei, L., Flogaitis S. (2011). Public administration in the Balcans: from Weberian bureaucracy to new public management. *Editura Economică.*

Myrdal, G. (1957). *Economic Theory and Under-developed Regions.* London: Duckworth.

North, D. C. (1955). Location Theory and Regional Economic Growth. *Journal of Political Economy,* no. 3, pp. 243–58.

North, D. C. (1990). *Institutions, Institutional Change, and Economic Performance.* Cambridge: Cambridge University Press.

OECD (2001). *Territorial Outlook.* Paris.

OECD (2009a). *Regions matter: economic recovery, innovation and sustainable growth.* Paris: OECD Publishing.

OECD (2009b). *Investing for Growth: Building Innovative Regions.* Policy Report. Paris.

Olbrysz, A., Zachariasz, I. (2015). Raport o finansowych skutkach polskiego systemu gospodarowania przestrzenią [A report on the financial implications of the polish spatial management system]. In: P. Kopyciński (ed.) (2015), *Samorządowa służba cywilna. Obszary metropolitalne. Zagospodarowanie przestrzenne. Badania nad kierunkami zmian w funkcjonowaniu samorządu terytorialnego w Polsce* [Local Self-Government Civil Service. Metropolitan Areas. Spatial Development. Research on the Directions of Change in the Functioning of Local Self-Government in Poland]. Cracow: MSAP UEK.

Pecqueur. B. (2013). Territorial development. A new approach to development processes for the economies of the developing countries. VI Congresso Internacional Sistemas Agroalimentares Localizados, May, Florianópolis, SC, Brazil.

Perroux, F. (1955). La notion de pôle de croissance [The notion of the growth pole]. *Economie Appliquée*, nos 1 & 2.

Pietrzyk, I. (2000). *Polityka regionalna UE i regiony w państwach członkowskich* [EU Regional Policy and Regions in the Member States]. Warsaw: PWN.

Pollitt, C., Bouckaert, G. (2011). *Public Management Reform a Comparative Analysis-New Public Management, Governance, and the Neo-Weberian State*. Oxford: Oxford University Press.

Potůček, M. (2008). The concept of the neo-Weberian state confronted by the multi-dimensional concept of governance. *The NISPAcee Journal of Public Administration and Policy*, Special Issue: A Distinctive European Model? The Neo-Weberian State, I (2, Winter).

Randma-Liiv, T. (2008). New public management versus neo-Weberian state in Central and Eastern Europe. Trans-European Dialogue 1: Towards the Neo-Weberian State? Europe and Beyond, Tallinn, 31 Jan – 1 Feb.

Romeo, L. (2015). What is territorial development. *GREAT Insights*, 4 (4, June/July), pp. 15–17.

Romer, P. (1986). Increasing and long-run growth. *Journal of Political Economy*, 94 (5).

Stead, D. (2013). Dimensions of territorial governance. *Planning Theory and Practice*, 13 (1), pp. 142–147.

Stead, D. (2014). The rise of territorial governance in European policy. *European Planning Studies*, 22 (7), pp. 1368–1383.

Storper, M. (1997). *The Regional World. Territorial Development in a Global Economy*. New York: The Guilford Press.

Tiebout, Ch. (1956). A pure theory of local expenditures. *The Journal of Political Economy*, no. 5, pp. 416–424.

Zaucha, J. *et al.* (2015). *Terytorialny wymiar wzrostu i rozwoju* [The Territorial Dimension of Growth and Development]. Warsaw: Difin.

10 The neo-Weberian approach as a public management model in urban areas

Michał Kudłacz

Activities of city administrations

The city is a unique organism, which, from the morphological and functional perspective, is characterised by an above-average concentration of institutions that contribute to socio-economic development, as well as by the presence of city-forming processes. This is what makes managing a city significantly different from managing local affairs in rural areas. Moreover, the traditional planning of urban development is not sufficient for solving today's wicked problems: what is effective in the case of relatively simple problems occurring in low-complexity systems fails to address problems which typically affect the highly complex ones. The technocratic and imperative approach no longer works. Complex systems operate in a non-linear manner, they are characterised by unclear, irregular causality and blurred space–time boundaries. Therefore, conventional and universal solutions are doomed to failure. Moreover, in systems whose key component is their varied social structure, it is difficult to determine the success criteria, since the various actors involved hold different values. In such systems, it is impossible to state that a given problem has been completely solved (Bendyk, Hausner, Kudłacz 2016).

Due to the fact that people and communities operate in a context of unlimited needs and limited development resources, one should recognise the dualism of local government activity. The overarching objective of public administration at the local level is to meet the collective needs of residents of a given territory. The word *administration* (from Latin *administrare* – to help, to serve) clearly underscores the subordinate role of local territorial structures with respect to the recipients of public services. These ancillary activities are implemented through public services (administrative, social and utilities). The performance of public tasks involves not only the observance of relevant statutory provisions, but also a focus on the quality and cost of public services, and measuring customer satisfaction (Bober, Kudłacz 2015).

Another important area in which local administrations play a key role is making their territory more attractive. The fact that cities operate in a context of unlimited needs and limited resources forces them to behave in ways directly adopted from the private sphere. Resource constraints affect not only the financial sphere (city budgets), but also residents, businesses and tourists. These resources determine the economic resilience of a city, contribute to the development of the local economy, and also constitute its tax base. For this reason, cities need to develop their infrastructure, functional resources, and have something to offer individual 'customer groups', which will enable them to retain their potential and attract new blood. This tug of war is city-forming in itself: cities never cease to develop as long as they can financially afford to engage in secondary investment (primary investment involves the capital-intensive provision of public services of appropriate quality).

City management models in theoretical terms

The science of urban management identifies three models of public management: bureaucratic, managerial and governance. Their distinctive features are compared with those of the emerging neo-Weberian model later in this chapter; this section focuses on selected aspects of these models.

The managerial model

Cities, due to their above-average growth potential, try to exploit it as efficiently as possible in order to achieve their own development targets. According to some researchers, cities also tend to be inhabited by creative individuals with a managerial disposition (Florida 2012). Under the managerial model, the city is treated like a company, with the mayor being its chief executive. The CEO is expected to deliver appropriate financial results by maximising the development potential, while rationalising costs, and to use every opportunity to achieve sustainable economic development. Business instruments are normally used for that purpose: marketing tools, strategic planning (exploring key resources and development barriers, making decisions regarding the direction of socio-economic development, quantifying objectives, etc.) and market surveys to identify the needs of the 'customers'. For each group of customers, city authorities prepare a unique set of tools to support their development. Stimulating the development of entrepreneurship and tourism belongs to the set of basic measures intended to improve the economic competitiveness of a city. The concern for financial performance of local governments stems from the following assumptions:

1   The richer the city, the more effectively it can accomplish its mission.
2   A city which successfully attracts resources has an opportunity to enter a positive development spiral (i.e. its resources act as magnets for new ones).

The key issue is how efficiently and how effectively cities can use their resources, which, in principle, are territorial and institutional in nature. The former aspect refers to the socio-economic, spatial and cultural resources available in a given territory and to the determination to use them in order to achieve a multiplier effect. The latter aspect involves actions to promote institutional development understood both as a process and as an objective, which are aimed at the optimal use of human, time and financial resources in order to effectively deliver public services to the residents of a given territory.

The entrepreneurial pragmatism of public administration conceals an autocratic form of governance. As is the case with commercial companies, decisions are taken by a small group of managers held accountable for their outcomes. Without undermining the assumptions of the bureaucratic model, the managerial model adds quantifiable elements (such as the financial results).

Tilburg is a city in the Netherlands (population approx. 650,000), which applied the managerial model in the process of its development. The city, divided into districts, operates like a holding company: very strong urban districts function independently; they have a wide range of decision-making powers regarding public spending and setting the directions for socio-economic development. Public administration at the district level is responsible for the delivery of public services of the highest possible quality. Its awareness of the micro-local potentials makes it fairly easy to rationalise its operating costs. The municipal administration acts as a coordinator. This model has been proven to deliver financial savings without compromising the quality of public services. It is worth noting that the managerial model focuses not only on efforts to generate savings, but may also contribute to maximising income by adopting a number of solutions from the commercial sphere. Consequently, cities where the managerial model predominates support management processes which economically and effectively recognise, anticipate, and meet the needs of 'customers' – residents, businesspeople and tourists. The managerial model is often described in terms of meeting the needs of residents and external stakeholders by offering them an economically appropriate set of tangible and intangible assets which facilitate development.

Public governance

'The performance of public authorities' has been continually present in urban development policy since the adoption of the managerial model. This parameter also constitutes the starting point for the search of new solutions which engage the various urban stakeholders in joint decision-making. Public governance modifies the process of public decision-making by integrating various social groups in determining the directions for socio-economic development. On the one hand, this is due to the objective, global processes with economic impacts: the economy is a network operating in various business and social relationships which contribute to the dynamics of socio-economic development of cities. The idea of public governance is pragmatic in its essence: the liberal public management model is applied not only for ideological reasons (right to freedom, right to decide), but also in order to improve the relevance and effectiveness of local administration's activity. For example, local governments should strive to become more effective in attracting new investors, or more broadly, in stimulating entrepreneurship. If city authorities wish to create optimal conditions for business development, they must first ask the entrepreneurs what they need. The dialogue with urban stakeholders is also important for micro-local communities. For example, solving the problems voiced by the residents of a given housing estate is possible if there is a platform for communication. This allows the city authorities to notice micro-local problems faced by residents and thereby to address them more effectively. Moreover, joint activities generate mutual trust, inspire further activities, motivate people to abandon their plans to leave the city (increasing social capital manifests itself as being rooted in a given place), but above all, make the efforts of local administrations more efficient. Cooperation with the environment, not only with public and third sector organisations, but also with businesses and knowledge-generating institutions, makes cities open, diverse, and dynamic. Structural diversification, responsibility, social diversity, networking and the intangible potential (culture) constitute the basic elements that increase the competitiveness of cities, their positive financial results, image and confidence.

The neo-Weberian approach and the bureaucratic model

The 21st century, especially after the outbreak of the 2007/2008 economic crisis, saw a gradual retreat from the neo-liberal economy in favour of a system in which the state and its agencies play a more active role. The trend was especially evident in Europe and in the USA. The increasingly radical views expressed publicly, protests against excessive openness and tolerance perceived as a threat by part of society – as a destructive policy leading to the loss of one's own identity – are manifest in many countries, and, naturally, they affect cities as well. Urban areas also exhibit another dangerous trend, a consequence of the public management model adopted by them, i.e. the conflict between societal expectations and the development policies pursued by the city authorities. The internationalisation and globalisation of development contributes to the blurring of spatial and temporal boundaries of cities and regions. In the industrial era, urban development was considered in the national (domestic) or possibly in its cross-border context. Currently, these external references have become much more complex. In the information age, big cities are the hubs of global and continental networks of flows and relationships. As a result of the post-industrial transition of economies, their employment structure has also changed – employees of the service sector replaced factory workers, industrial districts gave way to office buildings, and manual work to mental and creative work.

On the whole, the interventions undertaken by municipal authorities indirectly stimulate city development. By dealing with specific aspects of city activities, they produce broader spatial and processual impacts. To that end, they must involve lateral rather than linear thinking, and, in particular, must address the issue of supply of certain resources from outside the city. The problem is that such a supply should complement the city's own resources, strengthen and mobilise them, instead of replacing or displacing them. Otherwise development becomes dependent on external inflows, which must eventually be depleted, leading to stagnation. The city cannot develop without such a supply, but it must be selective in order to preserve its capacity to use and develop its own (internal) resources.

The complexity of development processes is mainly due to the fact that they require resources which do not belong to the social actors who initiate these processes, or are not directly produced by them. Moreover, all our activities involve the use of environmental resources. For example, today, we are experiencing the dramatic consequences of a structurally inefficient use of certain resources, especially in agriculture, fishing or forestry. Even though wasteful exploitation has not been completely eliminated from these sectors, its manifestations and effects are well understood and predictable. If we approach the functioning of the city from such a perspective, we will notice the importance not only of the scale of flows (current income) generated by the available resources, but also of the fact that these flows contribute to the deployment and development of those resources, in particular those that specifically promote certain flows (Bendyk, Hausner, Kudłacz 2016, pp. 133–135).

The neo-Weberian public management model, understood as a greater influence of the state and public administration on market and spatial planning processes, implies increased activity at its every level. At the state level, public administration primarily develops appropriate procedural frameworks and conditions for the various solutions developed at the lower levels of territorial organisation. The model also emphasises the importance of the state and local governments in building the territorial competitive advantage. At its core is the belief that the neo-liberal paradigm of socio-economic development not infrequently disappoints. Consequently, the neo-Weberian approach is, to a certain extent, founded on the criticism of the previous paradigms, and generally considered to respond better to emerging needs.

The neo-Weberian approach to managing public affairs differs in its assumptions from Max Weber's model of ideal bureaucracy, although the latter undoubtedly draws on the former. The differences are due to the vast amount of experience amassed by public administrations over more than 100 years – since the end of the 19th century until the end of the first decade of the 21st century. In fact, the various public management paradigms can be interpreted as responses to the shortcomings of the previous concepts. However, the successive paradigms often contained assumptions adopted from the preceding ones. Thus, in practice, no paradigm or model exists in its pure form. More often than not we are dealing with hybrids – even the neo-Weberian public management model is endowed with prominent managerial and participatory elements. (Kudłacz 2016, pp. 170–172).

The distinctive features of the city management models discussed so far are summarised in Table 10.1.

The neo-Weberian approach in the context of managing metropolitan areas

The features of public management characteristic of the neo-Weberian city model are present in a number of areas of the local economy for a variety of reasons, which are listed below.

1 *Improving public safety.* Innovative solutions based on modern technologies are intended to improve public safety. Examples include modern video surveillance systems feeding into the city crisis management centres and rescue services. The terrorist attacks which occurred in 2015 in Paris and in Brussels, stimulated efforts in this area.

Table 10.1 Institutional structure, human resources and activities in public management models

	Bureaucratic model	Managerial model	Public governance	Neo-Weberian approach
Institutions	Horizontal and vertical division of the public administration system; public administration operates on the basis of a complex system of precisely defined legal provisions, detailed procedures for both the official and the customer	Flexible institutional structures: local government units that deal with the implementation of public objectives by e.g. commercialisation of property, and adopting free-market principles. Important criteria for assessing the quality of institutions: cost, time, process effectiveness and individual performance	Specialised units involved in the performance of public tasks. Specialised entities acting with the key city stakeholders. Institutions aim to bring together local government, commercial entities and the public. Institutions involved in the creation and development of platforms for the exchange of ideas with the residents	Structural and processual flexibility which enables the authorities to achieve public objectives. Solutions typical of the bureaucratic and managerial models, which means that the most important value in the operation of local government is to maintain public order and safety using modern techniques and technologies
Officials	Impersonal, professional, apolitical and objective officials observe procedures and oversee the provision of public services to customers	Managers in an enterprising, rational, pragmatic, but also creative way perform their tasks in order to maximise the benefits: minimise costs, maximise revenue, achieve the set objectives	Animators of events, social activists working 'in the field', people engaged in cross-sectoral consultations, open to dialogue. Experts, for which one of the important performance measures of local administration is the effectiveness of public tasks, which increases thanks to the joint efforts of different social groups	Public officials, acting for the common good, to which individual claims should be subordinated. Experts and professionals who engage in personal development for the common good: the organisation and the city's territory
Activities	Transparent, equitable (do not disfavour any social groups irrespective of their social status) in accordance with procedures set out in detail by legal regulations	Anticipating future states, recognising the needs of key stakeholders, taking steps to increase competitiveness, develop entrepreneurship, tourism, maintain a positive balance of migration; efforts to improve the quality of public services by rationalising their costs	Use of financial and non-financial tools in cooperation with key stakeholders in the city. The city becomes a partner, coordinator, initiator and arbiter of efforts to inspire cross-sectoral initiatives. Implementation of activities promoting trust in local municipal administration	Use of modern techniques and technologies also in the infrastructural, procedural and legal sense to maximise economic benefits for the city and prevent political instability. Ensuring order and public security even at the cost of limiting civil liberties. Common good is the highest value

Source: Own study.

2   *Strengthening administrative procedures and control mechanisms.* The public finance sector and partners cooperate with public entities in order to limit the incidence of unethical behaviour, fraud, corruption, mismanagement and unfairness in entities which have an impact on the socio-economic potential of cities.

3   *Counteracting space shredding.* One of the dimensions of the market economy is opportunism: short-sighted policies reflect attempts to foster rapid development. The focus on long-term objectives and preservation of scarce resources were sometimes missing from the managerial model. The neo-Weberian model is meant to prevent market entities from maximising their operating costs at the expense of the resources held by the city. Urban space becomes subject to top-down regulations, e.g. common spaces in city centres have precedence over private interests and cannot be appropriated for particularistic benefits.

4   *Professionalisation of city administration.* This is possible thanks to modern technology and a natural consequence of digitisation – one of the dominant processes in the modern economy. The development of e-government reflects a certain tendency in the development of e-services provided by public administration, but continuous improvement of city administration and the use of modern tools for public service delivery are more important. The administrative staff no longer consists of officials, but of specialists performing high-quality operations in their respective areas of responsibility.

5   *The need to strengthen the city's capacity to resolve disputes.* Conflicts of interests lead to disputes among the city's social actors. The mosaic of social groups and personality profiles means that in practice, it is impossible to create a development vision which is always consistent with the expectations of all the residents. The neo-Weberian model assumes that in conflict situations, public authorities make the final decisions even if they infringe on certain local interests.

6   *The need to strengthen the capacity of social and economic actors to co-operate.* Businesses, the media, cultural institutions, universities, NGOs and society at large must work together to strengthen the urban functions. Under the neo-Weberian model, the responsibility for fostering cooperation rests with city authorities and their subordinate services.

As was already mentioned, urban development policy shows a strong presence of characteristics of the three public management models: bureaucratic, managerial and public governance. The proportions of their dominant features to a certain extent depend on the individual leadership qualities of local government executives (mayors), their charisma and the political context (e.g. the mayor's rapport with the city council) against the background of a realistic assessment of the city-forming resources (social, institutional, infrastructural) at their disposal.

To wit, there are presidents-officials – formalists who prefer legalism to unconventional actions, and strictly observe procedures that restrict the dynamics of change in the morphological and functional fabric of city, which often provides an alibi for their lack of initiative. By contrast, mayors-managers try to make the institutional structure of their city more flexible, attach above-average importance to its financial performance and do their utmost to stimulate economic recovery, which is essential for the development of the city in general; but, as was noted above, in certain circumstances, giving entrepreneurs too much leeway can be disastrous. Mayors-community workers want to boost socio-economic development by sharing power, adapting it to the will of the majority, although in practice it is rather the will of the loudest or the will of those who could be bothered to vote. It is worth noting that the neo-Weberian approach incorporates all the above-mentioned features, since, chronologically speaking, it is the latest in the series of public management models. The neo-Weberian model does not reject all the features of public governance, but public consultations are organised on a strictly-if-necessary basis, i.e. if they are in the city's best interest. The authorities are aware of the need to generate income for the city, but not at any cost, and certainly not at the expense of social issues. First of all, the city is supposed to meet the expectations and needs of all its residents, not just those of the privileged social groups called 'the metropolitan class'. The neo-Weberian model applied in cities is thus based on the bureaucratic foundations of public administration, which does not necessarily entail lengthy procedures or a general wastage of time and effort mentioned by Weber. (It is not true that the ideal model of bureaucracy in the 19th century was, in principle, ineffective in terms of time and labour; these issues were simply regarded as irrelevant at the time and, as such, were not considered as either tangible or intangible operating costs of public administration.)

Instead, the models and styles of public management likely to be applied in cities of the future will combine the features characteristic of the previous management models more closely linked with the economy of values, and therefore include development-inspiring relationships and socially responsible solutions which do not lead to an irreversible depletion of resources.

Conclusion

The neo-Weberian approach does not herald a return to the model of ideal bureaucracy, but rather constitutes an adaptation, a shift in emphasis, using the achievements of other public management models and modern technologies in order to realise the idea and vision of a stable and sustainable city.

The theoretical deliberations and empirical research reveal fascinating correlations among the different approaches in public management. Such correlations emerge among the models rooted in the same (neo-liberal) ideology and among the models embedded in different ideologies.

The neo-liberal public management models have had a strong impact on the rules and mechanisms of public management, which was particularly noticeable in big cities (Harvey 1989). The application of these models resulted in a reorganisation of management rules and in the adoption of techniques typical of business operations. They involved the economisation of municipal activities, privatisation of municipal resources, far-reaching changes in the public service provision system, mechanisms for contracting services and outsourcing. The application of the neo-liberal management models, especially NPM, has also led to redefining the relationships between municipal governments and citizens. The latter were renamed 'customers' on the assumption that they were interested primarily in high-quality public services. The negative implications of too much focus on the economic and technological aspects of public management constituted a kind of founding principle for public governance. The latter, while respecting the basic rules and mechanisms of NPM, expanded the range of instruments available to public management thanks to the network logic of public governance, further decentralisation of power and public resources, consultation and civic participation mechanisms. An important feature of public governance are alliances built by local governments with their social and economic partners in order to mobilise the resources necessary to achieve the objectives set out in the political process (Mazur 2016, p. 281).

The neo-Weberian approach arises from the continental culture and its strong attachment to the idea of an active, intervening state which assumes responsibility for the provision of public services, and combines it with a model based on a large administrative apparatus characterised by legalism, professionalism, hierarchy and observance of procedures. The key element of this model is an elaborate system of administrative law. The model has already evolved to include, among other things, certain values and public management tools associated with the neo-liberal approaches to public management.

The trajectories of modernisation processes are never identical. Even if identical objectives and similar mechanisms are mentioned in the declarative sphere, their practical applications vary by country and by outcome. Their main determinants include path dependence, the political and social context, and the dominant administrative culture. The notion of convergence of public administration modernisation efforts appears to be unjustified if only for the lack of empirical evidence. Moreover, the said modernisation processes involve the accumulation of features typical of distinct public management models. This phenomenon is particularly significant in big cities, which constitute multidimensional conglomerates of diverse values, attitudes, interests and coordination mechanisms which partly enter into functional relationships with one another, and partly remain in conflict (Mazur 2016).

Bibliography

Bendyk, E., Hausner, J., Kudłacz, M. (2016). Miasto-idea – Nowe podejście do rozwoju miast [City-idea: A new approach to urban development], in: *Open Eyes Book*, Cracow: Fundacja GAP.

Bober, J. *et al.* (2013). *Raport o stanie samorządności terytorialnej w Polsce. Narastające dysfunkcje, zasadnicze dylematy, konieczne działania* [Report on the State of Local Self-Government in Poland. Increasing Dysfunctions, Essential Dilemmas, Necessary Actions], Cracow: MSAP UEK.

Bober, J., Kudłacz, M. (eds) (2015). *Analiza instytucjonalna miast na prawach powiatu z oceną realizacji standardów kontroli zarządczej* [An Institutional Analysis of Cities

Operating as Counties and an Evaluation of the Implementation of Management Control Standards], Cracow: MSAP UEK.

Harvey, D. (1989). From managerialism to entrepreneurialism: the transformation in urban governance in late capitalism. *Geografiska Annaler* 71B, no. 1: pp. 3–17.

Florida, R. (2012). *Rise of the Creative Class,* New York: Basic Books.

Kudłacz, M. (2016). Ocena neoweberowskiego paradygmatu zarządzania publicznego z perspektywy procesów gospodarczych [An evaluation of the neo-Weberian public management paradigm from the perspective of economic processes], in: S. Mazur (ed.), *Neoweberyzm w zarządzaniu publicznym. Od modelu do paradygmatu* [The Neo-Weberian State in Public Management. From a Model to a Paradigm?], Warsaw: Scholar.

Mazur, S. (Forthcoming). Contemporary models of public management: The city perspective, in: Kudłacz. M., J. Hausner (eds), *Functioning of a Metropolis in Poland. Economy, Space, Society*, Warsaw: CeDeWu.

Conclusion

The neo-Weberian concept of state and its implications for public management

Paweł Białynicki-Birula, Jakub Głowacki and Jacek Klich

Introduction

The aim of this chapter is to review and summarise the neo-Weberian concept of state, to discuss some of the consequences of the adoption of the neo-Weberian paradigm in public management and public policy, and to highlight the potential areas for further research. These topical areas determine the structure of this chapter, which consists of three sections. In the first one, the principles of the neo-Weberian state are briefly discussed. The second one contains an evaluation of the approach in question to public policies – economic, innovation, labour market, industry, health care, regional, and urban development planning – with a view to reforming state structures and public management mechanisms. In the third section, the areas for further research on the neo-Weberian concept of state are suggested.

The neo-Weberian concept of state

The neo-Weberian state (NWS) stands in opposition to new public management (NPM), based on neo-liberal principles, and draws on the achievements of traditional public administration (TPA) also known as the Weberian bureaucracy. The reforms of the late 1970s and 1980s fundamentally rejected the Weberian model, and ultimately led to the emergence of NPM. An important factor which contributed to this change was the argument about the 'overload of government,' which gained substantial traction in the 1970s and reflected the belief that governments had a limited capacity to meet their citizens' rising expectations and that the traditional policy tools were ineffective (Torfing *et al.* 2013). As a result, the public policy sphere needed to adopt certain solutions characteristic of the private sector, including the idea of the market as a key coordination mechanism, and to apply managerial methods. Hence NPM should be interpreted as a response to the shortcomings of the traditional bureaucracy and associated with a clear preference for market-based and corporate management methods (Białynicki, Klich 2016).

The NWS, in turn, responds to the perceived shortcomings and failures of NPM, which include: disregard for the distinctive features of the public sector, unjustified discrimination and repudiation of the state, and low effectiveness in achieving its objectives (Dunn, Miller 2007). In particular, the neo-Weberian approach opposes the glorification of market-based management methods and their uncritical transfer into the public sector, typical of NPM. In this respect, it rejects the forced marketisation of the public sector, a process which not only ignores the unique nature of the latter, but also undermines its ideological foundations (Mintzberg 1996). In opposition to NPM, the neo-Weberian approach attempts to redefine the role of the state – a strong entity which assists its citizens, who, at the same time, constitute a major source of its legitimacy (Pollitt, Bouckaert 2011). The NWS also aims to modernise the state apparatus in order to make it more professional, efficient and citizen-friendly. The state is supposed to be a distinctive actor with its unique rules, methods, and culture. Private-sector solutions are treated as ancillary components.

The neo-Weberian approach draws on the Weberian tradition, but it cannot be simply identified with it. In fact, it constitutes a synthesis of the Weberian administration with the NPM principles and charts, a unique course to the modernisation of the state. Hence the concept of NWS constitutes an attempt to take advantage of the Weberian tradition in the context of the modern state and public organisation. It represents the choice of an enlightened and professional hierarchy, appropriately modernised in comparison with the centralised bureaucracies of the early 20th century, which were deemed incompatible with the rapidly changing conditions of the present (Pollitt, Bouckaert 2011). The neo-Weberian approach offers a vehicle for ideas about how to modernise the state, including public administration (bureaucracy) by making it more professional, efficient and citizen-friendly. In short, it is a kind of reaffirmation of the state as the principal public policy entity responsible for solving both internal and external problems due to its political, organisational and management potential (Drechsler 2009).

Such a reaffirmation of the state and its administrative apparatus is associated with the call for a fundamental reorientation, modification or modernisation of the traditionally understood (Weberian) hierarchy with a view to creating modern and efficient public management structures. Yet it certainly comes closer to viewing the state and its policies in terms of instrumental rationality rather than in terms of the logic of self-regulation typical of market mechanisms.

The neo-Weberian approach, therefore, strongly favours the state and expects it to pursue an active public policy. The organisation of both society and the state is mainly seen as a result of the activities of administrative élites and governments, not of social interactions (Lynn 2008/09). The proponents of this model emphasise the importance of the 'state machinery' in steering social processes with a special focus on the importance of power relations in administrative systems, which implies the prominence of the hierarchical coordination method recommended by state-centred theories (Pollitt, Bouckaert 2011). In this sense, it invokes the so-called conventional steering perspective, in which government was treated as a superior entity responsible for the rational management of society. The difference, however, is that in the NWS, social actors play a more active role. The creation of a professional culture to ensure the quality of operation of the state and its administration takes precedence over the market mechanisms proposed by NPM. The pragmatic aspect of the neo-Weberian approach manifests itself in an effort to achieve the fundamental objectives of public systems and to eliminate those of their functions that do not serve these objectives. It organises public policy in a way that assumes a certain degree of independence of individual organisations or communities in defining their own visions, missions and goals, which combine to form the general objectives of the system.

The NWS is a critical response to NPM on the part of European countries with well-developed welfare systems. The concept of NWS is thus not universal, but may apply only to the group of countries referred to in the literature as the continental European modernisers (Lynn 2008/09; Dunn, Miller 2007). In the modernisers' view, the state is an irreplaceable integration centre with a legal personality and a value system which cannot be reduced to such characteristics of the private sector as efficiency, competitiveness or customer satisfaction.

In their analysis of the NWS, M. Ćwiklicki and S. Mazur (Chapter 1 this volume) point out that the phenomenon can be understood in three ways: (1) as a model of state; (2) as a public management model; and (3) as a type of administrative reform. In the first sense, it is a specific set of institutions, functions and values embedded in the European culture, which implement the principles of democracy and the market economy. From this perspective, the desired model of state implies a departure from the neo-liberal vision of social order and the restoration of its strong position in its dealings with both the private sector and civil society organisations. The state as a sovereign actor in internal and external relations is expected to participate actively in social and market processes. In the second sense, the NWS is a set of reasonably coherent concepts, theories and management mechanisms drawing on the Weberian tradition. It assumes that the public sector has a specific organisational culture, and that public agencies operate professionally, efficiently, flexibly and responsibly. The model in question is contrasted with the dominance of managerial mechanisms, which marginalise the public sector. At the same time, the NWS takes advantage of certain positive features of NPM as an antidote to the weaknesses of bureaucracy or procedural democracy by using auxiliary market and participatory mechanisms. In its third sense, the neo-Weberian approach maps out a specific direction of change involving the transformation of state structures and public management mechanisms. The associated process of institutional reform advocates an ongoing modernisation of the state and its administrative apparatus. In this perspective, the NWS contests the reforms undertaken in the spirit of NPM and invokes the German or continental tradition, which manifests itself as path dependence.

The neo-Weberian state and public policies

The analysis of selected public policies from the perspective of the neo-Weberian approach fails to provide clear and unequivocal conclusions, which is mostly due to methodological issues. The descriptions of public policies employ non-uniform methods, which stems from the principle of methodological individualism. A brief recapitulation of relevant findings is provided below.

Economic policy

T. Geodecki set out to answer the questions whether the current economic reality and economic policies pursued in the context of the strengthening heterodox trends in economic theory justify the observation that we are facing the transition to a new public management model, and whether such a new public management model can be called the neo-Weberian approach (neo-Weberian state), as was suggested by Pollitt and Bouckaert. The attributes of this approach include an active involvement in the formulation of economic policy objectives, professional recruitment, employment stability, rate of overlap of work for the state with employment in the private sector, comparability of wages in administration and in business, prevalence and the amount of bribes as well as the attractiveness of employment in administration. The author gives affirmative answers to both questions on the basis of his literature review. Without undermining his arguments, however, it must be noted that there are few published studies on contemporary (i.e. after 2000) industrial policy undertaken in the neo-Weberian spirit. This shortage of relevant research and publications also affects the analyses of other public policies.

Innovation policy

Innovation policy is constantly evolving and, for this reason, it tends to comprise interventions in various fields, including research and development, technology, infrastructure, regional and educational policies. As is documented in the literature, the innovation policy tools proposed by NPM and public governance have proven to be partly ineffective. The global financial crisis of 2007/2008 resulted in increased expectations of state intervention in the economy in general, and in innovative activity in particular. According to P. Kopyciński, the concept of NWS may offer new solutions which reflect changes in the perception of innovation and innovation policy better than MLG, allowing for their more effective coordination. The neo-Weberian approach becomes even more attractive when we take into account the fact that the basic rationale for intervention in the field of innovation is not so much the neoclassical paradigm of market failure as primary systemic problems.

Labour policy

M. Frączek begins by defining the nine characteristics of labour market policy (LMP) from the neo-Weberian perspective, and then goes on to apply them to Poland's experience in this field. His analysis leads him to the conclusion that LMP in Poland shows a number of similarities with the neo-Weberian public management model. However, it also exhibits mechanisms and instruments typical of other models of public management and, therefore, the existing model of employment policy in Poland can be described as a hybrid one. According to the author, Poland is particularly open to the neo-Weberian approach. The presence of certain key features of the neo-Weberian model may provide an impulse for positive changes in the labour market, because it may offer a different perspective on the processes taking place in LMP without sacrificing the tried and tested mechanisms offered by other public management models. It must be mentioned, though, that LMP analysed from the neo-Weberian perspective has received only modest coverage in the literature.

Industrial policy

Ł. Mamica points out that globalisation has led to the perception of the state as the only entity capable of responding fairly effectively to certain undesirable phenomena associated with this process.

The 2007/2008 crisis was a milestone on the way to empowering the state in the area of economic and industrial policy in line with the neo-Weberian approach. It must be remembered that the approach does not stipulate any minimum level of state involvement in the sphere of regulation, but treats the state as a 'guarantor of social order and partner for markets and society' (Pollitt 2008/09, p. 14).

Consequently, state intervention in the economy is no longer considered (narrowly) to interfere with free-market mechanisms. The fact that public funds have been used to save banks, insurance companies or even entire industries from bankruptcy not only increased the pressure on the state to become more involved in the economy, but also showed that it is the only entity that can effectively restore balance in the markets. The crisis has also led to increased interest in sectoral activities. State-led industrial policy began to revive the neo-Weberian approach in public management, which, according to C. Pollitt and G. Bouckaert, constitutes a 'reaffirmation of the role of the state as the main facilitator of solutions to the new problems of globalisation and technological change' (2011, p. 118).

These actions are consistent with the neo-Weberian concept of state, which emphasises 'the modernisation of financial control systems so that they are able to more forcefully express the general political and strategic priorities in the process of resource allocation' (Pollitt, Bouckaert 2011, p. 82). The analysis of Poland's industrial policy over the last quarter of a century leads the author to the conclusion that the state has become the main stimulator of structural change and development in the economy.

Health policy

The state by necessity plays a major role in the health care system understood as all the organisations and institutions whose primary purpose is to preserve, improve or restore health, and all the resources used to that end. J. Klich reviews the characteristic features of such diverse health care systems as those functioning in France, Germany, Great Britain, Denmark and the Netherlands. He concludes that the neo-Weberian elements are present in all of them, although to varying degrees. The analysed countries seek to improve the transparency of their legislation, which is becoming more oriented to the patients' needs and to the results achieved by the service providers. Health policy is predominantly legalistic, the relationships between stakeholders (mostly health care providers and patients) are regulated by law, and standards are defined in the process of negotiation and consultation. Stakeholder relationships are intense and constantly developed. Private organisations have a large (and still growing) share in the provision of health care services. The role of market mechanisms is significant, or even dominant (e.g. in the Netherlands), but the mechanisms of organisational and systemic learning are barely visible.

Territorial policy

P. Kopyciński attempts to answer the question whether the MLG mechanism provides sufficient tools to meet the contemporary challenges and problems faced by regional policies or efficient territorial management requires new solutions, such as those offered by the neo-Weberian approach. The author concludes that MLG fails to respond adequately to the demand to strengthen the powers and clarify the responsibilities among the different public authority levels, and that the elements of NWS identified by Politt and Bouckaert (2011) better address the territorial policy issues. A stronger executive branch responsible for territorial policy should take advantage of the positive features of the bureaucratic system and incorporate the elements of the neo-Weberian approach into territorial governance.

Planning city development

M. Kudłacz discusses public management in urban areas and concludes that the traditional approach to planning city development cannot adequately respond to processes characterised by extreme complexity and non-linearity, as well as unclear causality. In his detailed survey of theoretical models of city management, the author juxtaposes the neo-Weberian approach with the worldwide process of transition towards a more conservative economy controllable in business and ideological terms. The desire to improve public safety, strengthen the administrative procedures and control mechanisms, limit 'public space shredding', professionalise municipal administration or reinforce the role of city authorities as an arbiter resolving disputes, and to strengthen its role in liaising with various social groups is reflected in a growing tendency to adopt more imperative tools. The author also identifies certain dangers inherent in the application of the neo-Weberian principles by mayors-officials unaware of what constitutes the city-forming potential or unique development resources held by their city. In his view, this may lead to a policy which emphasises procedures and control mechanisms.

Discussion and conclusions

The foregoing analyses of selected public policies justify the conclusion that the neo-Weberian public management model characterised on the one hand by hierarchy, specialisation, standardisation, depersonalisation, stability and political neutrality, and on the other hand by efficiency, effectiveness, quality and empowerment may be used to shape and implement public policies. Such a conclusion, however, has two caveats.

First, one needs to remember the modest theoretical (conceptualisation of the neo-Weberian model) and empirical (political and economic practice) literature dealing with the topic at hand. This is understandable, since the neo-Weberian model is still in *statu nascendi*. As such, however, it cannot produce strong inferences and almost precludes generalisations.

Second, the usefulness of the neo-Weberian model in the design and implementation of public policies must be analysed in context, which is provided by various attempts to cope with the consequences of the global financial crisis. The entire economic and industrial policy, as well as the others analysed above, demonstrate that only the state has the capacity to take effective remedial action and the potential to restore the disturbed balance. Therefore, the crucial role of the state and public administration in mitigating the effects of the crisis can be neither undermined nor relativised. This, however, begs two questions.

The first one might be: Can and should the key role of the state be maintained in times of sustained economic growth and macroeconomic stability? This question is also justified on the grounds that in periods of relative equilibrium, certain representatives of the world of economy and finance advocate the abolishing of the International Monetary Fund as an important stabiliser of the system (Bird, Rowlands 2016, pp. 2–4). It appears that an affirmative answer to this question depends on whether convincing arguments can be found to demonstrate the superiority of the neo-Weberian model over other models and approaches in public policies in the context of sustainable growth, which implies the need for extensive and well-documented research.

The other question appears to be somewhat paradoxical: If the state had not failed in its legislating and regulating functions, would it be necessary to involve it and its resources in combating the consequences of the global financial crisis? One may produce convincing arguments in support of the view that the primary causes of its global reach were not market failures, but state failures. Such a perspective, in turn, would undermine the validity of the neo-Weberian model and its constitutive principles. Taking a pragmatic stance, which assumes that both market failures and government/state failures are objective in nature (i.e. they are impossible to avoid), in order to demonstrate the superiority of the neo-Weberian model, we would first have to prove that state failures lead to losses/disturbances of lesser magnitude than do market failures.

In this study, we have interchangeably used such terms as the *neo-Weberian approach*, the *neo-Weberian model*, and the *neo-Weberian paradigm*. The principle of scientific accuracy requires us to take a stand in this regard. Mazur (2016, p. 234) argues that the neo-Weberian public management model does actually exist, but he notes and briefly characterises the theoretical challenges facing the neo-Weberian paradigm, including the following:

- heterogeneity of the concept;
- ambivalence towards network management mechanisms;

- weak conceptualisation of multi-level governance;
- vaguely outlined relationships between flexibility and stability;
- poorly outlined conceptualisation of individual public management mechanisms when applied in combination;
- weak conceptualisation of forms of organisational learning.

The neo-Weberian approach combines a host of features of the Weberian tradition of thinking about the state (centrality of the state, hierarchical management mechanisms, stability and predictability, civil service ethos) with the elements of market-oriented public management (efficiency, economisation, competition) and public governance (participation, consultation). For this reason, it remains difficult to describe and qualify consistently.

Advances in information technology, the ever-increasing amount of information and the free mobility of people, goods, services and ideas enhanced by the globalisation processes result, among other things, in a growing complexity of the world around us and in the strengthening of the emerging networks. The importance and impact of networks as a coordination mechanism on the processes of public management has been steadily increasing. Regrettably, there is no literature offering comprehensive and clear analysis of the neo-Weberian approach. Analysts tend to conclude that there is a strong tension between the network-based management mechanism and the hierarchical one in the neo-Weberian approach.

Apart from the phenomenon of networking, scholars of public management continue to show significant interest in the concept of MLG. This phenomenon is reinforced by the easier and faster access to information, which results in more intense contacts and deepening interdependence (with all their attendant consequences). The proponents of the neo-Weberian approach note the negative effects of MLG, but have yet to offer a satisfactory conceptualisation of the mechanisms behind it.

Likewise, due to its eclectic nature, the neo-Weberian approach fails to provide a clear-cut answer to the question concerning the relationship between stability (of legal regulations, employment in the civil service) and flexibility (changes in the environment or anticipation of social phenomena). In the context of dynamic change characteristic of the second decade of the 21st century, the hierarchical and procedural logics must be combined as seamlessly as possible with the capacity to respond swiftly and effectively to the emerging new conditions. There is good reason to believe that the adaptive potential of political, economic and social systems will to a greater extent determine the competitive advantage of nations.

Even though the hierarchical, procedural and centralised public management mechanisms occupy a central place in the neo-Weberian approach, the amount and quality of theoretical reflection on them are disappointing. The present conceptualisations of the interdependence among the various mechanisms of public management tend to be simplified and one-dimensional.

The issue of organisational learning in public administration has not been given much attention either. Its analysis in the context of selected health policies leads to the conclusion that the practical achievements are far from satisfactory. More research in this area, concerning e.g. the low efficiency of learning in strongly hierarchical organisations, would certainly enrich the theoretical basis of the neo-Weberian approach.

The neo-Weberian approach shows more promise as a model of state. A wide range of developments, especially globalisation and advances in information technology, supply arguments in favour of strengthening the position of the state in the political and economic systems.

Globalisation also promotes and strengthens the position of transnational corporations (TNCs) in the processes of production and exchange. As a result, TNCs wield progressively more influence on national economies (Kordos, Vojtovič 2016), including the sectors considered to be crucial to state security (Yang, Dong 2016). These processes lead to the reduction of state control over the economy and over such sensitive areas as health care (Gilmore, Peeters 2013). Bearing in mind that the global capital and goods transfer network made it possible for the US sub-prime mortgage crisis to spill over to other countries and continents, the issue of strengthening the role of the state as a regulator and effective sovereign is likely to win popular support.

The progressive digitisation of all the spheres of life, the virtually unlimited access to network-based data and its ever-increasing volumes (Big Data) mean that the issue of IT security is becoming increasingly paramount. The concept embraces military, energy, communications and banking security from the perspective of the entire state, as well as that of individual citizens. The only entity that is in a position to ensure information security (and negotiate successfully with corporations that manage social networks) is the state.

In the light of the above considerations, the neo-Weberian approach may be considered as a useful tool for describing, designing, and implementing public policies, which may gain in importance due to the processes of globalisation and progress in ICT. The approach, however, is still nascent, which makes it an interesting field for researchers, with a high yield potential.

The neo-Weberian state can be shown graphically in the context of other approaches and trends along a time axis. Figure C.1 shows the evolution of public administration systems. From the point of view of the level of structural formalisation, they waver between two conflicting standards. On the one hand, there is the extremely liberal model, which derives from anarchist doctrines and is primarily based on free-market and business mechanisms. On the other hand, the extremely autocratic paradigm is associated with the absolute power régime. Over the last 100 years, the characteristics of public administration models comprised features of both these extremes in varying degrees. Max Weber, when devising his ideal bureaucracy paradigm, specified strict rules intended to ensure the efficiency of the entire system. The implementation of these rules and practical experience (mainly in the Bismarck era) showed, however, that his model is not always effective. In response, a new paradigm – new public governance – was developed, whose basic assumptions stood in opposition to Weber's model. Public administrations in the USA and in the UK in the Reagan–Thatcher era tested this particular paradigm in practice. It turned out that this model was not perfect either. Hence a compromise solution was developed, which in its transitional form was called *multi-level*

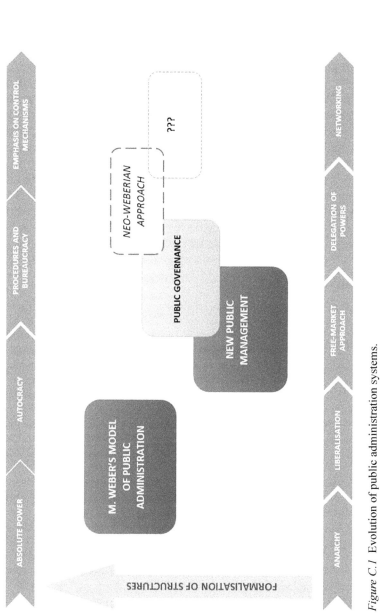

Figure C.1 Evolution of public administration systems.

Source: Own study.

governance, or in its version that to a greater extent emphasises certain aspects of procedures and control mechanisms, the *neo-Weberian approach*. It should be noted that neither multi-level governance nor the neo-Weberian approach completely reject the hallmark assumptions of the previous models. Instead, they adopt those that have proved to be successful in practice.

It is worth asking whether the neo-Weberian model constitutes a borderline point in the sense that the next paradigms will either lean towards a free-market model or emphasise the key role of the state. The dynamically changing environment further complicates any attempts to answer this question. In 2016 there was a clear shift towards a strong, national state, which was illustrated by Brexit, the election of Donald Trump as President of the United States, tightening immigration policies in a number of countries and increasing popularity of nationalist parties. Ideology translates into tangible public policy instruments, which tend to be based on prescriptions and prohibitions rather than on trust. The polarisation of society diminishes social capital and leads to the adoption of stricter rules of operation for public administration.

The neo-Weberian approach may reflect the need for a greater formalisation of public administration structures and for a stronger position of the state in order to protect the interests of individual countries and their citizens more effectively. As always, only history will tell whether the neo-Weberian state turns out to be the right answer to the challenges of the 21st century.

Bibliography

Białynicki, P., Klich, J. (2016). Specyfika krajów neoweberowskich na przykładzie działań podejmowanych w reakcji na globalny kryzys finansowy [The specificity of the neo-Weberian countries: A case study of actions taken in response to the global financial crisis], *Zarządzanie Publiczne* (forthcoming).

Bird, G., Rowlands, D. (2016). *The International Monetary Fund. Distinguishing Reality from Rhetoric*. Cheltenham; Northampton, MA: Edward Elgar.

Dreschler, W. (2009). The rise and demise of the New Public Management: Lessons and opportunities for South East Europe, *Uprava*, vol. 7, no. 3, pp. 7–27.

Dunn, W. N., Miller, D. Y. (2007). A critique of the new public management and the neo-Weberian state: Advancing a critical theory of administrative reform, *Public Organization Review*, vol. 7, no. 4, pp. 345–358. http://doi.org/10.1007/s11115-007-0042-3.

Gilmore, B., Peeters, S. (2013). Understanding corporations to inform public health policy: the example of tobacco industry interests in harm reduction and reduced risk products, *Lancet Online*, 29 November, p. 14.

Kordos, M., Vojtovic, S. (2016). Transnational corporations in the global world economic environment, *Procedia – Social and Behavioral Sciences*, vol. 230, pp. 150–158.

Lynn, L. (2008/09). What is a Neo-Weberian state? Reflections on a concept and its implications. *NISPAcee Journal of Public Administration and Policy*, Special Issue: 'A Distinctive European Model? The Neo-Weberian State', vol. 1 no. 2, pp. 17–30.

Mazur, S. (2016). Zakończenie. Od modelu w kierunku paradygmatu? [Conclusion. From a model to a paradigm?], in: S. Mazur (ed.) *Neo-weberyzm w zarządzaniu publicznym.*

Od modelu do paradygmatu [The Neo-Weberian State in Public Management. From a Model to a Paradigm?]. Warsaw: Wydawnictwo Naukowe Scholar, pp. 228–236.

Mintzberg, H. (1996). Managing government, governing management, *Harvard Business Review*, May-June.

Pollitt, C. (2008/09). An overview of the papers and propositions of the first TransEuropean Dialogue (TED1). *The NISPAcee Journal of Public Administration and Policy*, Special Issue: 'A Distinctive European Model? The Neo-Weberian State', vol. 1. no. 2, pp. 9–14.

Pollitt, C., Bouckaert, G. (2011). *Public Management Reform: A Comparative Analysis: New Public Management, Governance, and the Neo-Weberian State* (3rd ed.). Oxford; New York: Oxford University Press.

Torfing, J., Peters B. G., Pierre J., Sorensen E. (2013). *Interactive Governance Advancing the Paradigm*. Oxford; New York: Oxford University Press.

Yang, Y., Dong, W. (2016). Global energy networks: Insights from headquarter subsidiary data of transnational petroleum corporations, *Applied Geography*, vol. 72, pp. 36–46.

Index

Taylor & Francis eBooks

Helping you to choose the right eBooks for your Library

Add Routledge titles to your library's digital collection today. Taylor and Francis ebooks contains over 50,000 titles in the Humanities, Social Sciences, Behavioural Sciences, Built Environment and Law.

Choose from a range of subject packages or create your own!

Benefits for you

» Free MARC records
» COUNTER-compliant usage statistics
» Flexible purchase and pricing options
» All titles DRM-free.

Benefits for your user

» Off-site, anytime access via Athens or referring URL
» Print or copy pages or chapters
» Full content search
» Bookmark, highlight and annotate text
» Access to thousands of pages of quality research at the click of a button.

eCollections – Choose from over 30 subject eCollections, including:

Archaeology	Language Learning
Architecture	Law
Asian Studies	Literature
Business & Management	Media & Communication
Classical Studies	Middle East Studies
Construction	Music
Creative & Media Arts	Philosophy
Criminology & Criminal Justice	Planning
Economics	Politics
Education	Psychology & Mental Health
Energy	Religion
Engineering	Security
English Language & Linguistics	Social Work
Environment & Sustainability	Sociology
Geography	Sport
Health Studies	Theatre & Performance
History	Tourism, Hospitality & Events

For more information, pricing enquiries or to order a free trial, please contact your local sales team:
www.tandfebooks.com/page/sales

Routledge
Taylor & Francis Group

The home of
Routledge books

www.tandfebooks.com

For Product Safety Concerns and Information please contact our EU
representative GPSR@taylorandfrancis.com
Taylor & Francis Verlag GmbH, Kaufingerstraße 24, 80331 München, Germany